MULTICULTURAL EDUC

James A. Banks, Ser

(continued)

To Generation Mixed:
the mixed-race children who allowed us to listen to them.

Contents

Series Foreword

This trenchant, informative, and engaging book is timely and significant because of the tremendous growth in the number of Americans who are reporting more than one race on the U.S. Census. This population grew from 6.8 million in 2000 to 9 million in 2010. During that period, the number of people who self-reported as both White and Black/African American grew by more than one million, an increase of 134%; those who self-reported as both White and Asian grew by 750,000, as increase of 87% (Jones & Bullock, 2012). The number of school-age youth who identify as mixed-race is also increasing (Root, 2004).

This book is based on a mixed-method study that consisted of interviews and dialogues with mixed-race youth, their siblings, and caregivers. Some of the teachers of the youth were also interviewed. When interviewing multiracial youth, authors Ralina Joseph and Allison Briscoe-Smith uncovered stories in which teachers did not recognize and acknowledge their preferred racialized identities, and who identified them as one race when they preferred to identity with two or more. These youth also felt they were not accurately represented or visible in the school curriculum. They shared with the authors many stories of their teachers not listening to them. Consequently, a major recommendation made by the authors and a concept that undergirds this book is that parents, caregivers, and teachers should *radically listen* to multiracial youth. Radical listening centralizes power inequities and involves hearing the "voices of those often silenced." Additionally, it enables educators and parents to "make space for the fluidity and changes of race, and take cues from the stories [youth] tell about their racialization," which in turn empowers caretakers and teachers to "embrace them as they are: in their changing, agentic, multiple identities."

In a classic and influential essay, Merton (1972) states that the perspectives of both "insiders" and "outsiders" are essential for social scientists to depict a complete view of social reality. Many outsider perspectives on interracial marriage and multiracial people have been institutionalized within social science, popular culture [in movies such as *Pinky* (1949) and *Guess Who's Coming to Dinner* (1967)], and in society writ large (Davis, 1991; Pascoe, 2009). This book provides original and compelling insider perspectives on multiracial families and the socialization of multiracial youth.

Joseph and Brisoe-Smith are compassionate insiders and mothers of mixed raced school children who are keen and perceptive observers. The authors integrate "not only theory and research but their own lived experiences negotiating race and racism for and with mixed-race children."

This edifying book illuminates and verifies many empirical findings about race and racial construction. Drawing upon the work of researchers such as Omi and Winant (1994), Joseph and Brisoe-Smith point out that race is a social construction, and that groups with economic and political power construct racial categories to privilege members of their own racial groups and to marginalize outside groups. The authors state that although race is a social construction, it has detrimental and strongly negative effects on racialized and victimized groups because within an institutionalized racist social and economic system, people respond to targeted racialized groups based on their perceptions and beliefs.

Joseph and Briscoe-Smith cite empirical studies by the Clarks (1950) and Aboud (2003) that refute the notion that young children are colorblind. They also describe the harmful pedagogical consequences that result when parents, caretakers, and teachers assume that preschool children are colorblind or unaware of race. Kenneth and Mamie Clark, in their seminal studies of young children that began in the late 1930s and continued to the 1950s, established that both African American and White children are keenly aware of the racial distinctions and evaluations made by adults, which they internalize. Both Black and White children in their studies exemplified a White bias. More recent research by Spencer (1982), Banks (1984), and Cross (1991) confirm the findings made by the Clarks in their classic studies. However, more research studies indicate that as they grow older, African American children develop more positive attitudes toward Blacks and express less White bias.

The major purpose of the Multicultural Education Series is to provide preservice educators, practicing educators, graduate students, scholars, and policymakers with an interrelated and comprehensive set of books that summarizes and analyzes important research, theory, and practice related to the education of ethnic, racial, cultural, and linguistic groups in the United States and the education of mainstream students about diversity. The dimensions of multicultural education, developed by Banks (2004) and described in the *Handbook of Research on Multicultural Education* and in the *Encyclopedia of Diversity in Education* (Banks, 2012), provide the conceptual framework for the development of the publications in the Series. The dimensions are content integration, the knowledge construction process, prejudice reduction, equity pedagogy, and an empowering institutional culture and social structure. The books in the Multicultural Education Series provide research, theoretical, and practical knowledge about the behaviors and learning characteristics of students of color (Conchas & Vigil, 2012; Lee, 2007), language minority students (Gándara & Hopkins 2010; Valdés,

2001; Valdés, Capitelli, & Alvarez, 2011), low-income students (Cookson, 2013; Gorski, 2018), and other minoritized population groups, such as students who speak different varieties of English (Charity Hudley & Mallinson, 2011), and LGBTQ youth (Mayo, 2014).

A number of the books in the Multicultural Education Series focus on *institutional and structural racism* and ways to reduce it in educational institutions, which is a significant topic because of the national and international protests and dialogues about institutionalized racism that began after George Floyd, an African American man in Minneapolis, died when a White police officer pressed his knee to Floyd's neck for more than eight minutes on May 25, 2020. One of these books focuses on race and mixed-race people: Jabari Mahiri's *Deconstructing Race: Multicultural Education Beyond the Color-Bind* (2017). Other books in the Multicultural Education Series that focus on race include Özlem Sensoy and Robin DiAngelo, *Is Everyone Really Equal? An Introduction to Key Concepts in Social Justice Education* (2017, second edition); Gary Howard, *We Can't Teach What We Don't Know: White Teachers, Multiracial Schools* (2016, third edition); Zeus Leonardo, *Race Frameworks: A Multidimensional Theory of Racism and Education* (2013); and Daniel G. Solórzano and Lindsay Pérez Huber, *Racial Microaggressions: Using Critical Race Theory in Education to Recognize and Respond to Everyday Racism* (2020).

As this adept and elegantly written book illustrates, the experiences of mixed-race youth challenge many established and institutionalized conceptions of race and racialization. This book describes how the racial identity of mixed-race youth in a diverse nation such as the United States is complex and fluid and does not have rigid boundaries. The racial identity of mixed-race youth is flexible rather than fixed because their racial identification is influenced by many factors, such as institutional context, age, phenotype, and the extent of social pressure to conform in a particular situation. A child whose parents are Black and White might identify as biracial at home and as African American at school because of her phenotype and identity with Black school friends. The authors cite significant research findings by Tatum (1997) and Gaither (2015) about mixed race youth. Tatum (1997) describes the identity of mixed-race youth as circular rather than linear. Research by Gaither (2015) indicates that it is important for mixed-race youth to be given the opportunity to self-identify because it increases their agency, motivation, and self-esteem.

This book not only describes the challenges that are experienced by multiracial youth in families and schools, but also details cases of radical listening that facilitates their identity development and clarification. It illustrates how teachers can radically listen to multiracial students and change schools in ways that will enable them to prosper. This book also explains how parents and caretakers can practice radical listening and structure home environments in which racially mixed children can be nurtured and

have their emerging identities affirmed. Educators and families who work
with multiracial youth will find this practical and illuminating book very
helpful and empowering in their work. I am pleased to welcome this book
to the Multicultural Education Series, which it will grace and enrich.

—James A. Banks

REFERENCES

Aboud, F. E. (2003). The formation of in-group favoritism and out-group prejudice
in young children: Are they distinct attitudes? *Developmental Psychology*, 39
(1), 48–60.

Banks, J. A. (1984). Black youth in predominantly White suburbs: An exploratory
study of their attitudes and self-concepts. *The Journal of Negro Education*, 53
(1), 3–17.

Banks, J. A. (2004). Multicultural education: Historical development, dimensions,
and practice. In J. A. Banks & C. A. M. Banks (Eds.). *Handbook of research on
multicultural education* (2nd ed., pp. 3–29). Jossey-Bass.

Banks, J. A. (2012). Multicultural education: Dimensions of. In J. A. Banks (Ed). *Encyclopedia of diversity in education* (vol. 3, pp. 1538–1547). Sage Publications.

Charity Hudley, A. H., & Mallinson, C. (2011). *Understanding language variation
in U. S. schools*. Teachers College Press.

Clark, K. B., & Clark, M. P. (1950). Emotional factors in racial identification and
preference in Negro children. *Journal of Negro Education*, 19, 341–350.

Conchas, G. Q., & Vigil, J. D. (2012). *Streetsmart schoolsmart: Urban poverty and
the education of adolescent boys*. Teachers College Press.

Cookson, P. W. Jr. (2013). *Class rules: Exposing inequality in American high schools*.
Teachers College Press.

Cross, W. E., Jr. (1991). *Shades of Black: Diversity in African American identity*.
Temple University Press.

Davis, F. J. (1991). *Who is Black? One nation's definition*. The Pennsylvania State
University Press.

Gándara, P., & Hopkins, M. (Eds.). (2010). *Forbidden language: English language
learners and restrictive language policies*. New York, NY: Teachers College Press.

Gaither, S. E. (2015). "Mixed" results: Multiracial research and identity explorations. *Current Directions in Psychological Science*, 24 (2), 114–119. https://doi
.org/10.1177/0963721414558115

Gorski, P. C. (2018). *Reaching and teaching students in poverty: Strategies for eras-
ing the opportunity gap* (2nd ed.). Teachers College Press.

Howard, G. (2016). *We can't teach what we don't know: White teachers, multiracial
schools* (3rd ed.). Teachers College Press.

Jones, N. A., & Bullock, J. (2012, September). *Two or more races population: 2010*.
2010 Census Briefs. United States Census Bureau. https://www.census.gov/prod
/cen2010/briefs/c2010br-13.pdf

Lee, C. D. (2007). *Culture, literacy, and learning: Taking bloom in the midst of the
whirlwind*. Teachers College Press.

Leonardo, Z. (2013). *Race frameworks: A multicultural theory of racism and education*. Teachers College Press.

Omi, M., & Winant, H. (1994). *Racial formation in the United States: From the 1960s to the 1990s* (2nd ed.). Routledge.

Mahiri, J. (2017). *Deconstructing race: Multicultural education beyond the colorblind*. Teachers College Press.

Mayo, C. (2014). *LGBTQ youth and education: Policies and practices*. Teachers College Press.

Merton, R. K. (1972). Insiders and outsiders: A chapter in the sociology of knowledge. *The American Journal of Sociology*, 78, 9–47.

Pascoe, P. (2009). *What comes naturally: Miscegenation law and the making of race in America*. Oxford University Press.

Root, M. P. P. (2004). Multiracial families and children: Implications for educational research and practice. In J. A. Banks & C. A. M. Banks (Eds.), *Handbook of research in multicultural education* (2nd ed., pp. 110–124). Jossey-Bass.

Sensoy, Ö. & DiAngelo, R. (2017). *Is everyone really equal? An introduction to key concepts in social justice education* (2nd ed.). Teachers College Press.

Solórzano, D. G., & Huber, L. P. (2020). *Using critical race theory in education to recognize and respond to everyday racism*. Teachers College Press.

Spencer, M. B. (1982). Personal and group identity of Black children: An alternative synthesis. *Genetic Psychology Monographs*,106, 59–84.

Tatum, B. D. (1997). *What are all the Black kids sitting together in the cafeteria? And other conversations about race*. Basic Books.

Valdés, G. (2001). *Learning and not learning English: Latino Students in American schools*. Teachers College Press.

Valdés, G., Capitelli, S., & Alvarez, L. (2011). *Latino children learning English: Steps in the journey*. Teachers College Press.

Preface

When we started researching and writing *Generation Mixed Goes to School* in the fall of 2018, most school-age children, including our own, left their houses each day, jumped onto school buses, walked to school with a sibling or neighbor classmate or two, and piled into carpools in anticipation of a full day of education in their school buildings. They filed into their classrooms to see, hear, touch, and even smell their classmates as they learned in small groups, asked questions of their teachers, and practiced taking notes. They played and fought together on playgrounds devoid of caution tape. They whispered secrets in each other's ears, shared special birthday treats around a classroom rug, and traded lunchbox delicacies in crowded cafeterias. We conducted our research dialogues for this book in sealed-off recording studios, nodding encouragingly as mixed-race siblings shared germy microphones and crayons along with their stories. We passed tissue boxes to sniffling pairs of parents and children as we gratefully took in their tales of struggle, of triumph, and of quotidian complaints of mixed-race family life. As they arrived at our listening parties, we hugged our Generation Mixed families, as we came to know our participants, who were born after the 2000 Census that ushered in a "mark one or more option." Together we shared a buffet-style meal and the results of the dialogues; the children and youth passed around a mic where they spoke first and last, their voices, young yet full of wisdom, ringing out clearly.

And then the whole world changed. In the early spring of 2020 we were completing revisions for the book when a global pandemic shut down all of our lives. For months on end we lost a daily tactile connection with all except our immediate families. Our work lives were translated on screen with (often) grainy visuals, and our home lives made us have to think through so many pieces of our lives we had taken for granted for so long. Communities of color didn't experience this pandemic equally. That same spring the Centers for Disease Control and Prevention (CDC) reported the "disproportionate burden of illness and death among racial and ethnic minority groups" due to COVID-19, including, in New York City, where death rates of Black people due to the illness reached a staggering 92.3 per 100,000 people, and Latinx people at 74.3, with whites at 42.5 and Asian Americans at 34.5 (Garg et al., 2020).

And then late that same spring the video of a white police officer kneel-ing on the neck of a Black man named George Floyd for nearly 9 minutes while he begged for his life went viral. His murder, and those of other African Americans such as Breonna Taylor and Ahmaud Aubery, ignited again what was already live in our country: a rage, grief, and resistance against racism. This book speaks to our time. It provides not only context and a backdrop to our world today, but also calls out what is needed: more listening. During the pandemic, during the moment of racial unrest, the United States struggles to practice what we posit is the essence of this book project: radical listen-ing. While you, our reader, will soon learn all about radical listening in our introductory chapter, here's what we want you to know right away: Radical listening is about slowing down to hear what a speaker intends as their mean-ing, not what you, the listener, are filtering through as your own desires.

Radical listening entails righting the wrongs of power. In radical listen-ing we take the mic away from those who jealously guard it, such as white adults in positions of power, and task them with listening. We give the mic to those who are often silenced, such as our minoritized children and youth, and we ask them to speak as well as listen. Radical listening is not about passively receiving information: The listener cannot simply remain content with accepting the speaker's story, particularly when the story iterated is one of power inequities. However, the listener can't immediately jump to action. Instead, they must persist in places of discomfort before moving to create change. That action is to interrupt the privilege or the injustice the story conjures, and that interruption must come from, and always be in consulta-tion with, the speaker. The listener must do this whether or not it is comfort-able or easy. Being in a global pandemic in the midst of yet another wave of racialized violence and its resulting uprising has provided the two of us with the opportunity to practice our radical listening not just in a professional sphere, but in a personal one within our households as a necessary part of our healing, our families' healing, and our daily dismantling of racism.

We wrote *Generation Mixed Goes to School* because this is the book that we need for ourselves and for our children and for our students, as scholars, mothers, and race and equity practitioners. We need it not just because of our nation's changing demographics, but also because of our racially hostile political climate. In the era of our 45th president we have both experienced an increase in requests for support on racial equity and have heard many educators and parents lament the lack of resources for mixed-race children. Ralina brings a critical mixed-race studies perspective alongside a knowledge of critical race theory, intersectionality, and communication studies to this project. Allison brings social, developmental, and clinical psychological per-spectives on how children and adults learn and discuss race.

Perhaps just as importantly, we both bring our lived experiences. We are mothers of color, both first-generation and multigenerationally multiracial, with mixed-race husbands, who are raising our toddler-through-high-school-age mixed-race children in our current educational system. This is a book written from the "inside" of these experiences—integrating not only theory and research but our own lived experiences negotiating race and racism for and with our mixed-race children. Just as decades of scholarship, most notably in sociologists Michael Omi and Howard Winant's (1986, 2015) groundbreaking formulation of racial formation theory, have demonstrated the paradox that while that race is an illusion, centuries of racialized violence have also made it a very real, embodied experience. Both of us negotiate the illusionary and very much nontranscendent nature of race in ours and our children's daily lives; that paradoxical perspective structures this book.

Generation Mixed Goes to School is the culmination of our scholarship over 20 years meeting our nearly 20 years of conversations. We have written this coauthored book entirely together with each of us touching every piece of every chapter; we write in one voice, a "we" even as one or the other of us has taken a first or last pass through the text. We wrote in a reciprocal braiding style, with Allison offering up the psychology strand, Ralina introducing the critical mixed-race studies strand, and the two of us together working in the third radical listening strand of the participant stories. Such braiding feels natural for us. We first met when we were assigned as roommates for a sleepaway dissertation race and gender workshop in 2002. As the only two women of color chosen for this retreat, we gratefully clung to each other as we shared our very different psychology and ethnic studies projects. Yet we saw ourselves in each other immediately; our friendship was fast and furious, and we chose each other as family: When we had children, we made it official by becoming godparents to each other's children.

As we began this book, our school-age children were in 1st, 3rd, 6th, and 9th grade, in elementary, middle, and high school, respectively. As we finish it, they are in 4th, 6th, 9th, and 12th grades, with a rowdy 3-year-old in their midst. We have counseled each other through their trips to the principal's office, their forays into racially segregated classroom spaces, racial misreadings by teachers, and racial exclusions by and of other children. Although we live in different cities, our children know and love each other as cousins whose racialized experiences echo their own. This book has been a labor of love for our families. We are deeply appreciative of each other and the sister friendship that has developed through this work. It has meant that we have had to learn how to manifest the principles of the book with each other—radically listening and enduring the friction, heat of being uncomfortable. It has not been easy, but it has been worth it. We eat, sleep, and breathe mixed race, and in this book we hope to give you a sense of how we create radical listening spaces to help foster our attempts to develop healthy mixed-race children.

We thank all of the individuals and communities who have helped us create this book. First and foremost, we want to express our heartfelt gratitude to our families. They supported us in our writing retreats, Zoom calls, and phone conferences that brought us together but took us away from them.

They answered our constant probing questions about every aspect of what it means to be a mixed-race kid in school today. They gave feedback for everything from questions for participants to full drafts of the book. Ralina would like to thank TJ, Naima, and James; Richard and Irene; Grandpi and Diane; Diana and Ed; and Janine, Wadiya, and Joy. Allison would like to thank her mother and father for providing the foundation to explore these issues of race and justice. And thanks to Mike, Alonzo, Ava Marie, and Aria for their motivation, inspiration, and support. Thank you to everyone who worked on the book, especially the CCDE family, and within that, Gina Aaftab, Meshell Sturgis, and Anjuli Brekke. We want to send a special thank you to Dr. James A. Banks for inviting us include the voices of mixed-race students in his highly esteemed multicultural education series. We are thrilled to have our book join the ranks of our very favorite education and social justice texts. Thank you, Laura Helper, for helping weave the heart of our argument through the heart of the work. This work would not have been possible without the generous participation of all of the Generation Mixed families who gave their time and their stories to us. We hear you and we thank you. *Generation Mixed Goes to School* is for all of you.

"It's hard speaking about race . . . especially when you're mixed because there are so many sides!"

Thirteen-year-old 9th-grader Aiyana, who identifies at school as either white and Black or mixed, and lists her races and ethnicities as Black and white, iterates a truism for race talk in this country: "It's hard speaking about race." She quickly follows up her pensive statement with an exclamatory one, noting to her 15-year-old, 10th-grader brother Gray, such race talk is "especially [hard] when you're mixed because there are so many sides!" Although race is filled with complexities and contradictions and constructions for all, answers to the questions surrounding race, the "what" and "who" and the "why" questions of identity, can feel particularly complicated for children and youth who are mixed race. These complications come about not because of an intrinsic sense of confusion inside of multiracial kids; rather, mixed-race kids, or to use the nomenclature of this book's title, Generation Mixed kids, experience a monoracial, or single-race, world that is confused about mixed race.

We are identifying Generation Mixed as those born after the 2000 Census, which included a "Mark One or More" option that allowed for both the self-identification and the demographic delineation of multiracial people. These Generation Mixed kids told us stories in which teachers regularly failed to recognize their full and chosen racialized identities; in which their media and history failed to represent them accurately (if at all); and, most importantly, in which most members of their school communities failed to listen to them. Some multiracial children and youth express frustration in talking about race because at school some are tokenized; others who are part white are sometimes granted a phenomenon we describe as white adjacency, or being given the proximity-privileges of near-whiteness; and still others, largely those who read as Black, suffer from the weight of implicit bias. Although some students experience home as a reprieve where race talk is easy, natural, and deployed as a way to uncover the unspoken scripts that play out in their school days, other students struggle with home lives in which their families refuse to accept their chosen racialized identities, or sometimes refuse to speak about race at all. In short, there is not just one story to listen to about Generation Mixed. In the words of historian Paul Spickard (2020), "The story of race has been written as if races were real, biologically discrete entities, not heuristic constructions of philosophers' minds. It has been written as if monoracial people—people who imagine they are racially pure—were the norm and multiracial people were anomalies" (2020, p. 6). In our book, Generation Mixed children share stories that violate the notion of "real, biologically discrete" race.

Multiracial people, the "anomalies" who see through to the fiction of race, and perhaps especially those mixed-race individuals such as Aiyana whose loose, golden-brown curls, honey skin, and round features belie easy racial classification, are asked the "what," the "who," and the "why" questions of race daily; such questioning, as Aiyana notes, can make it challenging to talk about complex contours of the very issue—race—that looms so large in so many of our multiracial and monoracial lives. In order to make this talk just a little easier, *Generation Mixed Goes to School: Radically Listening to Multiracial Kids* doesn't just present the stories of students like Aiyana; we strive to radically listen to Aiyana. In radical listening, we go beyond merely telling the stories of participants.

We aim to not only hear the stories the children and youth participants want to share, but to hear them in the ways they seek to share them; we strive to filter out the desires we hold as listeners, researchers, teachers, and parents, and fully uplift the voices of the youth and children. Although we do not claim representativeness as our sample is small, the stories we highlight aren't random ones—they resonate with what it means to be a member of Generation Mixed today. In radical listening, which is our theory, method, and intervention, we present our participants' voices alongside scholarship in psychology, education, and Critical Mixed Race Studies, drawing a cross-section of work in ethnic studies, history, communication, sociology, literature, anthropology, political science, and more. As psychologist Sarah Gaither (2015) writes, "Trying to force multiracial research into monoracial research boxes is not the path that will allow innovation. It is time for research to adapt to changing demographics—much like multiracials continually adapt to their surroundings" (p. 117). We carefully curate and situate the scholarship from which we draw, as it too has experienced the impact of racism that our youth and child participants describe. We hope that the book you are beginning will illuminate the challenges and opportunities that mixed-race youth and children experience today in our educational environments, so that your own race talk widens and deepens as you begin radically listening to multiracial kids.

RADICAL LISTENING AS THEORY: CREATING
A CHILDREN-AND-YOUTH-BASED FRAME

We didn't begin this book planning on using radical listening as our central framing device. While we always knew that we wanted to animate these pages with mixed-race children, youth, their families, and teachers, we were going to dedicate the first half of the book to articulating their problems in light of the scholarship, and the second half of the book to solutions neatly packaged as "mixed-race conscious spaces." We were intent on giving people the tools to create those spaces. Although we designed our book in a fairly conventional fashion, we conducted our research untraditionally: We arranged for conversational interviews in which the youth and children participants got to choose their conversation partners, choose from a list of prompts, and direct their own conversations. Furthermore, our first level of data dissemination, or how we shared out the results of our research, was in the form of community events where the youth and children participants shared out their own clips to their friends, family, and members of the greater Seattle community. This was in the very academic year that we conducted our research dialogues, sometimes just weeks after. None of this was conventional. And after our first very unconventional event we went back to the literal drawing board and reframed the entire book in accordance with the themes that we heard our participants speaking both in our recording studio and in the community gathering.

The community event where we shared out the clips is named Radical Listening, a key component of a program Ralina runs called Interrupting Privilege at the University of Washington's Center for Communication, Difference and Equity (CCDE). We soon realized that what this session sought to accomplish was actually what we were seeking to achieve in our book. As we revised the manuscript by following themes from the Radical Listening sessions, we constructed a book that listened more carefully; we sought to create an *intervention* of radical listening that was driven by the wants and needs of the child and adolescent participants, and not by our agendas. This meant not just legitimately having the words of the students guiding our book, but also interrogating all of the moments in which scholars were not holding the students' words with the care that we deemed necessary. It also meant teaching our readers listening processes throughout its pages.

So what is radical listening? First, listening is not the same as hearing. Although hearing is involuntary and physiological, truly listening is both voluntary and emotional. One doesn't simply take in sound as your ear does in hearing; to listen, we must filter out the distraction in order to create meaning. In radical listening, as defined by the colleagues of critical education scholar Joe Kinchloe, who coined the term in 2009, we must "consciously valu[e] others by attempting to hear what the speaker is saying for the meaning he or she intends, rather than the meaning the listener interprets through his/her own view of the world" (Winchell et al., 2016, p. 101). The phrase "radical listening" has been adopted by practitioners across disciplines as diverse as business and psychology, as, for example, psychologist Carol Gilligan ran a center at NYU (which at the time of this printing is no longer in existence) called "radical listening," a branding of her listening method guide of psychological inquiry, a primarily gendered form of political resistance (Gilligan, 1982; Gilligan & Richards, 2018; Gilligan et al., 1991). In the tradition of critical education studies, "radical listening affords opportunities for new awarenesses and mutual culture to be collaboratively generated" (Winchell et al., 2016, p. 101). Kinchloe's colleague Ken Tobin expounds on this idea: "The goal" of radical listening, he writes, is "fully understanding what was said and considering its potential. Rather than focusing on pitfalls and shortcomings, the focus of radical listening is on making sense and exploring possibilities" (Winchell et al., 2016, p. 101).

The "radical" in radical listening centralizes issues of power: One is listening for power, and in particular, power inequities. Radical listening aims to hear the voices of those often silenced. This means realizing that we must train our ears to hear what is spoken and what remains silent. Radical listening for power and difference means that when we take in individual stories (as well as those that are slow to be iterated), that we must hear not just discrete experiences, but oppressive histories, unequal structures, and repressive institutions.

Different disciplines prize listening for power and difference with terminology other than radical listening. Media studies scholar Tanja Dreher (2009) uses the phrase *political listening* to denote how listening with an ear toward power pushes us toward a "justice which sustains difference" (p. 448). For rhetorical theorist Krista Ratcliffe (2005), the phrase *rhetorical listening* denotes listening "to hear people's intersecting identifications with gender and race (including whiteness), the purpose being to negotiate troubled identifications in order to facilitate cross-cultural communication about any topic" (p. 17). Communication scholar Wendy Chun (1999) writes that the listener "must constantly ask, 'what is being elided in my identifications with the speaker?'" (p. 139). Tobin calls radical listening a "revolutionary action" that "create[s] conditions for learning from the other by being with the other, and learning from difference by valuing difference as a resource for learning" (p. 101). All acknowledge that radical listening is also far from easy; education scholar and Kinchloe colleague Tricia Kress notes that "learning to listen for difference can be challenging because difference is often a destabilizing force (at least initially); instability is problematic when trying to implement . . . reforms" (quoted in Winchell et al., 2016, p. 105). Part of the difficulty of radical listening is that "these spaces leave us vulnerable; they expose us as constantly in process, and reframe so-called battle grounds as fields of listening and learning" (quoted in Winchell et al., 2016, p. 105).

One would expect that the clinical psychologists would be adept at this type of radical listening, and their literature full of insights about it. And indeed, while many traditions of therapy and engagement have similar elements of close and active listening, radical listening as we define it here remains absent from much of the literature. Radical listening in psychology, with a focus on race and power, is perhaps most aligned with the widely held concept of *cultural humility*. Cultural humility is a term that has become so ubiquitous in clinical–therapeutic spaces that many forget to attribute its origin to Dr. Melanie Tervalon, a Black pediatrician who worked at Children's Hospital Oakland, and her coauthor Dr. Jann Murray-Garcia, a Latina pediatrician across the Bay at University of California San Francisco (Tervalon & Murray-Garcia, 1998). They coined the term to push the field beyond the core concept of *cultural competency* (Sue et al., 2009); they sought to illustrate that well-trained physicians did not necessarily need to be fluent in other cultures as much as to be open to them. Cultural humility shares the same foundation as radical listening, of needing an open, curious, and expanded attitude in order to be of service. As they state, "Cultural humility incorporates a lifelong commitment to self-evaluation and critique, to redressing the power imbalances" (p. 117). We argue that radical listening is a practice of cultural humility.

We remain inspired by the work of so many scholars around listening, most notably the critical education theories of radical listening by Kinchloe and colleagues, the listening theories of media and communication scholars Chun, Ratcliffe, and Dreher, and the clinical psychological models of cultural humility by Tervalon and Murray-Garcia (1998). However, in the CCDE's radical listening projects, including this Generation Mixed one, radical listening remains different from all of these. In this book, radical listening attends keenly to how power shapes *racialized* difference; our particularly explicit focus on race (and its intersections) is how we are different from the critical education theories and critical listening theories, and closer to that of Tervalon and Murray-Garcia (1998). However, in addition to the attention we pay to power and racialized difference, we also focus on radical listening as not just listening differently, but slowing down, and moving into action.

Thus, we articulate radical listening as a three-step process:

1. cultivating a nonjudgmental and focused listening and curiosity about the meaning of the speaker's words while attending to overarching (and sometimes barely iterated) scripts of racialized power and inequity;
2. encouraging what we call *friction*, which we explore later in this chapter. Friction is the process of slowing down, of uncomfortably

confronting one's own assumptions in the listening process, and
finally;

3. moving into action as a form of interrupting the inequities you have
   heard iterated. The action that the listener moves into must always
   be in consultation with the speaker.

By radically listening, we are able to foundationally understand how
mixed-race identity development happens. Such knowledge helps us anticipate, affirm, and embrace mixed-race children's identities as self-chosen,
fluid, and changing. Radical listening allows us to hear all of the ways in
which different children experience racialized violence differently. Radical
listening readies educators to interrupt bias in the ways that their students
both need and want. As educators and parents, we must encourage and
make space for the fluidity and changes of race, and take cues from the stories our kids tell about their racialization.

Radical listening also allows us to hear how mixed-race children and
youth use the second feature of radical listening, *friction*. In her comprehensive book on implicit bias (a phenomenon we will explore in depth in
Chapter 3), social psychologist Jennifer Eberhardt (*Biased*, 2019) mentions
the idea of friction as a necessary step to reducing bias. Both in her book
(p. 186) and in a talk where she and Allison copresented (personal communication, August 2019), she describes friction as the process of slowing down, pausing, and providing additional time between our automatic
reactions and our actions. Eberhardt uses an example of her work with the
widely used community/social networking platform Nextdoor.

Although Nextdoor is intended as a tool to build community, facilitate
relationships, and support, it is also plagued with overt biases and painful experiences of racial discrimination. The common example Eberhardt
provided was that of a "concerned neighbor" signaling that someone was
"suspicious," which led to neighbors calling police or even vigilante involvement. Many times "suspicious" was code for Black. This led to many incidents of racial bias against people in their own yards, neighborhoods, and
homes. Nextdoor consulted with Eberhardt to see how these biases could be
reduced. They worked together to create *friction*. They developed a system
where if someone was going to report "suspicious behavior," the platform
required them to slow down: Users had to answer several questions to encourage them to reflect on their own assumptions and what confronts them.
They were asked to become uncomfortable. Were Nextdoor users seeing
someone as "suspicious" because of their race? Were they operating from
bias? This slowing down was uncomfortable for users because it pointed out
their bias; that was precisely the point. As radical listening requires attention to power, friction is a way of attending to that power.

Friction implies both slowing down and heat. When we utilize this term,
we often show it by rubbing our hands together, implying the movement of

two objects opposing each other, a way to stay warm or maybe start a fire. In this case friction is the heat between our assumptions, our automatic ideas, and what we are listening to. This slowing down can be painful, requires additional time, and as we frame in this book, is a fundamental step of radical listening. As we will talk about later in the book (see Chapters 4 and 5), persisting in the discomfort as a teacher or a parent is the challenge that requires deep introspection; radical listening enables that discomfort. We are building on Eberhardt's concept to state that in the case of mixed-race children friction necessitates a type of radical listening where one's desire cannot be for sameness, as Wendy Chun notes. Friction might feel like a flip of power; this is where you learn from your student or child. Friction entails unabashedly race-based curiosity, fostering multiracial racialized communities, both in schools creating affinity groups through what we deem fictive mixed-race siblinghood, and at home providing spaces for multiracial identity play. Radical listening allows us to hear how mixed-race children and youth want for members of school communities to center relationships with them and always be conscious of power differentials, particularly those that are racialized. Finally, radically listening to mixed-race kids allows us to embrace them as they are in their changing, agentic, multiple identities.

Chapters 1 through 3 in *Generation Mixed Goes to School* focus on teaching you the skills of points one and two (listening and friction), while Chapters 4 and 5 begin to speak about point three (action). Before you can spring to action, as point three guides you to, you must fully understand the landscape of inequality. As we move to the three points of radical listening, let's uncover radical listening as a method and an intervention.

RADICAL LISTENING AS METHOD AND INTERVENTION: COLLECTING AND SHARING STORIES

In every step of our research project, from design through execution, we aimed to listen first and foremost to our children and youth, and thus, achieve some form of agency for our participants in the process. As education scholar Michael Wyness (2012) writes, "[g]iven the status of children as incompetents and dependents in earlier social scientific research and practice," scholarship today must seek to "recenter the position of children as individual rights-bearing agents." Wyness goes on to write, "The agentic child is the participating child" (p. 439). We didn't want our interlocutors to feel as though we were taking their stories in order to use them for our own selfish purposes; we wanted for them to tell us their stories so that together we could share out their knowledge in order to change their school communities for the better. They were aware of our intention and took the chance to exercise this agency before, during, and after our radical listening sessions.

Specifically, *Generation Mixed Goes to School* employed a community-engaged, mixed method of interviews and dialogues about mixed-race identity development between youth, their siblings, and caregivers. We also interviewed the teachers whom they identified as being ones who listened best. We advertised for kindergarten through 12th-grade age students who had parents from different racialized backgrounds, and who wanted to come to the university to have a conversation with a sibling, parent, another family member, teacher, or a member of their school community (such as a coach). We were careful not to send out a call for "mixed-race" or "multiracial" students because we did not want to impose that identity on students with multiple racial backgrounds who might choose, instead, to name their identities in monoracial ways. We sent our flier through a variety of networks including Families of Color Seattle (FoCS), the University of Washington's College of Education, the Center for Communication, Difference and Equity (CCDE) at the University of Washington, and various other schools and nonprofits that serve students of color. We ended up with a good number of respondents simply by word of mouth.

We had no trouble recruiting participants in very multiracial Seattle. Although Seattle is 15th among U.S. metropolitan areas for size, the population of mixed-race people is the fourth largest in the country, after New York, Los Angeles, and San Francisco. Furthermore, Seattle boasts the second-highest percentage of people who identify as two or more races; for comparison, the city with the highest percentage is Oklahoma City, where more than 50% of people who claim that category identify themselves as having both white and Native American background. This is different from Seattle where there is not a particular multiracial combination that is more popular than all others (Balk, 2016). As of 2018, King County, where Seattle is located, reports 10% of children under 18 as being two or more races (Washington State Office of Financial Management, 2019). Anecdotally, our participants described having multiple multiracial friends, with some of the participants describing all of their closest friends as mixed race. Thus, as opposed to the work that paints a picture of mixed-race children and youth suffering from "racial isolation" (Chang, 2015; Jackson & Samuels, 2019), our work illustrates a Generation Mixed experience when a multiracial identity is exceedingly common.

From these conversations, we recorded 18, in-depth conversational interviews between a school-age mixed-race student and a parent or guardian, or two mixed-race siblings. No one brought a teacher or coach to participate. With the teen and tween siblings, sometimes a parent or parents would join the siblings for the end of the interview. The two of us were both present for the majority of the interviews, and when we did marathon back-to-back dialogues one of us would step out of a session so we could stay fresh as listeners. In addition, because of travel restrictions Ralina was only able to interview the teachers and administrators, with whom she held more conventional one-on-one interviews at their schools. However, we consulted extensively after each interview, and even when the two of us weren't physically present, we poured over the audio and written transcripts of the sessions together.

We didn't set up typical interviews, with the two of us asking a series of questions of our interviewees. Instead, as we invited the participants to bring in a trusted conversation partner, our mixed-race youth and children came to our interview studio with siblings, parents, an auntie, and a cousin. We provided them with a series of conversation prompts such as "how did you learn about your racial identity?," "what do you think other people think about your racial identity?," and "can you remember and describe a time when you saw people treated differently because of race at school?" You can see the entirety of the prompts in Appendix A, and before the end of this chapter you will have an opportunity to practice responding to some of them with a partner. Although we did begin by introducing the questions to the participants, we also encouraged them to have conversations with each other.

We used 16 of the 18 interviews for the book (two of the children were so shy that they only whispered to their mothers in our presence). These stories animate the book. You'll see as the book unfolds that when the pairs were siblings, they jumped easily to all kinds of questions, including what for the parent–child dyads proved to be difficult and probing questions of race. When the dynamic included an adult and no sibling, the conversation took longer to come around to such honest conversations of race. In keeping with our radical listening methodology, we interviewed teachers and administrators who our participants named as the ones who most made them feel as though they belonged in their school communities.

Not only were the interviews unconventional, but so was the dissemination of the information from the interviews. After we conducted the interviews, we shared the stories in three public, intergenerational listening sessions about Generation Mixed. You can hear a selection of those clips at the website of the University of Washington's Center for Communication, Difference and Equity (ccde.com.washington.edu). These sessions had several parts: teaching radical listening, practicing radical listening, listening to clips, sharing out reflections, and open mic testimonies, questions, and answers. The audience comprised our Generation Mixed families and friends, participants in the CCDE Interrupting Privilege project, CCDE friends and supporters, and University of Washington students, faculty, and staff. The attendance ranged from approximately 50 to 75 people, with anywhere from 8 to 10 Generation Mixed participants and their families.

The didactic portion of the evening primed us all to be radical listeners. Then the room shifted to practicing those radical listening skills as mixed-race students' voices rang out in edited clips. In the first session, themes included the "What are you?" question, "Choosing Identification," "Sticking

Figure I.1. A Slide from the First Listening Session, Autumn 2018 (Artwork Courtesy of Meshell Sturgis)

WHICH BOX DO I CHECK?:
THE WHAT ARE YOU QUESTION

"I don't actually like that question. It's a device that people use to sort other people."

"If they ask me [what are you] it gets me in a different mood."

"I've started to think of my racial identity not as a binary but as a spectrum."

"It's hard speaking about race. Especially being mixed because there are so many sides."

with Your Team," and "Not Other" (Figure I.1). Each table discussed the clips, and then we opened up the conversation to the whole room with the rule that student participants had license to speak first. In fact, our rule was that any child or youth in the space could "cut the line" and grab the mic. We knew we wanted a child-centered space, but we weren't sure if our plan would work. Indeed it did! At the first session, in fact, not one adult spoke. The mic traveled from child to child, with the teenage participants speaking the most. And, throughout the sessions, the children and youth participants ruled the spaces, with even the youngest ones grabbing the mic to share their thoughts. The adults practiced their radical listening.

WHO WE INTERVIEWED

So who are these Generation Mixed kids? The children and youth who bring our book to life are the United States' newest generation, dubbed Generation Z by others (although we must note this is not a term that any of our participants themselves used). Since the global pandemic of 2020 and the ubiquity of the videoconferencing platform Zoom, they have been called "Zoomers." This generation is more racially diverse than any generation of the past. The 2010 Census reported that about half of children under the age of 5 in the United States are racial or ethnic minorities (United States Census Bureau, 2012). The mixed-race kids of this generation were born into the presidency of Barack Obama, our 44th president, a mixed-race

African American man who sang the praises of interracial unity. They are buoyed by newfound representation and language that gives both images and names to their identities: They have multiracial celebrities and stars to look up to, and names to identify under whether they are "biracial," "multiracial," "mixed race," "Blasian" (Black and Asian) Hapa, or "Whasian" (white and Asian).

We are surrounded today by more discussions of mixed race, and more explicit conversations on multiracial imagery than ever before. The sitcom *Mixed-ish* is a case study in the commonplace nature of mixed race today. In the 2010s, the television network ABC had well established itself as the network that brought diversity to mainstream family entertainment with *Modern Family* (wealthy white family with gay, transracially adopted, Latinx, Asian American members, Lloyd & Levitan, 2009–2020), *Black-ish* (wealthy Black family, Anderson et al., 2014–present), *Fresh Off the Boat* (middle-class Asian American family, Huang et al., 2015–2020). *Mixed-ish*, a spin-off of *Black-ish*, is an origin story of oldest daughter Rainbow growing up with a Black mother, white father, and two younger siblings in the 1980s (A. Anderson et al., 2019–present). The show's storylines ham-handedly constrain young Generation X Rainbow's racialized identity choices in ways both convergent and divergent with the stories our Generation Mixed children describe. In every episode of season one up until the season finale Rainbow struggles through middle school identity choices as imprimaturs of her "Black" or "white" identity, while in the last episode after experiencing explicit anti-Black racism she comes to the realization that while she would be seen as Black, and more than simply seen, racialized, a term we will go into in the next section, that she is also mixed race; indeed that she is mixed-race African American. Despite the awkwardness of how the show handles race, the primetime showing of *Mixed-ish* feels, in some ways to these Generation X authors, nothing short of revolutionary: Mixed race is now common enough to enter into the ultimate hallmark of mainstream Americana—sitcoms.

Thus, Generation Mixed kids hear versions of their stories on television, in social media, in activism. But they do not necessarily hear them echoed or affirmed by their teachers and administrators. And despite a boom of multiracial imagery, Generation Mixed children and youth are coming of age during the era of a 45th president who marked his presidency by activating a barely dormant white supremacy and riding the waves of an explicitly virulent racism little seen in the lifetimes of their parents. Their own young lives have seen an uptick in race-motivated hate crimes from when President Obama left office to the 45th president taking over the White House. According to the FBI, race-motivated hate crimes in 2016–2018 are 56% higher than in 2013–2015 in Washington state where we conducted our research. Nationwide over the same period of time, race-motivated hate crimes are up 33% (FBI, n.d.). Not only have these crimes increased, but so has the exposure children have to the viral images of these crimes. Death after death of a Black person at the hands of police escalated to the viral broadcasting of George Floyd being murdered while calling for his mother and gasping "I can't breathe." The set of challenges this generation of mixed-race children faces is different than the challenges faced by previous generations of multiracial folks. Some of their schools have educational policies that support antiracist curriculum and race-based affinity groups, but many of their schools fail to provide either curricular or extracurricular supports that even acknowledge the demographic diversity within their walls.

This is the generation of "digital natives," or those who were born into technology, who live their lives equally in person and on social media. Although they may consume fewer hours of television than Generation X, typically their parents' age, and Baby Boomers, typically their grandparents' age, they are more adept at using smartphones as a central hub for television, games, social media, and more (Turner, 2015). This means that they not only consume representations of themselves as young mixed-race people, but also are exposed to uncontrollable images of viral death, hatred, disaster, and human-made atrocities. It is not that this generation is new to coping with trauma and violence and hate; it is the scale at which these things are now available, and lacking the ability to control what they see, that is new. This group of children and youth are likely to have watched the murders of Philando Castile, George Floyd, and others over and over again within the palm of their hands.

But this generation is also not remaining complacent about the racialized violence that they are witnessing. The murder of George Floyd, coming on the heels of so many other viral murders of Black people, sparked protests and uprisings around the world. Youth are attending and often leading these marches and rallies. Even before the great protests of 2020, Generation Z, and certainly the members of Generation Z that we interviewed from the Seattle area, were likely to have participated in youth-lead walkouts and national protests about Black Lives Matter and other forms of racialized violence, including climate change. These children and youth are also part of a generation of activism and the visibility of that activism in large scale. They are tackling issues of racism, gun violence, climate change, gender discrimination, trans representation, to name just a few. Not only are they witnessing mass protests internationally, but young people are leading these movements.

These are also children who have had their educational experiences fundamentally upended by COVID-19. They have had their major milestones radically altered by shelter in place, with virtual classes, prom dresses only worn for the camera, and even drive-through graduations. They have had to miss out on so much: the touch of a friend, and the "normal" occasions of playing, going out, and kicking it on the field. The landscape of childhood and adolescence looks very different for this generation not only due to violence, technology, and a global pandemic, but also the ways in which this generation has tackled these challenges with innovation, determination, and grit. The radical listening of this book allows us to understand to these kids. This work is not about hearing the stories of how mixed-race kids fail as the passive recipients of inequitable educational systems or racism, or even how the system fails them, but rather about how they fight inequalities as agents of change and power. And how we can uplift their words and fight hard for them. (See Appendix B for a chart of the students whose stories you will hear in this book.)

LANGUAGE, TERMINOLOGY, AND RADICAL LISTENING AS EPISTEMOLOGY

In using the phrase "mixed race" (which we use with a hyphen when deployed as an adjective, and without a hyphen as a noun), we are making the very deliberate choice to center what we understand to be a problematic concept in 21st-century U.S. life: race. Although we have introduced the concept of race already, as it is central to the construction of our book, we want to underscore it here. And yet, like so many scholarly conversations about race, this one must begin with a disclaimer. We understand that race is constructed. It's not real. Sociologists Michael Omi and Howard Winant summed up this paradox in their formulation of the notion of racialization (1986). Racialization holds the reality that race has no biological basis. It was something fabricated in order to exploit differences and create and consolidate white privilege, which happened most effectively by creating and consolidating Black and brown disenfranchisement. We use the term "racialization," or the adjective "racialized," in order to illuminate Generation Mixed participants' paradoxical experiences of race. But it also bears very real weight in our world. Furthermore, when we say "mixed race," which we use interchangeably with "multiracial" and occasionally "mixed," we mean two different racialized groups, that is, some combination of Black, Latinx, Native American, Asian American, and white; not, for example, Irish American and German American (which we would read as white). We use the term "minoritized" instead of "minority" to denote "power relations in the construction of the so-called minority/majority divide . . . [w]hereas minority means smaller in numbers, minoritized means smaller in power in a racialized economy that systematically denigrates people of color" (Joseph, 2017, p. 3307). Indeed, we use the more established term "people of color," and not the newer BIPOC (Black Indigenous People of Color) simply because it was emerging in popular parlance when we were completing our final edits.

But the term that you will hear the most here is race. Race perhaps should more accurately be known by what Karen E. Fields and Barbara J.

Fields (2012) call *racecraft*. "Racecraft," Fields and Fields write, is "distinct from *race* and *racism*," in that it "does not refer to groups or ideas about groups' traits. . . . It refers instead to mental terrain and to pervasive belief. Like physical terrain, racecraft exists objectively; it has topographical features that Americans regularly navigate, and we cannot readily stop traversing it. Unlike physical terrain, racecraft originates not in nature but in human action and imagination; it can exist in no other way" (Fields & Fields, 2012, pp. 18–19). Fields and Fields enter into their compelling book of the same name by using the case of mixed race to illustrate that the concept of race has, and continues to be, a manipulable fiction. The authors note, for example, that the contemporary terms "biracial" and "multiracial" ("us" terms claimed by contemporary people asserting mixed-race heritage) "rehabilitate," in their words, the anachronistic and racially antiquated terms "mulatto," "quadroon," and "octoroon" ("them" terms applied to people assumed to have mixed-race heritage) (2012, p. 2). Fields and Fields go as far as designating those who utilize the descriptor of "monoracial," or those coming from a single racial background, as those who trade in "recycled racist fiction" (p. 3), meaning that all conceptions of race must acknowledge multiraciality. Following Fields and Fields' logic, perpetuating the fantasy of "mixing" races propagates the fantasy that race must be real.

As the concept of mixed race cannot exist without a claim to the very reality of race, we acknowledge that, for better or for worse, claiming mixed-race identity does further solidify the idea that race is a reality. In writing this book we are saying that mixed-race children's identities are different enough from other children's racialized identities to dedicate a study to them; our scholarship thus participates in the project of making race more real, which is the process of racecraft. However, like Fields and Fields, we see and lament the connections between race and racism. As scholars we are incredibly skeptical of reifying race in the language that we use to racialize ourselves and our children.

But at the same time, refuting racialization is also refusing to see how power operates. Race is here, whether or not we want it. As parents of mixed-race children and as race facilitators, and in the case of Allison, as a psychologist, we also understand the necessity of having access to racializing language that feels as though it fits. Racialized labels, particularly those that are self-determined, can provide access to agency. Thus, when we describe the participants in this project we will describe them in two ways, both of which have been determined by them: We describe them with the racial label(s) they tell us that they use in and out of school, and we will describe them with the list of races/ethnicities they filled out on the demographic forms for us (or in the case of the very young children who were not filling out the paperwork themselves, the labels they told their parents to put down for them on the demographic forms). We have also used the pseudonyms our participants (or in some cases, their parents) chose for themselves. Although we would not go as far as categorizing this research as Youth Participatory Action Research (YPAR), as the students themselves were not involved in research production, tenets of YPAR that direct researchers to radically listen to students guided us (Anyon et al., 2018a; Caraballo et al., 2017).

Nevertheless, our attempts at careful language can only attempt to approximate a snapshot moment of the incredible fluidity that multiracial people enact on a daily basis when it comes to racialization and racialized labels; we also understand that while we invited students to identify the ways in which they identified racially/ethnically at school and asked if that label changed in any school context, our writing cannot capture that full complexity. Our research was limited to conversations and dialogues we had in a controlled (studio) setting, online, telephone, and in-person correspondence after the interviews, and the children's and youth's participation in radical listening session(s). As such, we did not engage in the type of participant observation that would allow us to see, for example, how a student might identify a shift in identity from context to context or multiple identities in action in a single space. We attempted to capture the fluidity of students' identities in their accounts throughout the book, but we could not accurately capture all of the hows and whys of those changes; the fluidity of mixed-race children's and youth's identities was simply too dynamic. We did our best. We identify our participants with language that transforms situationally, that changes and shifts (almost) as often as race itself changes and shifts.

Articulating multiple racialized identities or becoming a "shape shifter," as historian Paul Spickard (2020) documents, isn't a new phenomenon, as "at different times in their lives, or over generations in their families, as they have moved from one social context to another, or as new social contexts have been imposed on them, [shape shifters have changed] their identities . . . from one group to another" (p. 6). Furthermore, as sociologist Miri Song (2010) notes, we have to understand that for mixed-race people, the racialization to which shapeshifting is a response is itself a "long-term albeit changeable, process in which they are shaped by a variety of factors, including parental upbringing, the ethnic composition of an individual's neighborhood and school and exposure to one's extended family" (p. 267). *Generation Mixed Goes to School* attempts to radically listen to multiracial children and youth in the middle of their changing process of racialization and shapeshifting. This book is a radical listening session about how Generation Mixed lives race in school.

GROUNDING OUR WORK IN CRITICAL MIXED RACE STUDIES

Although we draw from psychology, education, and critical race scholarship, our work exceeds the boundaries of each of those categories. As such our work also fits into the subfield of Critical Mixed Race Studies (CMRS). To situate our work in CMRS, we must first historicize what comes before Critical Mixed Race Studies, which is to say, mixed-race studies (before the prefix "critical"). Current CMRS scholars, including literary theorist Cedric Essi (2017) and sociologist Miri Song (2017), cite anthropologist Jayne O. Ifekwunigwe's (2004) edited collection *'Mixed Race' Studies: A Reader* as presenting a fundamental insight into the three moments when mixed-race people move in the literature from being objects to subjects to actors (2004, pp. 8–17). The first, the Age of Pathology, is the moment at which racist pseudoscientists demeaned mixed race as a disastrous entity. The second, the Age of Celebration, is when the pendulum swung back the other way, as scholars reclaimed personhood for those of multiracial descent (Root, 1992; Root, 1996; Spickard, 1989; Zack, 1995). In this "coming out" moment of mixed-race studies, the redemption (if not heralding) of the multiracial subject was key. A number of the authors described their personal, not just intellectual, cleavages to mixed race: Some of these authors self-identified as mixed race, and some self-identified as interracially married partners and parents of mixed-race children. In other words, they have a very personal stake in the work. For them, the scholarship was a tool for justifying and celebrating the existence of multiracial people. The third, the Age of Critique, is the current, CMRS era, where even greater numbers of multiracial authors (and those who aren't mixed race are often interracially partnered and parenting mixed-race children; in other words, they have a very personal stake in the work) produce scholarship on a myriad of topics related to mixed race.

The Age of Celebration produced a good deal of scholarship on the visual aspects of being mixed race, or "looking mixed," which has really acted as a proxy for looking "racially ambiguous." In *Bulletproof Diva* (1994), essayist Lisa Jones delineates all of the questions denoting racial ambiguity, that mixed-race people continually field, from "what are you?" to "where are you from?" to "who are your people?" Literary theorist Hortense Spillers (2011) notes that racial ambiguity, which she deems "looking that way," is "probably about seven centuries old by now" (pp. 2–3). Such historicizing is key as it pokes a hole in the positioning of mixed-race people as new, unique, and never before seen. However, the historical fact of multiraciality doesn't prevent contemporary questioning about "looking that way." Indeed, as literary scholar Molly McKibbin (2018) argues, "Racially ambiguous people are asked to identify themselves, but their self-naming is an arduous task because of a number of factors, including the desire to belong or be accepted as however they label themselves and the lack of vocabulary available to label themselves within the first place" (p. 69). As we will explore in this book, our participants certainly had the desire to be accepted as themselves, but most of them had a wide variety of self-naming options at their fingertips.

Much scholarship in multiracial studies worked through this notion of the "what are you?" question, to the extent that one of the founders of multiracial studies, psychologist Maria P. P. Root (1996), authored a still well-circulated "Bill of Rights for Racially Mixed People" that defends those with so-called ambiguous looks from having to delineate their racialized identities publicly (p. 7). Myra S. Washington posits that Root's "Bill of Rights," "rhetorically positioned Blacks as trapping biracial people into Blackness through enforcement of the one-drop rule" (Washington, 2017, p. 8). Such barely concealed anti-Blackness was at the heart of both the multiracial movement and multiracial scholarship. Although this work was important in many ways, especially in terms of providing a platform to listen to self-identified multiracial voices, because the work centered personal choice to the exclusion of other issues of power, such as institutionalized, historic, and even, to a certain extent, interpersonal racism, some Critical Mixed Race Studies scholarship points out its serious limitations (Joseph, 2013; Sexton, 2008).

The third, the Age of Critique, is the current, CMRS era, where an even greater number of multiracial authors produce scholarship on a myriad of topics related to mixed race. CMRS emerged around the turn of the 21st century as a generation of multiracial scholars began to critique the first generation of multiracial studies scholarship that was largely celebratory or descriptive in tone and politic, but that rarely centered questions of power. The "critical" prefix signifies a focus on "power" as it does in other scholarly movements; there was a similar transition from "ethnic studies" to "critical ethnic studies," for example. The mixed-race studies, Age of Celebration, authors largely emerged from a pre-*Loving v. Virginia* moment, whereas those from CMRS, Age of Critique, are largely from a post-*Loving* moment, the Supreme Court decision that made interracial marriage legal in all 50 states.

In other words, Critical Mixed Race Studies is a movement of scholarship where mixed-race people make the full transition from objects to subjects to actors. CMRS, Myra S. Washington notes, analyzes how "the social conditions and boundaries trumpeted by early participants in the multiracial movement and mixed-race studies has exposed an uncritical embrace of whiteness and the call for the erosion of solidarity within communities of color" (Washington, 2017, p. 11). Put another way, the Age of Celebration embraces mixed-race subjects without questioning the power behind what being mixed race entails (Daniel, 2002; Root, 1996; Spickard, 1989), while the Age of Critique asks the question "what does it mean to be mixed race?" (Elam, 2011; Ibrahim, 2012; Nishime, 2014) and even, as mixed-race people are given greater opportunities to identify under a category of "mixed," "what are the pitfalls of choosing this category?" In particular, "how do we understand those that rely upon anti-Black racism?" (Joseph, 2013; Sexton, 2008; Washington, 2017).

The first question of definition might seem like a silly, obvious, or self-evident one, but given the porousness of race, it's a good one. An easy answer is that a person should be designated as mixed race if their parents are from different races, or even more specifically, from two different races. In other words, a mixed-race experience is one of being a first-generation multiracial individual born to two monoracially identified parents. But there are so many problems inherent in this essentializing formula. What if, for example, a mixed-race child is adopted by parents of a phenotype similar to theirs so they don't read as "differently" raced than their family? Are they any less mixed race? What if a mixed-race child is multigenerationally multiracial, or in other words, if their grandparents, great-grandparents, or other ancestors have been multiple races, even if their parents would choose the same box on the Census? Are they any less mixed race? Can we make room for histories and communities such as Black American ones that developed in strength because of the *one-drop rule* of hypodescent for African Americans (which counted those with any Black ancestor as Black), and thus have always been multiracial? How about using that very same one-drop rule as a source of strength and pride in Black community identification, instead of demonizing it as multiracial activists in the Age of Celebration did (Williams, 2006)? Can we make room for racialized experiences of multiplicity as articulated in Latinx or Native American communities, where race/ethnicity aren't cleanly and clearly delineated in the same manner as the one-drop rule? Keeping all of this in mind complexifies understandings of mixed race as emerging solely from a first-generation experience of two parents of two different races. And yet, holding all of these questions in tension gets us to the place where we can actually approximate real-life multiracial experiences.

Critical Mixed Race Studies, as a subfield, asks questions just like these. CMRS boasts a national conference and a journal of the same name. In the premier issue of the journal, ethnic studies scholar Andrew Jolivette (2014) writes that Critical Mixed Race Studies must resist "binaries—like right, left, conservative, liberal, Muslim, Christian, immigrant, citizen." Jolivétte's article, titled "Critical Mixed Race Studies: New Directions in the Politics of Race and Representation," asserts that such binaries "only serve to separate us from knowing who we are as a people" (2014, p. 152). Eliding such binaries means, as the Age of Critique authors demonstrate, that we can hear the stories mixed-race children and youth want to tell us about themselves. And hearing such stories—radically listening to them—is harder than it might seem because there is so much projected onto mixed race—the ultimate race cypher. As communication scholar LeiLani Nishime (2014) asserts, "Multiracial people [are invoked] as an emerging racial category to argue that they act as a stepping-stone to a race-free future" (p. 2). Put another way, by communication scholar Jasmine Mitchell, "The mixed-race body has been used to construct a racelessness that permits a liberal color blindness coded in white normativity" (Mitchell, 2020, p. 224). Thus, stories of mixed-race children and youth refute the fallacy of color blindness masquerading as a desire for whiteness. As artist and activist Louie Gong (2013) puts it, "Mixed race isn't post-race. It's not less race. It's more race . . . [I]n order to dialog about mixed race, we need more understanding. It's not a dialog to forget about issues of race" (p. 17).

We are working with the idea that understanding mixed race as more race, or what historian Greg Carter (2013) writes of as "an abundance of race" lets us engage with the structuring and multiple ideologies of racialization. We can then reject, again in Carter's words, "racelessness, color-blindness, or postraciality," and instead form a "racial identity [as] a preliminary step towards antiracist activity" (p. 227). In a similar vein, literary scholar Michele Elam (2011) explains, "Mixed race prompts us to consider that race, too, is an image that is never perceived as 'one thing' or the possession of just one person. Rather, mixed race functions as a relation among things and people" (p. 161). What Carter and Elam suggest is that mixed race does not have to be the way out of discussions of race, but rather, a way deeper into them. Deeper into race talk means deeper into Blackness, or deeper into Latinxness or Asianness or Nativeness; not deeper into whiteness, or as we will discuss in Chapter 2, not deeper into white adjacency. For subjects with African heritage, for example, literary scholar Sika Dagbovie-Mullins (2013) posits a Black multiraciality can be understood as "black sentient mixed-race subjectivity that includes a particular awareness of the world, a perception rooted in blackness" (p. 2). In the care we take with writing mixed race, race and power, we are also cautious about not conscripting multiracial children to a "special class" or reifying race in a binaristic fashion.

At the same time, we acknowledge that for those unaccustomed to mixed race, there is not something about mixedness, and even first-generation mixedness, that causes pause. Jackson and Samuels, citing Hamako, describe this pause as "*monoracism* or racism specifically targeting individuals and families who are racially mixed" (p. 2) (Hamako, 2015; Jackson & Samuels, 2019). That pause is an instantiating experience of some multiraciality. There is something about the experience of being asked "what are you?" in the classroom, on the playground, in the lunchroom; about being thought of as the white (passing) charge and not the child of your Black mother; about never being told by a teacher "you look so much like your dad!" These are not the only experiences of mixed race, but these are some that aren't largely typical in monoracial–majority schools, and so we need to thoughtfully, consciously listen to them. Such moments of racialized misrecognition or racialized confusion are where one can hear how race operates. These are the moments that make clear that nothing is self-evident about race. To call on the language of Fields and Fields, the racecraft is obvious. This is not to say that monoracial people do not experience such self-conscious race thought. Indeed, the non-multiracial Black, Native American, or Latinx child who is the only child of color in their class might not be asked "what are you?," but they might be asked "what are you doing here?" in not so many words every day of the school year. Such questioning might prompt similar levels of internal questioning such as "am I supposed to be here?," or put another way, "do I belong?" Just as these questions are inherently racialized, classed, and gendered, they also point to the porousness of race. Our approach here is not to exceptionalize mixed-race experiences of racialized difference and exclusion as monoracism alone, but to listen to mixed-race experiences as part and parcel of larger system processes of discrimination that differentially impact all children of color.

WE HOPE YOU WILL LISTEN TO OUR BOOK

As you move into the body of *Generation Mixed Goes to School*, we want to underscore that radically listening to Generation Mixed provides teachers, parents, and all who care about multiracial children and youth with a crucial insight: that these children are living the contradictions of racial formation theory. On the one hand, we hear the youth tell us that they are skeptical of race as a formation and their racialized identities flow freely with the porous nature of race. Race is always in flux for them. Such porousness is not just theoretical: It's embodied. Indeed, as 19-year-old college sophomore Oyin and her 15-year-old high school sophomore brother Olu ask in one story (see Chapter 2), if they can change racialized identities at various points in their schooling from identifying at school as Filipino to Black to Blasian, what can race mean? In other words, their changing racialized identities in changing spaces reflects the truism today that race is a construction.

On the other hand, mixed-race children and youth instinctively, strategically, and at key moments identify monoracially as the situation dictates. They understand the stakes of when singular, sometimes more politicized identifications must take precedence over multiple, sometimes more personal identifications. They are cognizant and critical of racism, and critique it when it is being deployed not just against them, but against Black and brown others in the classroom. They understand when teachers are using them as convenient "anchors" who bring a proximity to nonwhiteness but also safely approximate whiteness, as we will hear in Chapter 4, listening to Japanese American and white brothers Takuji, a 16-year-old 11th-grader who identifies as white and Asian at school, and Hiro, a 13-year-old 8th-grader who identifies as Asian. Our mixed-race youth see racism and its intersections operating not just interpersonally, but structurally, and historically as well. Thus, these children speak out against color-blind spaces not because they don't like the idea that color blindness is about "seeing everyone equally," but rather because they don't like the fact that color blindness is about seeking proximity to whiteness. Schools are not empty of race, or places where race ceases to matter. These kids tell us that race matters—race matters at school—and it matters in the ways that aren't entirely legible to those who do not know how to read multiple racialized identities. Radically listening to mixed-race children and youth, we hear them affirm the insight from the father of cultural studies Stuart Hall's (1998): identities are not "armor plated" against one another (p. 168).

The 1967 ruling in *Loving v. Virginia* legalized interracial marriage, and destigmatization followed. In 1970, a handful of years later, the U.S. Census reported that only 1% of babies living with two parents had parents from different races. As of 2013, 10% of babies living with two parents had parents from different races (Parker et al., 2015). And as we illustrated earlier in this chapter, in certain geographic areas, such as the Seattle Metropolitan Area where we conducted our research, the numbers are far greater. Moreover, Critical Mixed Race Studies scholars such as literary scholar Michele Elam (2011) and political scientist Kimberly Williams (2006) note that this population, historically, was here long before the courts and the Census recognized it. Nonetheless many school communities have yet to incorporate mechanisms for how to best listen to and then serve this historically sizable and publicly more visible demographic.

When we set out to write this book, we were struck by a statistical disparity: In 2012, 82% of K–12 teachers nationwide were white women, whereas 49% of children were children of color (U.S. Department of Education, 2016, pp. 5–6). We wondered how the teachers were able to listen to or hear children who said, "it's so hard speaking about race," as Aiyana did in the opening to this chapter. Thus, this book relies on the wisdom of mixed-race children we had the privilege of getting to know, to help answer the following questions: When the treatment of mixed-race children is largely contingent on the slippery notion of "a racialized look," how can school communities, partnerships of teachers, parents, and children fully hear, or radically listen to, mixed-race kids? And second, how do we help teachers follow the advice of 19-year-old college sophomore Oyin who identifies as Blasian?: "If you make more of a connection with your students of color then they won't feel as ostracized when they're in class, they'll trust the teachers more. Then there'll be a whole ring of respect." Oyin seeks to be listened to, and through the process of being listened to, to belong. Furthermore, Oyin emphasizes that white teachers shouldn't be afraid of kids of color, a notion a number of our participants touch on in their sessions; just as teachers encourage students to ask informed questions when they don't know the answer, Oyin says, "I'm going to tell you teachers to ask [mixed-race students] questions too."

Generation Mixed Goes to School radically listens to and weaves together stories of mixed-race children and youth, teachers, and caregivers with perspectives and research from social and developmental psychology, Critical Mixed Race Studies, and education. We listened for how children learn about race; what educators can do to foster antibiased classrooms; how race is both constructed and yet very real; and the role that race plays in structuring educational experiences. Although some other resources are available to educators, parents, and researchers on addressing bias, creating equitable classrooms and enacting race-based dialogue, this book is unique not only in that it brings together these multiple conversations, but also in that it will explicitly address issues of mixed-race children from multiple disciplines. *Generation Mixed Goes to School* investigates how implicit bias affects multiracial kids in unforeseen ways, impacting those who are read as children of color or not; how the silencing and invisibility of mixed-race experiences often create a barrier for mixed-race kids to engage in nuanced conversations about race and identity in the classroom; and how teachers are finding powerful ways to make meaningful connections with their mixed-race students. In addition, this book breaks out of the Black–white binary, a critique of some work on mixed race (Guevarra, 2012; King-O'Riain et al., 2014), to include the perspective of mixed-race children from Asian American, Latinx, and Native American backgrounds; it also diverges from scholarship on mixed race by providing the perspective of children who come from two or more communities of color, and not simply those who are from white/people of color backgrounds.

Our chapters follow this logic: In the first chapter we center how mixed-race children see, hear, and understand race through a process called racial socialization. In the second chapter, building off of racial socialization, we listen to how mixed-race kids experience change—that's often unseen or misunderstood—in their racialization, and yet they script their own stories despite others "cognitive dissonance" when they encounter them. In the third chapter we listen to how despite their efforts to be seen and heard, many mixed-race children and youth, particularly those who are part Black, experience implicit bias in school. The fourth chapter shares stories of how mixed-race children's racialized identities can be supported at school with teachers and through school supports such as affinity groups, and the fifth chapter listens to how some multiracial families struggle with racial literacy, and others practice it daily. Each chapter provides hands-on exercises for how to radically listen to mixed-race children and youth in the process of change-making.

We want to note that the participants spoke race clearly and consistently; perhaps this was because of the limitations of our questions or the way in which we narrated our topic. They came to answer a call about school-age youth with multiple racial backgrounds, for example. Although we are intersectional scholars and we listened for moments of students' intersectional intervention, our book here emerges from our students' stories, and the stories speak race. Although gender, or sexuality, or class might be woven in at various moments, they focused on race and we followed suit. Accordingly, the pages that follow will help you not only radically listen to mixed-race children as they develop racial identities, but as you develop your own skills to create healthy, antiracist school environments in which teachers, parents, and others listen to and benefit all children.

Throughout the book we share stories of success and challenge from children, youth, and family members speaking to their teachers and class-mates. Many of these stories focus on the ability or failure of members of a school community to listen to a child's self-identified mixed-race heritage. These stories illuminate how school communities can develop skills of radi-cally listening to mixed-race kids. We are writing this book for classroom teachers, teacher education students, administrators, and families—in short, for all of the people who are thinking about, constructing, and maintaining school communities as well as engaging in the day-to-day interactions with our mixed-race kids. Our goal is to help kids be heard. *Generation Mixed Goes to School* asks: How do we take this moment to listen to mixed-race kids, fully and completely as they tell their own stories, and to fully and completely hear how their stories speak back to their racialization in a racist world? We hope you will radically listen.

RADICAL LISTENING WITH YOUR CRITICAL FRIEND

Each chapter in this book will include a radical listening exercise, and you will end this chapter practicing the first one. As we mentioned earlier in this chapter, radical listening is a key component of Ralina's Interrupting Privilege program. In this program each participant has what's known as a *critical friend*. We hope that you can read this book with a critical friend; even more than that, we will give you exercises in each chapter to do with your critical friend. But first, how do you pick your critical friend? Think about choosing a person who can support you with care; think about a true interlocutor who isn't scared to tell you when you are wrong, when you're not being vulnerable, or when you're not being truthful.

The critical friend model was developed by the Annenberg Institute for School Reform at Brown University, and it's intended as a feedback mecha-nism in challenging work; critical friends help us see the blind spots that we have difficulty seeing ourselves (Appleby, 1998; Cushman, 1998; Bambino, 2002). Feedback from critical friends can come in three different modes. The first mode is that of "warm" feedback, whereby a critical friend gives encouraging, enthusiastic statements intended to bolster the work of their critical friend. In order for people to hear a critique, they must first under-stand that their work has been appreciated, even in some small mode. This first level of engagement is intended as a means of pure support and is neces-sary before any additional critique can happen. The second mode response is that of a "cool" and more impartial form of feedback, which might be in the form of asking questions. In the third mode of feedback, a critical friend provides "hard" feedback, which is challenging in nature and might in fact contain explicit concerns. Each of these forms of feedback builds on the previous mode, and we believe that the "cool" feedback must only happen after "warm" and that the "hard" feedback" must only happen after both "warm" and "cool" feedback sessions (even if those are brief). Critical friends help us process through difficult feelings. In order to make a substantive change in your life you must have a space to process and a supportive person with whom to process. We are hoping you will find both as you embark on this book.

You will partner with your critical friend for each chapter's radical listening exercise, which will contain prompts that correspond to the topic of the chapter. After reading and thinking about them, please take turns with your critical friend by sharing out your thoughts. Specifically, you will carry out the following Interrupting Privilege version of serial testimony from whiteness studies scholar Peggy McIntosh's critical education project (McIntosh et al., 2015). First, set your timer for 2 minutes and determine who will go first in the speaker order. Each speaker will answer the same prompt without intervention from the listener. The speaker is to answer the question as fully as possible, without concern over how one's words will land with the listener. The listener is to listen as fully as possible, without concern over how what the listener is saying fits with or diverges from their own points of view. For this very first radical listening exercise, as part of heading into the body of the book, you and your partner will respond to some of the dialogue prompts that we gave our Generation Mixed participants:

- What have your parents taught you about race and your racial identity?
- What have your teachers taught you about race and your racial identity?
- As a parent, what do you think you are teaching your kids about race?
- As a teacher, what are you teaching your kids about race?

Please discuss, and then read on!

CHAPTER 1

From (G)race to Race

Racial Identity Development and Mixed-Race Kids

Race is neither a transcendental topic across geography, across class, nor, as you will see in our research, across age. Jaylen, a 9-year-old 4th-grader who identifies at school as Asian and has Filipino, Korean, Native American, and Chinese American heritage, answered our question, "Do you guys understand what race is?," by eagerly responding, "Yeah! It's something when you do dinner or something and then when you do church."

His wise 10-year-old, 5th-grade big sister Mila, who also identifies as Asian at school and has the same ethnic background, quickly cuts him off by exclaiming emphatically, "That's not race! That's grace! Color! Skin color!"

Not deterred, Jaylen pipes back in with one word quickly tumbling over the next. His race, he says, to answer the next question of how he understands his own race, is "a tan, Asian skin color, kind of black, I don't know what I have."

Not to be outdone, Mila adds that her race is "like a yellowish white kind of, a dark tan."

We ask if Jaylen has ever had that question before, and he says that he has "never before" gotten that question. But Mila says that she has and when people asked her, "I usually tell them about my parents. I tell them that my dad is mixed and my mom is Korean."

As Mila says she sometimes forgets the specificities of their father's background, Jaylen chimes in helpfully saying, "He's Filipino, he's Native American. And then he's Asian." Jaylen pauses just momentarily, continuing, "And then he has a lot of relatives." Although Mila responds after hearing this list by saying, "I think I am just Asian." Jaylen agrees with some extrapolation, "I think I am Asian American and then different kinds because I have a long, long line of family."

Another mixed-race brother–sister pair, 15-year-old Grayson and 13-year-old Aiyana, who are African American and white, and tell us they identify as both mixed or Black and white at school, do not need to be prompted to ask if they understand race; in fact, such a question would have resulted in their incredulous balking at us. These two describe how they understand their race partially by describing how they respond to the ubiquitous "what are you?" question that Critical Mixed Race Studies scholars have document-ed as the *ur* inquiry for those read as racially ambiguous. Both Grayson and Aiyana agree that their canned answer to those who ask about their race is to say that they are "a mix between African American and white." However, Grayson explains that although his answers are consistent, his interrogators respond differently to this answer as different people read his identity differ-ently. In his previous school, for example, a large, predominantly Black public middle school, he was racialized as white by his peers, whereas at his current school, a small, predominantly white private school where he attends high school, he is racialized as Black. Aiyana notes that Grayson is asked about his racial background far more often than she because, as she puts it, most people "actually assume that I'm white." In contrast, Grayson describes how he is forced to narrate his racialized identity through the "what are you?" question way too often for his taste, as, in his words, "it's a device that people use to sort other people into sort of like"—and here he pauses as Aiyana completes his thought for him, saying, "boxes."

These two sets of siblings' conversations offer glimpses into the com-plexities of racial identity development for mixed-race youth and children. In the first pair (who are 9 and 10 years old), Jaylen is so unaccustomed to talk-ing about race that he first confuses "race" and "grace," but with his sister Mila's clarification, both children quickly begin talking about how they un-derstand both their parents' and their own racialization. In the second pair, the adolescents (who are 13 and 15 year years old) toggle between a sophis-ticated conversation of their own internal understanding of their multiple racializations and an articulation of how their racial identities are read by outsiders. In both sets of siblings, one recalls being asked about their racial background, and one does not. Race emerges as an easy topic of conversation for all four mixed-race siblings, and by radically listening to their experiences we will hear what these kids need in order to feel as though they belong: We hear the ways in which the friction of race—or how ideas surrounding questions of race and racialization should cause us to slow down and listen more—meets the fluidity of multiracial experiences. In this chapter we lay the groundwork for radically listening to what it means to be a member of Generation Mixed, illuminating racial development models, and thinking about what existing models can tell us about mixed-race kids. Furthermore, in addition to radically listening to our Generation Mixed students, we also radically listen to the scholarship on mixed-race children and youth that, as we will see, is just beginning to hear the complexities of multiraciality.

HOW DO YOU UNDERSTAND RACE?

Social developmental theory gives us a foundation to understand how children make sense of race. Although racial understanding varies according to a child's age, geographic location, class, gender, context, temperament, and more, the field of psychology has pointed to some basic and common cognitive processes by which children make sense of race (Aboud & Doyle, 1996a; Aboud & Doyle, 1996b; Bigler & Liben, 1993). Understanding them will help us contest common prevailing ideas about children's "race-lessness" or rather, ideologies of color blindness that espouse the notion that children are a *tabula rasa* when it comes to race. In actuality, children are "scientists in the crib" (Gopnik et al., 1999) and are often trying to make sense of the racialized world around them. In the following exercise you will explore this foundational notion.

Radical Listening Exercise: Remembering Race, Listening to Race

As with all of your radical listening exercises, you will do this exercise with your critical friend. This exercise will serve two purposes: (1) You are going to have the opportunity to think deeply about your own racialization, and (2) you are going to have the opportunity to try a second radical listening exercise. Let's begin this exercise with an experiment: *Think back to your first race-related memory—the first time you remember hearing about race, encountering it, noticing it. Try to engage your sensory memory.*

After you have conjured your memory, set a 2-minute timer for the first speaker. Share it in as much detail as possible with your critical friend. Fully describe your thoughts and feelings, and don't worry about what your listening partner might think about your story. In other words, please try not to anticipate their invalidating your story, having guilt about hearing it, or even resonating with it. Simply share it. For the listeners, please focus your full attention on the words of your partner. Try hard not to evaluate or judge their experience, or do anything outside of fully hearing it. Remain silent during these 2 minutes, giving affirmation such as head nods or "um hmms" where it feels comfortable. But try not to frown, or shake your head, or otherwise register nonverbal disagreement with the story. If your partner gets stuck in attempting to tell the story, you can ask them encouraging, dialogue-building questions such as "tell me more," "what's that like?," and "please help me understand." By the same token, avoid dialogue-halting questions such as "well," "but," or "what about?" This is an exercise in affirming stories that are often hard to speak: our first stories about race. Here are your prompts as you conjure that first race-related memory with your critical friend:

- What do you see? Hear? Smell? Touch?
- How old are you?
- Is this a positive or negative memory?
- Who is there—your friends, family, or strangers? Are you at school, home, or another place?

- Did you process it immediately after it happened with a loved one, or did you keep it all bottled up inside?

Take another moment to reflect on this memory. If you "can't think of anything," what do you think this lack of an early race memory means about the role of race in your life? Note if your first contact with race comes much later for you than in childhood.

Welcome back!

As facilitators and professors, we have brought this exercise to thousands of people in the classes, talks, and consultations that we give on race. When we ask people to share their first race-related memory, we tend to get two kinds of answers. One large group of people indicates that they remember their first race-related experience as happening when they were between the ages of 2 and 9. This first group has tended to grow up in heterogenous, diverse spaces, where from a very young age they encountered people who were racially different from them. Then there is another group, who have their first race-related memory much later, maybe in late adolescence or early adulthood. This latter group, on average, is made up of those people who grew up in predominantly homogenous contexts in which one race was present or dominant. This group includes those people who grew up in another, more homogenous country and immigrated to the United States later in their lives. This latter group helps us think about how race is constructed for people who immigrate to the United States. They are often thrust into the particular "American" context of race, which is markedly different than that of their country of origin.

This exercise helps participants immediately challenge the notion of color blindness or "racelessness" of children. Children are, in fact, noticing and paying attention to race very early; they are not doing it in the same ways that adults do, but they are noticing race. And mixed-race children, particularly those who are first-generation multiracial or who are raised by parents of two different races, might, in fact, be "doing race" in some markedly different ways simply because their caregivers look different. But to get to the important studies about how mixed-race children "do race," one first has to wade through some formative studies in psychology that examined monoracial children and their racialization.

SEEING DIFFERENCE/HEARING DIFFERENCE

One way that race works is through a notion of being racially aware. Neville et al. (2000) write that those with racial awareness understand the reality of racial hierarchies as well as the idea that color blindness is a fallacy. In other words, if you have racial awareness, you can address the real-world reality of racialized difference as well as the real-world issues of racism. One mother described how she observed racial awareness growing in her own daughter. Emily, who participated in the dialogue with her 12-year-old, 7th-grade daughter Mara, described how she observed Mara's process of racial awareness grow as she moved through elementary school: "I just noticed her talking about [race] more. I noticed her noticing it more." Emily continued, giving Mara credit for the observations around race she was most likely doing, even if it wasn't in direct conversation with her mom: "She most likely always notices it, but I heard her verbalizing it more." Emily, who is white, and Mara, who identifies as African American at school, moved through the interview together in ways that illustrated not just Emily's sensitivity to Mara's racial identity, but her keen sense of racial awareness.

As we noted in the Introduction, the research on the basic processes of race, including racial awareness within mixed-race children, has been scant at best. The majority of scholarship in psychology has examined race-based developmental processes solely within monoracially defined Black and white populations (even if we understand the historical multiraciality in Black American populations, in particular; again, we are thinking through the racialization of first-generation multiracial children). However, one study by psychologist Sarah Gaither and her colleagues recently sought to investigate how mixed-race infants—in other words, those who grow up in homes with parents or caregivers of multiple races—might fare on tests that rate prolonged gazes. This initial work suggests that when infants have ready access to caregivers who are of different races, their processing of racially diverse faces is different than children who see less racially diverse faces (Gaither et al., 2012).

In previous work, babies have been found to be able to better distinguish faces from within their own racial group, but not those of other racial groups—this is called the other-race effect (ORE) (Bar-Haim et al., 2006; Kelly et al., 2005; Sangrigoli et al., 2005). However, the ORE was found to *not* be true for 3-month-old mixed-race Asian and white infants. In other words, one preliminary investigation of mixed-race babies provides initial evidence that these children are processing faces *differently* than their monoracial peers. The researchers noted that they were the first to examine biracial children and that the majority of previous work had not only examined monoracial infants, but infants who lived in nondiverse, homogenous locations. All this means that what little evidence we have about how mixed-race infants may be processing race is that it is different from how monoracial infants in homogenous settings are processing race. The word is still out on what might cause such differential processing, although it's important to note that the study's authors hypothesize that diverse context matters (Gaither et al., 2012).

DIFFERENCE AS BAD VERSUS DIFFERENCE AS SPECIAL

The conversation thus far has indicated that children are not "raceless," and in fact they are seeing race and noticing difference very early. In talking with parents, white parents in particular often express a concern that if they or their children notice racial difference that will automatically translate into their children seeing difference as bad, or wrong—that talking about difference encourages bias. In fact, this concern often stops parents from talking about race. In countless engagements with parents we have heard, "But I don't want them to notice that there is a difference." Or, "won't pointing out that their skin color is different make them feel bad?" Sometimes they say, "Teaching children about racial differences feels like teaching them to be racist." This equating of difference with bad is not a *fait accompli*. Rather, talking with children, and radically listening to their observations about difference, is vitally important because it gives parents an opportunity to interrupt the moments before observing difference becomes equating difference with negativity. And listening to children talk about difference can illustrate, as one of our 7-year-old interviewees illustrates, that it can also mean *extra special*.

When Yuriko, a Japanese American and white 7-year-old in the 1st grade sits down to share her experience with Ann, her Hawaiian, Japanese American mother, Eliot, her Hawaiian, mixed-race Japanese American and white cousin, and us, she enjoys talking about difference. Yuriko tells us, "I like being different so everybody's not like the same. Everybody's not the same hair color, not the same voice."

Ann then asks her, "What do you like about being different?"

Yuriko responds, "I like to be different because I like to be unique in my own way."

Ann asks back, "Is that something that you would communicate to your teacher?" and the little girl says in assent, "Mm hmm."

"What would you say?" Ann follows up.

The little girl says self-assuredly, "I would say I like to be unique in my own way."

Ann tells us that Yuriko's small private school is quite homogenous, and that her daughter was one of the only children of color who attends it. As a result, their family worked hard to connect Yuriko to her Japanese American and Hawaiian heritage. In addition, their conversations of difference also meant that their race talk also converged frequently around the topic of mixed race. Eliot came to the interview as well and freely shared experiences that were perhaps decades in the future for Yuriko.

Another young Generation Mixed participant, 5-year-old Caleb, also participated in frequent talk of race and identity with his family, and particularly with his mixed-race Vietnamese American and white mother Linda. Linda, who is a teacher by profession, arrived at the interview with a big bag full of snacks and activities for Caleb, who smiled readily and was intrigued by our small sound studio. Caleb, whose father is also a teacher and also mixed-race Asian American, in his case Japanese American and white, exhibited his fond affection for and closeness to his mother by sitting alternately on her lap and stroking her leg. While, as is appropriate for a 5-year-old, he spent much of the interview coloring and passively listening as his mother shared stories with us, he perked up in the interview when his mother told us one of his favorite tales. Linda prefaced what she was about to tell us with "I have a funny story" as Caleb excitedly nudged her on. Linda narrated:

> A few years ago, about 3 years ago, he was in day care. One of the things that I've tried to start to do is celebrate Tet, which is like the biggest holiday for Vietnamese, it's their New Year. So, he had his *ao dai*, his costume. We got red envelopes, and I went on YouTube, and I learned how to say Happy New Year in Vietnamese, which is—and I'm going to totally butcher it—but it's *Chúc Mừng Năm Mới*. We would say that and we practiced it and went to day care. So everybody sat in a circle and Caleb passed out his red envelopes to all his friends. Miss Denise said, "Okay, Caleb. Did you want to tell your friends Happy New Year? Or do you want to tell your friends something?" And he looked at her with kind of a quizzical look, and he goes "*Uno dos tres*, Happy New Year." And she just busted up laughing. It's one of my favorite stories. I was like, "Okay, obviously we need to work on this a little bit more."

As she tells us this story, we all break into laughter: We are taking our cues from both Linda and Caleb. Caleb, clearly pleased with this story, and grinning broadly, turns to his mother and says, "Can you tell that story again?" Linda smiles at him, says "later," and goes on to tell us that this is one of his favorite stories. However, this story could have been told differently. Caleb is grasping that he has race, but he identifies it incorrectly as he knows he's supposed to say a phrase in another language, but he gets the wrong one. Although Caleb and Linda could have narrated this story as one of cultural failure, as one of shame and Caleb's (and even Linda's) inability to perform race correctly, instead they show how sometimes we simply "need to work on this a little bit more," and also, lovingly laugh at ourselves in the process. They bring joy into racial socialization, even when it goes "wrong."

Thus, as modeled by Ann, Eliot, Yuriko, Caleb, and Linda, recognizing racial difference is not a cause for alarm. Quite the opposite, in fact. For years, studies have found that children like Yuriko who recognize differences from an early age show a stronger general ability to identify subtle variances between categories such as color, shape, and size—which, in turn, has been linked to higher performance on intelligence tests (Aboud, 1988). Furthermore, researcher Frances Aboud (1988) has found that children between the ages of 4 and 7 who show this advanced ability to identify and categorize differences are actually less prejudiced. This cognitive flexibility is the ability to understand that things and people can be part of multiple groups and multiple categories; in other words, someone exhibiting cognitive flexibility could assert that a person could both be in the "smart" category and the "Black" category. Cognitive flexibility develops over time for all children.

As for mixed-race children specifically, Sarah Gaither's work again seems to indicate that the "work" of seeing and noticing multiple races actually translates into differential cognitive processing, in other words, greater cognitive flexibility. In her research on adults, Gaither et al. (2015) found that when multiracial adults were primed to think about their multiple racial identities, they demonstrated more flexibility and creativity than monoracial adults. Furthermore, work by Gocłowska and Crisp (2014) has shown that the challenges that multiracial people face of thinking in multiple ways in regard to identity might have benefits. Their work found integrating two identities that might be at odds enhances creativity. Likewise, Gaither's initial data with multiracial children found that those who were encouraged to think about their multiple identities demonstrated *more* cognitive flexibility and creativity than those who weren't primed to think about their mixed race. In other words they were able to solve more problems and score higher on creativity tests than those who were *not* encouraged to think about and pay attention to their multiple identities (Gaither et al., 2019). Hughes et al. (2006) write that, "By asking children to reflect earlier on during development about their multiple identities, children could experience a positive form of affirmation and shift how they see outgroup members in their social worlds."

The opportunity here is to discover what researchers learn in an experimental manipulation, encouraging kids to think about their identities, and what could be done by actual parents and teachers, in relationship with children. Parents and teachers encouraging children to think about their racial identities, talking with children about their different racial identities, and radically listening to all matter of their race talk, is a particular form of racially aware parenting and teaching that refutes color blindness. Confirming this idea, Hughes et al. (2006) "suggest that 'colorblind' parenting and educational strategies are not necessarily effective; instead, conversations that facilitate open discussions about racism and intergroup conflict may be more beneficial" (Hughes et al., 2007). Our Generation Mixed participants, as you will see throughout this book, wanted to share their voices in these very types of open discussions.

CHILDREN'S BRAINS AND RACE

The research on how children notice race should encourage adults who work with children to support children in noticing difference and engaging in difference as a way to move toward more flexibility and understanding.

As we see with Linda and Caleb, Linda is modeling loving acceptance of where Caleb is developmentally. We also need to appreciate that while young children and even adolescents are asking, watching, or learning about race, they are doing so with children's perspectives and children's brains. We cannot import our adult understanding, which often means our adult fears of race, into a child's mind. We need to hold the notion that children and adolescents are developing and changing and that their brains and understandings are growing. It's important that we appreciate the ways that brain development affects children's understanding of race.

For example, there is a common developmental task called conservation that may be at the heart of understanding how young children make sense of race. In this task a child is shown two glasses of a colored juice. Both of the glasses are of the same short and fat size, shape, and dimension (see Figure 1.1). These glasses have the same amount of juice inside of them. The children are asked to indicate which glass has more juice, or if the glasses have the same amount. Children in the experiment respond that they understand that both glasses hold the same amount of juice. Then after indicating they know the amounts are the same, they are asked to watch while one of the shorter, fatter glasses of liquid is poured into a very tall, skinny glass; after this, the liquid in the skinny glass is higher than in the original short, fat glass. Children are then asked the same question: Does one of the glasses have more juice in it, or do the glasses have the same amount? Most children under the age of 7 or 8 *fail* this task. In other words, very young children say that the taller, skinnier glass actually has more liquid in it. They have failed to understand conservation, meaning that they don't understand that changing the physical properties of an object doesn't mean an actual object itself.

Canadian researchers Anna-Beth Doyle and Frances Aboud (1995) take this understanding of child development and conservation and apply it to how children learn about race. For example, if children haven't mastered conservation, they don't understand that race is conserved, or that race can't be given, altered, modified, or shared. Often many of the ways that children play with race are along these lines of development. Doyle and Aboud (1995) have discovered that children under the age of 8 tend to think of race as something flexible that can be altered or shared—by, say, laying in the sun and getting darker or touching someone's darker skin and having the color rub off.

Aggie, the mother of one of our participants, told a story that illustrates the way that conservation works with mixed-race children in particular. Her son, 10-year-old 5th-grader Kai, identifies at school as Black and Mexican, and comes from a Black, white, and Mexican background. Aggie, who is African American, told us:

> We talk a lot about race at home, and the kids knew from very little
> that they were Black, white, and Mexican. I remember when he was

Figure 1.1. Cartoon illustrating the process of conservation (Artwork courtesy of Meshell Sturgis)

about 5 or 6, a day after we had gotten home from a swim class Kai said, "Mama, Mama, I figured it out! This part [*here Aggie gestures to Kai pointing to the darker-tanned part of his leg*] is where my Black is. And this part [*here Aggie shows how Kai pulls up his pants to reveal the whiter part of his thigh*] is where my white part is. But I just can't figure out where the Mexican is."

Aggie laughs and says, "We laughed so hard at that together, and he gets a kick when I tell that story. His sister really loves to hear it."

Young Kai's thoughts on race provide a classic example of how children are trying to make sense of race by thinking of it as something that is purely associated with skin color, and that "lives" in certain parts of the body. This example also gives an opportunity to deeply listen to how mixed-race children might be engaging in this process. Kai is very literal in his thinking about where his "Black, white, and Mexican is"; his literal thinking reveals his social cognitive processing of race. Children, just like infants as the ORE research shows, are learning how to make sense of the racialized world around them. Although limited, initial research indicates that mixed-race children are engaging in developmental processes of noticing race, they have differential cognitive processes due to their access to multiracial exposure and may even have access to increased cognitive flexibility and creativity when they are encouraged to think about their multiple social identities (Gaither et al., 2012, 2015, 2019).

WHAT ABOUT YOUR FRIENDS?

Twelve-year-old 7th-grader Lucy, who identifies as mixed at school and comes from a Black and white background, told us something that we heard multiple times in our conversations with Generation Mixed kids: "Yeah, a lot of my friends are mixed, like a lot." We have focused on the early foundation of children's development and brain, but another element we want to listen to is children's social worlds. Children's peers are deeply impactful for their understanding of themselves and the racial world around them. For children under the age of 7, race—or, rather, physical traits like skin color, facial features, and hair texture that act as proxy for race—are simply signs that someone is in some way different from themselves, similar to gender or weight. And, neither noticing difference nor being drawn toward sameness is "bad."

Indeed, it's neither unusual nor unhealthy for kids to gravitate toward the familiar so early in life. Katz and Kofkin (1997) found that, by the age of 3, children will start choosing to play with people of their own race more than people of a different race, while research by Aboud (2003) finds that children around the age of 2 begin choosing peers of the same racial group. Choosing same-race peers is evaluated by assessing propinquity measures (how close you choose to sit next to someone), sociometric choice measures (where children are given pictures of different-raced kids and asked with whom they want to be friends) and naturalistic observations (where researchers count whom children interact with on a playground or at a school setting). All of these indicators show that beginning around ages 2 or 3 children start choosing to associate with the same race (and often the same gender) peers. In this early developmental moment, peers become a big socializing factor. Are there other groups of mixed-race children with whom to associate, or children of color with whom to even become peers? What does this mean for mixed-race children who may or may not have the ability to make friends who "look like" their racialized phenotype? Certainly, as we will learn through the section on racial identity, many factors affect how children see themselves. We also need to consider what does choosing same-race peers mean for mixed-race children.

When we listened to the youth in our study, we often heard statements like Lucy's. Some children made this comment in a declarative fashion, while others in the course of the interview seemed to stumble on it. Tatiana, an 8-year-old Black, white, and Mexican girl who identifies as Black and white at school pondered out loud to us, "Well, most of my friends are brown." When we asked her what "brown" meant, she elaborated, "Well Malie is brown like me—Mexican, Black, white, and maybe Hawaiian, and Lana's parents are different colors, and Maria is brown and her daddy is Mexican and her mother . . . I think is brown Asian." Here we can listen in on Tatiana's emerging ideas about skin color, and how it's connected in fundamental ways to race, nation, ethnicity, and her own mixedness. We also see how Tatiana identifies herself as racially similar to her diverse "brown" peers.

As we do have little literature to draw on for mixed-race children and racial socialization, we will draw heavily on that of other children of color. The literature on racial socialization illustrates that something interesting starts happening early on for Black children. After choosing same-race peers initially, at around age 3 Black children begin choosing white peers with whom to associate more often. Why would this be true? Some theories suppose that children, very early, are learning the lessons of who is supposed to be desirable. Let's turn to a seminal research study that teaches us more about this: the doll study, conducted in 1954 by two African American psychologists, Mamie Phipps Clark and Kenneth Clark (see Figure 1.2). This study is remarkable not only because of its consequential findings, but because it was the first psychological study to be used as part of a Supreme Court case, the landmark *Brown v. the Board of Education of Topeka, Kansas*. The Clarks' study was used to demonstrate how spurious the notion of "separate but equal" (the legal precedent established in an 1896 Supreme Court case, *Plessy v. Ferguson*) truly was, and indeed how racial segregation had devastating psychological impacts on children. In this study Black and white children were given Black dolls and white dolls and asked to ascribe a host of positive or negative words to the dolls (smart, good, nice versus bad, mean, dumb). The majority of children, both Black and white, labeled the white dolls with positive attributes and Black dolls with negative

Figure 1.2. Dr. Kenneth Clark Observing His Famous Doll Study (Photograph by Gordon Parks)

attributes. Then the children were asked to indicate which doll they looked like. If you watch the videotape of these interactions, you will see that many of the Black children become uncomfortable when asked this question. They have just listed a host of negative terms with the Black dolls, and they realize, in that moment, that these same terms apply not just to dolls, but to them. In turn, they found that a high rate of Black children actually chose the white doll. At the end of this study the authors conclude:

> It appears from the data that coincident with the awareness of racial differences and racial identity there is also the awareness and acceptance of the existing cultural attitudes and values attached to race. It is clear that the Negro child, by the age of five is aware of the fact that to be colored in contemporary American society is a mark of inferior status. (Clark & Clark, 1950, pp. 349–350)

The Clarks performed this seminal research more than 70 years ago, and yet it is still relevant today. In fact, this study has been reproduced multiple times in popular realms. For example, in 2014 television journalist Anderson Cooper hired a psychologist to replicate this study (with some modifications) to see how things had changed. These modifications included asking children to indicate which child on a continuum of skin colors matched a particular attribute. They found, on the whole, that in 50 years racial attitudes of young children weren't much different.

What we see here from this research is that young children are not only learning how to notice race, but they are learning very quickly how people are treated according to race. As the research indicates, this learning may affect peer selection and how children see and understand themselves. Again, we are faced with the absence of literature in particular of mixed-race children within the research with only few studies looking explicitly at how these phenomenon work with multiracial children. Through the course of listening to the participants of this book, we heard very clearly that there was another level of deeply impactful peer influence: that of a sibling.

WHAT ABOUT YOUR SIBLINGS?

Learning about race does not only occur within friend groups; it occurs immediately within the structure of the family unit. One of the many unexpected results from this project was the strong theme of siblings speaking race to each other. Although many siblings of all racial and ethnic backgrounds ponder how they look alike and look different, when each of those markers means looking like different racialized identities, such interpretations of phenotype hold additional weight.

In their dialogue, two African American and white sisters, both of whom identify as mixed at school, describe to us how they are constantly thinking and talking about how they are racialized in similar and different ways from each other. Lucy, the younger, 12-year-old 7th-grader, who frequently gets told that she "must be" a member of a variety of races and ethnicities other than the ones from which she comes, shares that in school, "it's hard for us to be sisters because people are always like, oh, you guys look so alike." Lucy disagrees, saying, "I don't think we look alike at all."

Gia, her 14-year-old, 9th-grade sister, interjects, "Some people say we don't look alike at all and others say we look alike, almost identical."

Lucy continues, "Yeah, um, but like people will come up to me and be like, um, like, 'oh what is she?' but they won't come up to Gia which I think is strange because if people think we look so alike, then why don't they say that to Gia too?"

When we ask Gia what she thinks about outsiders asking her sister about her racial background but not asking her those questions directly, she responds, "I don't think it's like an exclusion thing. I think it's just that they don't know [what race I am] and don't want to offend anybody." Later in the conversation Gia explains that her read on these folks is that racializing her as white also provides whites with an excuse for their racism. She explains, "And so maybe if I just don't acknowledge that like maybe there is a person of color in the room then maybe we can just keep going [without acknowledging our racism]." For Gia, not being identified as a person of color (although she is very clear to not explicitly say "passing as white") can be more comfortable in school settings because, as she puts it, "I'm kind of like, like Lucy, I'm kind of shy so I kind of don't like being called out, that [being called out as a person of color, i.e., to connect to a character in a book on the basis of race in English class] would make me super uncomfortable so I'm kind of glad [my teachers and classmates] don't [see me as a person of color]." She also adds, "But I feel like maybe other people wouldn't be [uncomfortable] and maybe might want to share their experiences too." Gia and Lucy's conversations throughout their interview illustrated that the two not only talked race easily with each other, but that their own racialization was developing in part through these conversations.

Although there have been few studies on multiracial siblings, just as listening in to Gia and Lucy's conversation reveals, scholarship indicates that mixed-race siblings play an important role in racialization. Sociologist Miri Song (2010), who studies Black–white and Asian–white mixed-race siblings in the United Kingdom, writes that "the language of race and racial difference is so firmly embedded in society that even when individuals deny the existence of ethnic or racial essences and differences within their families, they often employ racial thinking and terms to talk about themselves, or to differentiate themselves from other family members" (2010, p. 266).

Although race remains an important topic, however, in her case study of 51 sibling pairs, Song does not come to major sweeping generalizations about racialization and mixed-race siblings as "although most siblings engaged in comparisons between themselves, in relation to various markers of difference (not unlike many nonmixed siblings), less than half of the sibling pairs . . . reported that racial and ethnic differences existed among siblings, and/or regarded such differences as significant and meaningful in their families" (2010, p. 269). For example, she describes how in one sibling pair she interviews, the signs of Blackness and whiteness remain signs of difference and not signs with judgment attached. Song notes that "specific gradations and markers of Blackness or Whiteness (such as friends and music, and also differences in skin color and build) were noted in describing their siblings, but these markers of difference were not regarded as problematic, or somehow divisive" (p. 276). However, this is the exact opposite of another family Song interviewed where the siblings note that various gradations of skin color and hair texture were indeed quite problematic and divisive within their sibling and family unit.

Song writes that a sibling's racial choices of friends and romantic partners do indeed inform the ways in which they racialize themselves and each other; but ultimately how a person looks will play the very largest role. In other words, if someone is racialized as Black or Asian by outside viewers, they will more likely choose a Black or Asian identity, and if they are racialized as white, they will more likely choose that identity. The exception is Black identity: A person who is part Black is more likely to identify as Black even if they are not readily identified as Black by outsiders. Song notes that geography plays a tremendous role in siblings' experience of racialization within families as well: The families who were the healthiest when it came to race, who, in other words, "were better able to resist hegemonic ethnic and racial discourses and categorizations" (including within their family units), were those who "lived in multiethnic contexts where being mixed or non-White was not unusual" (2010, p. 281). Ordinariness, or not being "the only" is a theme that will continue throughout the literature and throughout the stories in this book. Radically listening to multiracial siblings allows us to both hear what is happening within families and connects us to this larger issue of racial socialization, or how children learn about race. Returning to another aspect of Linda and Caleb's story shows us what this looks like in practice.

RACIAL SOCIALIZATION

If we go back to Linda and Caleb's story from earlier in the chapter, they give us an opportunity to listen in on racial socialization, the process by which parents communicate and teach their children about race. The field of psychology often describes racial socialization as something that parents *do* to their children, and also predominantly focuses on a "whether it happens or doesn't" approach (Anderson & Stevenson, 2019; Hughes et al., 2006; Hughey & Jackson, 2017). Leaders in the field Hughes et al. (2006) and Anderson and Stevenson (2019) have tried to complicate this process, by elaborating on types of socialization and also what is required of "skillful socialization." However, the field has yet to catch up to be able to fully describe what Linda and Caleb are doing together.

Racial socialization is the process by which parents communicate about and teach their children about race and racism (Hughes et al., 2006). By and large psychology finds that racial socialization happens more often, and more explicitly in families of color rather than in white families (Bronson & Merryman, 2009). The majority of the work, as is consistent with the psychological literature, has examined this phenomenon only in white versus Black families. Research finds that racial socialization contributes to stronger ethnic and racial identity and provides a host of benefits such as increased self-esteem, ability to cope with racism, academic achievement, and overall better psychological adjustment (Anderson & Stevenson, 2019; Byum et al., 2007; Hughes et al., 2006; Neblett et al., 2008; Scott, 2004). The field as a whole is working to articulate racial socialization beyond mere parents' "do it or don't" description. For example, Hughes et al. (2006) and subsequent studies have articulated four types of socialization in an effort to elaborate and differentiate the process: minority socialization (the preparation for bias), cultural socialization (the transmission of cultural knowledge, beliefs, and values), egalitarian socialization (also known as color-blind socialization), and no socialization (Hughes et al., 2006; Priest et al., 2014).

The empirical literature on how parents are racially socializing their mixed-race children is nascent. A 2014 review by Priest et al. of 30 years of racial socialization research and the resulting 86 studies found only two that addressed racial socialization within multiracial families (Priest et al., 2014). More recently, Jackson et al. (2019) found eight studies, many of which focused on socialization within the context of transracial adoption—by white parents of a child of color. They conducted a study to address this gap by interviewing parents of mixed-race Mexican American youth and found that parents used more overt socialization messages (talking about their racial and ethnic identities explicitly) about cultural and minority status than previously reported (2019). However, Jackson and colleagues' review and work highlight that these limited studies find contradictory information about how parents racially socialize their mixed-race children. Some studies, contrary to theirs, find parents silent, subscribing to color-blind approaches to socialization (Hughes et al., 2006; Rauktis et al., 2016). In 40 years of research on racial socialization, there is scant research focusing on the racial socialization that happens with multiracial families; furthermore, the majority of those articles focus on the socialization within transracial adoptive families. Thus, as we do not have a robust body of pre-existing literature, we feel privileged to radically listen to the voices of our multiracial families as we add to this literature.

To situate racial socialization with one of our Generation Mixed families, let's again return to Linda and Caleb's story, and explore how her role as a teacher and as a mixed-race person undergirds her role as a mother to a mixed-race child in this story. As we listen to Linda, we find that this is not some insignificant, uncomplicated story, but rather a story rooted in her own personal reflection, trauma, and resilience. Their story, in particular, also helps us to understand the role of children in constructing racial socialization—in fact, in demanding it. Linda is mixed Vietnamese and white and describes not having access to her Vietnamese father and his family as they remained in Vietnam while her mother returned to the United States to raise her. She describes being raised in predominantly white spaces, understanding herself as white and having little access to aspects of her Vietnamese heritage and culture. She understands her separation from her father as being abandoned by him and has had to reconcile that hurt and separation through the years. She then became a teacher at a school where she taught many students of color and mixed-race children as well. Linda explained, "It really wasn't until I started working at [a] high school [where] . . . my students taught me [about race]. They have such rich heritage, you know? They taught me so much in terms of that."

Then, Linda notes, when "I had Caleb, that I was like 'This part of me I haven't explored,' [so] . . . I was like, 'I need to understand my Vietnamese heritage for the sake of him.'" Furthermore, within the context of her family unit, Linda also describes how her mixed-race Asian American husband's racialization also affected her: "my husband, his story is he also would tell you he's identified as white growing up. His mom is Japanese, his father is white. . . . His grandmother, so my mother-in-law's mom, was in the internment camps in Idaho. Lots of trauma there. You were told when they came out of the camps, 'You don't want to identify as Japanese. That is a big no-no.' . . . Language, customs, culture, so much was lost." Her son's physical appearance also adds to the way in which she narrates her process of racial socialization: "Even him, even Caleb, you can tell maybe a little bit in the eyes, but really you could say that he's white and people wouldn't question it."

Because of all of these factors, of teaching at a racially diverse high school, of having her own son, of having a partner with a similar racial but different ethnic, cultural, and historical mix, and of having a son who can possibly pass for white, Linda explained that "it . . . hasn't been until recently these last few years that we have started making sure that we have conversations about it, making sure that [Caleb] has . . . [doesn't finish thought]. So, I feel like I'm a late bloomer. I feel like I'm learning about this part of me right now as an adult." But of all these factors, what Linda highlights the most here, and throughout the conversation, is that while her child ignited her purposeful racial socialization, the children she served sparked the need to engage in these conversations about race and identity.

Racial socialization within psychology is rarely conceptualized as discursive, recursive, or even bidirectional. This process is often merely defined as "what we say to our children." However, we can hear a bidirectionality in Caleb's request, "Can you tell that story again?" Linda tells this story both as a response to our question, and because she knows this is a story he likes, and a story he has requested. Linda also demonstrates another important, often ignored portion of racial socialization: the need to know oneself. Linda decides to investigate her own heritage and celebrations and looks for resources. She purchases the celebratory outfits, the special envelopes, does the research in the outlet available to her, and courageously tries on something that does not quite feel like it is not her own, or as she says, "I'm going to totally butcher this but . . . ," and here she makes the case that she will be vulnerable in her efforts toward her own racial socialization for the sake of her son. Lastly, and most relevant for this book, she brings this socialization to school. She is not only doing it for the broader group of children at the school so they can learn about Vietnamese culture, but so they can hear Caleb's full story, to enable him to have a space where all parts of his identity can be recognized. She is aiding her child's school in helping to radically listen to him as a mixed-race child, even as he doesn't always get all of the pieces of his racialization "right."

Indeed, while children are noticing, playing with, and engaging with race, research indicates that most parents, unlike Linda, are resoundingly silent. This leaves children on their own to pick up and learn about race from the fundamentally racialized and racist society around them (Bronson & Merryman, 2009). For example, in Allison's work at a preschool, the staff wanted to discuss an incident in which a 3-year-old white girl in the play space was refusing to clean up. When the teacher directed her to clean up, the child said, "I don't clean up, only brown people clean up." The teacher, who was herself "brown," was stung by the child's comment but was able to react with kindness and by reaffirming the values of the school. She told the child, "We all clean up here. We all help to make our community nice for others." Later the teacher revisited the incident with the child, asking her why she thought only brown people cleaned up. She replied, "Well, we have a brown lady who comes to our house and she cleans up, and the guys who clean up the yard are brown and they clean up, and you are brown and you clean up." In other words, this child was narrating her lived experiences, which had already communicated a lot about race. We encourage people to radically listen to children, as this school community did. This means listening radically even and perhaps especially to the youngest of children, to hear how they are making sense of race. Such sense-making will be difficult and uncomfortable. Indeed, as we explore further in the next chapter, such moments of discomfort are ones we encourage as moments of friction. But it's up to adults to both listen and then speak to their questions to help them learn how to read and react, and to guide our children toward antiracism in a dialogic process. This guidance is the moment of interruption we will discuss further in Chapters 4 and 5. In this example, the teacher (a seasoned teacher who had been thinking a lot about equity and justice) took a breath and redirected the child to clean up. She pointed out how not all brown people at the school were solely responsible for taking care of public spaces. In effect, the teacher slowed down, encouraged flexible thinking, and still got the girl to clean up.

The stories and the science of this chapter point to the fact that mixed-race children, like all children, see race. We have to begin here, with this foundational information, because it is so compelling for so many to reiterate ideas of color blindness or the racial transcendence of children. Many people hold onto the specious hope that if kids simply won't notice race then maybe racism will simply go away. As we will see in Chapter 5, this hope is iterated sometimes implicitly and sometimes explicitly in the ways in which families parent their children; after all, some families use their own multiracial composition as proof that race doesn't matter. Yet, as we listened to the Generation Mixed children and youth, they let us know that they can see race, they are noticing race, and they are trying to make sense of race. They are playing with race, and they are co-constructing their understanding with their siblings and their friends. As we end this chapter, we want to encourage you to go back to that first exercise about your first race-related memory and ask yourself to think about: What did you hear in that memory? What were you told or taught by others about what happened? Who listened to you if you ever talked about race?

CHAPTER 2

Changing Team(s)

Mixed Kids' Agency in Choosing, Moving, and Sticking with Racialized Identities

Hiro, a 13-year-old, 8th-grade boy, tells us, "Usually when I'm talking to people, usually I just say I'm Japanese." This explanation of his racialized identity, he says, matches up with his majority–Asian/American friendship group at school as identifying in a racially similar way is part of how he tries to "make a connection." However, his interior definition is more complicated, as "when I'm talking to myself in my head I say Okinawan and white and American." Each of those individual pieces are, in his words, "all very important to me." Hiro utilizes his racialized identity strategically to make and maintain friends, or in part by simplifying what others might read as his complicated racial background: He takes an easier approach with the shorthand of a singular racial label.

Twelve-year-old 7th-grader Kema explains that sometimes she tells people who ask "what are you?" that she's simply "mixed," but if they press her for more information that she'll give them the whole story of "Black, white, Indian." Kema likes the idea of being mixed as an end-game answer in itself and doesn't like to have to explain. Kema articulates the racialized identity she wants, even if people do not understand her answer. Olu, a 15-year-old 10th-grader, tells us that he "is African American and Filipino," but back in elementary school, "I would say I was Black, because my friends they were mostly Black. . . . Kind of forget about the Filipino side." But now in high school, at a predominantly white school, if "someone asked me like what my ethnicity is I would just tell them I am African American and Filipino." This answer isn't acceptable to some folks, though: Olu reports that "the kids that I told them that they were like, 'Oh, I just thought you were just Black.'" His response, he recalls, is "'I say, 'No, I'm Filipino as well.'"" That is also not satisfactory, he says, as others want to have to have the last word about how they see his race: Then they would say probably, "Oh, I can actually see your eyes and stuff." His final answer, he recalls, is: "I would just be like, 'Well, okay.'" Olu expresses his racialized identities in different ways at different stages.

As we explore in this chapter, for multiracial kids, making such strategic choices in racialized identification is not about "using" race in a way that feels inauthentic to them, but rather performing race in a way that illustrates its fluidity.

Percy, a 13-year-old 8th-grader who identifies as Filipino and comes from a Filipino and white background said in a story you will hear later in this chapter, he always identifies as Filipino, which to him means loyally sticking to a team. At the same time, as other children and adolescents such as Hiro and Olu show us, those teams might change, or as Kema illustrates, they might choose a team that few people know or understand. Simply, when given the space and choice, multiracial children will script their identity in multiple ways. Sometimes perhaps the choice is about simplifying an answer; sometimes it might be about making or maintaining friends; sometimes it might be about connecting to family; sometimes it might be a political decision. Regardless of motivation, all of these articulations of identity are a valid part of a mixed-race child's experience. The question is: How can schools—and parents—really listen to what children are saying about their experiences? In addition, how do schools and families foster an antiracist critique, particularly for children who are part white, light-skinned, and/or white-passing in a world in which whiteness amounts to ultimate privilege?

In this chapter we explore how mixed-race students' explanations of the racialized identity labels that they might offer up at different times, spaces, and with different groups, provide us a window into the complexity and fluidity of racial identity for multiracial individuals. As we discussed in Chapter 1, we have the empirical foundations that show us children, even young children, are able to notice, and be affected by race. They also have the ability (and are in fact compelled by social pressures) to create racial identity(ies) as we hear from the stories in the book thus far. Although the models of monoracial identity development have served psychologists as the initial foundation for understanding how mixed-race children are making sense of their racial identity, those models cannot account for the variation, movement, flexibility, agency, or complexity we hear about from actual, multiracial kids. In the following pages we more deeply examine how mixed-race racial identity development theories elucidate processes of mixed-race racial identity development. In the last chapter we listened to the ways in which mixed-race children, like all children, experience and begin to engage with racial socialization. Now let's radically listen to how mixed-race children desire *choice(s)* in their racial socialization—when they "change teams" by choosing a new-to-them identity, switch racialized identities, or stick with a singular racialized identity—and hear the consequences of what happens when that desire remains unheard by members of their school communities.

But First, a Radical Listening Exercise in Salient Identities

This is a remembering, sharing, and listening exercise on the topic of salient identity. As in the last chapter, you will do this exercise with your critical friend. Please have a 2-minute timer ready to go. Please read through this section in its entirety and then begin the exercise. As we prompted in the section exercise in Chapter 1, in order to model radical listening, each partner will speak, uninterrupted, one at a time, about the topic on the table. This time, that topic is: your own identity.

Think back to when you were the age of either a child that you now serve, or a child that you are raising. At that time, what was the most salient part of your identity? That is, what was the part that was the most important? It might or might not be the most celebrated aspect of your identity as a child. Although it might be the most valued, it might also be the most shameful, or even the most hidden. Think in terms of these phrases, "when I was 10 I was an athlete," or, "in 3rd-grade I was the class clown," or "at age 15 no one knew I was depressed." Invoke that memory now.

As you do, ask yourself, what did adults say or do to support, validate, or listen to your most salient identity? You might think "that coach really helped me see that my huge growth spurts meant I wasn't just tall and gawky but strong and powerful." Or, "That teacher laughed with me at my jokes when I desperately needed a teacher to value me instead of sending me to the principal's office." Or, "That school counselor could tell that I was hurting and gave me the support I needed to make it through middle school." Conversely, what are the things that adults did to invalidate your salient identity? You might recall a coach who "told me I could never go pro" after an especially disappointing loss that precipitated your quitting the team. You might remember "that teacher kicked me out of every class" because you had a reputation that preceded you as a class clown, even though you rarely cracked a joke in her class. You might think "that counselor who told me I should just 'cheer up' in middle school stopped me from asking for the help I needed to get for too many years."

This exercise reflects on how some aspects of our identity remain seen and heard, and others remain unseen and unheard. But more importantly, the exercise shows how identities can at times be seen, heard, and *valued* and at other times, ignored, dismissed, and *invalidated*. If you recall one particular adult who made you feel supported, talk for another minute to your critical friend about that person. Conjure them up to your partner, describing them, and their particularly effective way of engaging with you. Finally, discuss this question: What did this particular adult do to make you feel supported? When we ask this question to audiences, one of the main replies that we get is that these special adults *listened*.

RACIAL IDENTITY DEVELOPMENT MEETS MIXED-RACE KIDS

We focus here on how we can listen to mixed-race kids describe the salience of their racial identities. We have examined the foundations for children's understandings of race, initial evidence about peer selection, and parental racial socialization. We now shift to how all of these factors affect a child's understanding of their identities. To begin, however, we are going to radically listen to the field of psychology as it attempts to speak to racial identity development. We will take a developmental approach, beginning with psychology's initial articulation of identity in the 1920s and follow it in the subsequent 100 years as it moves toward articulating models of mixed-race identity development.

Let's begin with the grandfather of the field of identity development, Erik Erikson. He was a German American psychoanalyst and developmental psychologist from the early 1920s, who posited foundational theories of child identity development. The field of psychology's approach to identity began with ubiquitous theories of identity development. For decades psychology assumed that all people underwent the same identity processes, and these processes did not include how people come to understand themselves in the context of race.

Coinciding with the civil rights movement, the field was pushed to address how race did after all affect identity, and, in fact, how people formed racial identities (Parham, 1993). In this initial wave of racial identity development theories, one of the first was the theory of nigresence, the process of identifying as Black (Cross, 1995 and Cross, 1991). This model was elaborated on by Black scholars, including Thomas Parham who coined the term "psychological storms" as a means of describing the process of racial identity development (Parham, 1993). Soon thereafter Dr. Janet Helms articulated a model of white racial identity, and scholars articulated identity development theories for other racial groups (Helms, 1995). For example, Ruiz (1990) created the model of Latinx development, which continues to be elaborated on (Pabón Gautier, 2016). Chang and Karl Kwan (2009) elucidate the continued development of Asian–American identity models, that, much like the Latinx models, address broad issues of nationality, colorism, immigration, and biculturalism, in addition to race.

The models of racial identity formation have common and overlapping themes. Some are stage theories, which means that a person has to master a task before moving on to the next stage. Each stage is posited as a hierarchically significant or "more progressed" stage (Erikson, 1993). An analogy would be that you can't do algebra before you master how to add. Identity theories have stated that you had to do stage 1 before you could do stage 2. Scholars leveled critique against the stage theory, arguing that not everyone had to "master" the same sets of experiences. This critique also challenged the linear and hierarchical nature of the stage model. In response, theorists began describing "phase" models. Phases imply movement between and overlap of experiences. Perhaps more connected to our own lived experiences, Tatum describes these "stages" or "phases" as moving up a spiral staircase where the walls often feel familiar.

Two models emerged to describe ethnic identity development broadly. James Marcia's (1966) model proposes orthogonal categories with exploration and commitment on each axis. The four quadrants describe each "status": (1) *moratorium:* explored but not committed; (2) *achieved:* explored and committed; (3) *diffuse:* unexplored and not committed; and (4) *foreclosed:* unexplored and committed (Marcia, 1966; Tatum, 2017, p. 123). Phinney's work on adolescent ethnic identity development was based off interviews, questionnaires, and research done on adolescents of different racial groups (although not with mixed-race folks). Similar to Marcia's work, identity exploration is central. Phinney's (1993) model includes three "phases": (1) *unexamined:* ethnic identity is not particularly salient; (2) *identity search:* active engagement in thinking about, defining, and understanding one own's ethnic identity; and (3) *ethnic achievement:* when one is committed to and has a clear sense of an ethnic identity (Phinney, 1993; Tatum, 2017, p. 237).

Regardless if identity is imaged in terms of progression in stages, phases, or movement upstairs, the models involve moving from a lack of awareness about race (a period of racelessness), into an event, or moment of recognizing race (an awakening to race). Theorists often describe these events or encounters, the moments of coming to race, as negative, and moments of encountering racism, exclusion, or questioning about one's identity, and as the catalysts for the searching about which these theories speak. The next stage/phase or step after the encounter is that of exploration. Exploration is best characterized by time spent getting to know one's identity, exploring it through community, learning and "trying on" aspects of group membership. There are phases/stages of denial, conflict, and reconciliation, and also of commitment to one's identity. Some models articulate an "end state" where one is "integrated" or has "achieved" a claimed identity (Parham, 1993; Phinney, 1993; Tatum, 2017). These end states often articulate that this arrival comes with not only a commitment to a racial identity but to understanding oneself as an intersectional person with multiple identities.

Identity models have proven helpful and resonant with many people's experiences. Janet Helms' model, in particular, has been widely used both in the context of training and supporting the development of culturally competent clinicians and in facilitating difficult race-based dialogues and racial-healing work (Helms, 1995). However, these models also face several critiques. Most of these theories propose that racial identity development does not begin until adolescence or early adulthood. However, this stands in contrast to the evidence that children are noticing, thinking about, and even making peer choices according to race early. Relatedly, these models presume a period of "racelessness"; however, many of the Generation Mixed children and youth tell us that they have never experienced a time when they didn't notice, recognize, or feel race.

Likewise, the idea that a specific, singular racial encounter is the catalyst for a person's self-examination is flawed: There hasn't been any data that indicates that such an event is necessary or sufficient for a person to begin reflecting. Lastly, and perhaps most related to the research on mixed-racial identity development, these models only articulate a person's movement between, back and forth and through these phases, levels, and stages as failure, regression, or some other negative judgment about failing to progress. Another idea has been put forth to help explain racial identity development. As a way of describing the movement within racial identity development, Tatum describes the process "is not so much linear as circular. It's like moving up a spiral staircase: as you proceed up each level, you have a sense that you have passed this way before, but you are not in exactly the same spot" (Tatum, 2017, p. 174). Radically listening to mixed-race children and youth, we can hear that flexibility and celebrate what these models fail to denote: the in-between, the back-and-forth, and the recursiveness of racialized identity for mixed-race kids.

A story from of our Generation Mixed participants helps illustrate such back-and-forth movement perfectly. Olu's sister Oyin, a 19-year-old college sophomore, who identifies herself at school as "Filipino and African American or Blasian," talked with her brother and us about her various multiracial identities throughout her K–12 experience. She notes that she both simplifies her race answers and changes them now that she's a sophomore in college. In fact, "I would say my answer would shift in the setting, even now." This has been true of all her schooling, she reports, as "I would say in middle school all of my friends were basically Filipino, so I identified as Filipino at that school. Because all my friends, we ate the same food, we listened to the same music, all that kind of stuff." As Olu's story in the opening of the chapter indicates, her brother, at this same school, at the same age, identified monoracially as Black (not Filipino), but for friendship reasons as well.

At the same time, Oyin explains, "If I were to go back to my high school setting and my high school self maybe as a sophomore, I probably would just say I'm Black." Such an identification was important to Oyin in "a predominantly white high school"—not for friendship groups as Olu said, but in her words, because "Black students really feel empowered when you say 'I'm Black,' when you're in a white setting, so I think most of the time I wouldn't be like, oh, 'I'm Filipino and Black.'" Instead, she says, "I'd be like, 'I'm Black.'" She adds, "Then I would, maybe, say, yeah, 'and I'm Asian.'" Her brother, again at the same high school, also has a different identity than his sister, and now responds that he identifies as both Black and Asian. At this moment, during her college life, "I feel like now as I've grown and I do still go to a white, predominantly white place I would say I'm African and Asian. I feel like it has grown over time, so now I can really appreciate both sides rather than just one." Both siblings' racialized identity changes over schools and over time; interestingly, it also differs from each other when they are at similar ages, although at the particular moment of their interview, with Olu in high school and Oyin in college, both identify the same: as Black and Asian.

For both Oyin and Olu, as so-called "multiple-minority" or "dual-minority" multiracials, questions of racial flexibility can be exceedingly multifaceted. Education scholar Sandra Winn Tutwiler notes that although other multiracial kids experience "authenticity tests," "the situation for minority-minority mixed-race youth . . . can be even more complex and more daunting [in terms of proving their] authenticity to both groups that constitute the racial/ethnic lineage" (Winn Tutwiler, 2016, p. 145). Layered on top of this is the idea that, as education scholar Mica Pollock (2004) argues, mixed-race youth become "one race" for their own convenience. In her study, "self-described 'mixed' . . . youth *became* single-race-group members in school, even as they negotiated so becoming every time they described themselves or others in simple racial terms" (2004, p. 33). Pollock calls the process of "youth's everyday strategic use of race labels," race-bending (p. 33). As opposed to adults, she explains, "Youth, far from accepting their nation's race categories wholesale, alternately contested and strategically accepted the ability of simple race categories to describe complex people" (Pollock, p. 33). In other words, "In describing themselves purposefully at times as members of simple 'races,' [mixed-race] . . . students temporarily prioritized simple, equality-minded 'racial' identification over complex, personal race identity" (Pollock, p. 33).

As we listen to the experiences of mixed-race individuals, we must consider how stories such as Oyin and Olu's make their way into racial identity models that were in no way constructed for them. In the next section we will discuss the models that scholars constructed to account for more dynamic versions of identity movement and also for when their racial identity is ascribed to them or for them through "checking a box," a phenomenon we will discuss later in this chapter. The problem with the literal or metaphoric box is that the choice of racialized identity it offers is often singular, not multiple. Indeed, a common experience for mixed-race children is that they constantly have to face external definitions of their racial identity and frequent requests to identify themselves racially, as we heard in the opening of this chapter (Urrieta & Noblit, 2018). Many mixed-race people experience the social pressures of having to "choose" a singular identity or a side, and they find this experience tiresome, stressful, and one that causes tension (Gaither, 2015). This "push and pull" on their identity deeply affects their racial identity formation and development (Rockquemore & Brunsma, 2002).

THE PSYCHOLOGY OF MIXED-RACE KIDS
AND RACIALIZED CHOICE

Although psychologists formed monoracial identity development theories, scholars in the field slowly began to investigate experiences of mixed-race folks. Yet with deepening research and listening to dynamic and multifaceted multiracial experiences, we found that these theories are often too limiting for what our participants tell us is their experience. Those models help us understand there is exploration, examination, movement, and at times commitment to racialized identity. However, we heard that many mixed-race children and adolescents experience added layers of complexity and movement, which include the racial ascription of others, or how others make sense of their racial identity, and contextual factors such as proximity, acceptance, and access to multi- and monoracial others.

As we know, the first wave of racial identity development theories focused on the experiences of monoracial groups. Even when multiraciality is the focus in psychology, then the predominant groups are multiracial Black–white individuals. Rockquemore et al. (2009) and Gaither (2015) offer critical analyses of these theories while highlighting their implications. Gaither shows that these theories come with the assumption of a "mixed race monolith," as if all of the experiences and processes of mixed-race individuals can fall into a singular theory. She argues that this is exactly why we know so little about how racial identity unfolds for multiracial individuals. With this in mind we can turn to what we do know from studies.

Thornton and Wason (1995) frame the history of mixed-race identity development theories in three waves. Just as in the Introduction we described the first wave in scholarship, writ large, on mixed-race people as being mired in the problem of mixture, the first wave in psychology is known as "the problem approach." This is marked by assumptions of mixed-race tragedy and deficiency, also known as psychopathology. Such theories have been endemic to the founding of this nation. From "as early as the 1600s, White North American settlers called mulattoes a 'spurious issue' and an 'abominable mixture' . . . [demonstrating that] mixed-race is therefore taboo from the moment of conquest" (Joseph, 2013, p. 11). Joseph notes, "The body of a mulatto or a mulatta has inspired considerable scientific debate over the course of American history" (p. 13). One of these so-called scientific queries surrounded fertility. Historian Thomas Gossett (1963) describes studies of mixed-race African Americans, largely conducted during the Civil War, to investigate the "hybrid degeneracy theory" in which "mulattoes—like mules—tended to be barren" (1963, p. 49).

Another social scientific theory exercised on mixed-race Black bodies decades later was that of the "marginal man," who sociologist Everett Stonequist described as exhibiting "nervous strain," "racial disharmony," a "clash of blood" and an "unstable genetic constitution" (Joseph, 2013, p. 17; Stonequist, 1937, pp. 145–155). In literature, the unstable mixed-race Black female character is known as the tragic mulatta figure (Ashe, 2007; Dagbovie-Mullins, 2013; Elam, 2011; Foreman, 2002; Joseph, 2013; Sollors, 1997; Streeter, 2003). Thus, theories of multiracial psychopathology have circulated not just in psychology, but across scientific, social scientific, and humanistic spheres, in popular and academic cultures.

Thornton and Wason (1995) note that the next wave of psychological research on mixed-race people takes the equivalent approach. This theory relies on notions of hypodescent, also known as the one-drop rule, that states basically that mixed kids experience racial identity formation and development just like black kids do. The third wave is that of the "variant" approach. Maria Root's foundational work in 1992 articulates this approach, as does Poston's (1990) biracial identity development model, arguing that previous theories are limited and problematic in their assumptions and implications. This third wave similarly uses ideas of phases/levels that progress from unawareness to learning and conflict to an achieved state. The so-called final destination of racial identity is that of a "biracial" identity. These variant theories argue that mixed Black–white children who choose to identify as Black have overidentified with one parent. Such theories frame choosing Blackness as problematic and not as optimal as other identity choices, and especially not as psychologically positive as the achieved biracial identity. Again, such work fits well with the classic mixed-race studies wave of scholarship that we discuss in the Introduction, the "coming out" moment of biraciality that occurred after the first wave.

The evolution of the theories has continued to shift as more listening happens. As such, Maria Root's later work (1996) alters her earlier theory and moves beyond these ideas of an achieved biracial state. She highlights the complex issues in "border crossings" of identity development, but still premises "multiracial" as a preferred identity that leads to greater psychological wholeness. Building on Root, Rockquemore et al. (2009) argue for a fourth wave of theory that they call the "ecological approach": (1) how mixed-race people identify varies; (2) context matters; (3) flexibility rules as the process of racial identity development for multiracial folks is not linear, predictable or in stages; and (4) identity changes over the life course. We will listen deeply to Rockquemore et al.'s ecological approach and so will explore each of these possibilities below.

Variability

First, the literature demonstrates that how mixed-race people identify not only varies but varies widely, as the range of labels that mixed-race individuals use to describe themselves is quite broad. Some of our respondents identify themselves through monoracial labels such as Black, African American, Asian, Asian American, white, Native American, as well as ethnic labels such as Japanese, Chinese, or Otomi. Other respondents used singular identity labels for ethnic identities that are themselves multiracial, such as Latina, Latino, or Latinx. Other respondents—and sometimes the same respondents but at different times—identify themselves with multiracial labels such as multiracial, biracial, Hapa, Blasian, mixed, and mixed race to name a few. Mica Pollock (2004) studied a group of mixed-race California high school students who she observed changed their race labels regularly in school settings: They "sometimes list[ed] multiple terms to describe themselves . . . sometimes creat[ed] new racialized words to describe 'mixed' youth accurately, and sometimes apply[ed] single, simple race labels to describe their own diversity." These students were, in Pollock's estimating, figuring out a way "strategically to cope with an already racialized, racially hierarchical world" (2004, p. 33). In other words, "They retained race labels as dominant descriptive tools, hinting that the contest of simple race categorization was simply too pervasive to be escaped. Students thus bent race categories in such debates rather than breaking them apart altogether" (Pollock, p. 40).

This varied identification is clear in Rockquemore and Brunsma's (2002) study, in which they investigated the types of identifications used by a large group of people with one Black parent and one white parent. This study found that mixed-race individuals categorized themselves in "at least six ways" (p. 351): the singular identity (either exclusively Black or exclusively white), the border identity (defining oneself as biracial), the protean identity (shifting back and forth between Black, white, and biracial), and the transcendent identity (rejecting all racial categories). Their study elaborates on the context that might undergird multiracial identity choices and the "push and pull factors" (p. 349).

Context

The second factor that affects racial identity development and identification is context. Brunsma (2005) highlights social class, social network, and phenotype as well-researched contextual factors. These three factors are profoundly interlinked and intersectional, exerting multiple pressures on identification. Findings indicate that higher social class leads to *less* identification with racially minoritized (in other words "lower") status. Put another way, for the Black–white respondents to the study, the wealthier a mixed-race person is, the more likely they are to identify with their white than with their Black background. Social networks often directly overlap with family network, neighborhood, and school, all of which are racialized in our highly segregated communities. The overarching finding of this research is that the larger the racially minoritized social network, the more likely the person is to identify with the minoritized community. Involvement with a whiter social network, in contrast, supports the identification of a person as white *or* also as biracial, rather than as a racial minority.

The third main contextual factor is phenotype. Looks matter when it comes to race. Such racial looks, education scholar Peters (2016) notes, are a part of a "visual grammar," or a way that orders us alongside racial readings. Peter continues, "how we look matters and classification practices are subject to individual understandings of what mixed looks like and how it ought to operate in an existing racial schema," or, in other words, how race is ordered (Peters, p. 58). Given that race is often understood and "read" as a physical set of features, it makes sense that how one looks determines racial identity. For part-Black individuals, some research states that the darker skin that a person has, the more likely they are to identify as Black. However, the research on the impact of skin color on racialized identity choice for mixed-race individuals has been conflicted at best (Gaither, 2015). Instead, as sociologist Miri Song (2017) writes, "The policing of group boundaries and membership, and who can or cannot claim a particular identity, . . . [occurs in] discourses about racial authenticity, (both on the basis of physical appearance or the demonstration of specific cultural attributes), notions of blood quantum and racial fractions, and racialized scripts of behavior to which children were expected to adhere" (Song, p. 115). We found that the children we interviewed played with such racialized scripts, or the expected ways in which they should act according to racial stereotypes, by sometimes participating in the game, sometimes opting out, and sometimes trying to change the rules.

Flexibility: Not Linear, Predictable, or in Stages

Rockquemore's research includes nonlinearity of the identification process, and that identity changes over time. Another way to think about these is as flexibility. The challenge inherent in racial identity models is that they are often based on data from a snapshot, a moment in time. As we have discussed, many theories articulate an end state where individuals achieve a particular identity at the end of a process. However, given that "mixed race youth are four times more likely to switch their racial identity than to constantly report the same identification over time," this end state is elusive at best, and most likely, inherently false (Rockquemore et al., 2009). When research looks longitudinally, and even retrospectively, mixed-race people indicate that their racial identities were more likely to have changed over time, rather than remain the same (Gaither, 2015).

Gaither states that identity flexibility is the "ability to freely and easily switch between or identify with their multiple racial identities at a given moment" (2015). Urrieta and Noblit's (2018) meta-ethnography also found that a central experience for mixed race people was that of "fluid identities." Mixed-race people in their study speak about this flexibility both as a challenge and as agency. Identity fluidity implies almost a minute-by-minute negotiation of race, the changing of identification dependent on context.

For children, in the midst of their development, the most salient contexts affecting racialized identity choices are age and school. Percy, a 13-year-old, 8th-grade boy, who is mixed Filipino and white and identifies at his large, predominantly white middle school as Filipino, participated in our interview with his similarly mixed mother Zita. Percy's biological father, who Zita notes, "doesn't really see him," also has the same mixed background. Zita is remarried to a white man with whom she has other children. In this particular interview Zita talked about her own struggles with being racialized in ways that didn't align with her own sense of self when she was growing up, and, in particular, feeling sensitive about not being "Filipino enough"—she describes being bothered by an externally motivated sense of labels. In contrast, Percy notes, "When I think about what I identify as I think about what I want, not what other people call me. So a lot of the time it's just like my personality to stand up for what's right." For Percy, "what's right" means identifying as Filipino.

Percy clarifies, adding an extended metaphor: "And I mean, if I'm going to identify as a Filipino I need to stick with it. It's like in sports, if you're, let's say you're from Seattle and then the one year the Seahawks win the Super Bowl you like them but when the Patriots win then you start liking them. You can't be a bandwagon [fan] and call yourself a real follower of the Seahawks or Patriots. It's like the same thing with me calling myself a Filipino. I can't just go and switch. I gotta stick with it no matter what happens."

However, in what Percy posits as "stick with your race" analogy, he illustrates that he was choosing his own racialization despite how others, including his mother, might identify him. This young athlete is Team Filipino. This was a tough interview, filled with tension and, at times, tears. As we noted in the previous chapter, in the sibling dialogues it was far easier for the siblings to talk about issues of race and racialization than it was in the parent–child dialogues. And yet, the one moment of levity in the whole conversation was when Percy iterates his philosophy of race: stick with your team. We heard Percy, and this statement has stuck with us. The agency that he uses to claim his identity as fully Filipino in his mixed-race body, and the complexity that the racial identity models try (and largely fail) to capture, are clear in this example.

SUPPORTING MIXED-RACE KIDS IN RACIAL IDENTITY
EVEN WHEN THEY DON'T "MAKE THE TEAM"

As parents and teachers we must understand that our children will be pushed and pulled by multiple factors to identify in ways that might be dissonant with theirs—and our own—racial identities. We must also understand that their identifications will change again and again. But there are things that we can do, ways we can listen that will help them to feel comfortable with their identities.

As you begin to imagine how to radically listen to mixed-race children, we also want to illuminate the times when adults have a hard time listening to kids and therefore end up invalidating their experiences. One way we are going to approximate this difficulty in listening is by hearing mixed-race people talk about the tensions they feel. For example, Townsend et al. (2009) asked 59 mixed-race undergraduates about the tensions they feel about racial identification. Unlike most studies, this study moved beyond a Black–white focus and interviewed students who were mixed Asian–white and Latinx–white in addition to Black–white. Specifically, it asked them to "think about a situation in which your biracial identity was brought into focus, caused tension, and made you feel pressure to identify with only one of your racial/ethnic heritages." Students reported experiencing the most tension about their self-identification when (1) others misread them due to their appearance not matching their interior sense of racialized self, and (2) they had to fill out forms and demographic questionnaires, especially those that only allowed them to only "check one box." For mixed-race folks these moments of identity discrediting can be common, and, for some, perhaps daily occurrences.

One of our participants, Kema, a 12-year-old 7th-grader, shared an assignment she had written for school the year before that had to do with this precise idea of misrecognition. For a Language Arts short writing assignment on personal stories, Kema recounts one experience where she struggled to be seen as both her perceived and desired racial identifications of African American and mixed race. She recalls that during her lunch period in the very beginning of the 6th-grade school year, various clubs advertised their offerings on folding tables around the edges of the lunchroom, from the Cooking and Gardening Club, to the Junior Jazz Ensemble, to the club she wanted to join, My Sister's Keeper, a club for Black girls.

Kema was walking around, perusing the various club options with her group of diverse friends. This confident girl was in a buoyant mood and laughing with her friends, so that when she approached the person manning the table, the African American male coordinator of the after-school programs, her chuckling trailed her to the table. When she tried to sign up, she writes that she was met with this statement:

"You can't sign up. This is for My Sister's Keeper. It's for African American students."

My face dropped and my thoughts rushed all around my head. *Does he not think I'm mixed?*

"Sorry," he said.

What if I'm not really mixed? Why couldn't I look like my brother?

"We really encourage you to sign up for another after-school class."

Curly haired, browner skinned, flatter nose, fuller lips? What am I . . .

After the thoughts quieted down, I scrambled for words. "Um, well actually I'm mixed. Um, um, um," I mumbled, face feeling heated up. "My parents are both mixed." I stammered, way too fast and quietly.

Her emotions, Kema writes, quickly traversed from joviality to anguish ("my face dropped") to confusion ("my thoughts rushed") to externalized questioning ("does he not think I'm mixed?") to internalized questioning ("what if I'm not really mixed?") to desire for other phenotypes ("Why couldn't I look like my brother? curly haired, browner skinned, flatter nose, fuller lips") back to questioning ("what am I?") and finally to embarrassment at the moment of speaking ("face feeling heated up"). Kema did not want to discuss the assignment with us, but she wanted us to read it, and to know and understand how she experienced exclusion because the way in which she was read at that moment in school—as white—was misaligned with the way in which she understood her own racialization—as Black and mixed. Moreover, the after-school coordinator prevented her from forming bonds with other Black girls. This is a way in which the school was complicit in encouraging light-skinned, racially ambiguous (or children who some adults read as white) mixed-race kids to identify with whiteness: by not heeding their minoritized self-identity. Not only was Kema's racialized identity not honored, but the after-school coordinator held up whiteness as the option she should pursue. This is the very opposite of radically listening to mixed-race students.

Kema's experience echoes an experience from the literature of "not being enough," or in her example, "Black enough." In a meta-ethnography that examined eight qualitative studies from the psychological and educational literatures, a common experience across studies was that of a mixed-race kid being rejected by monoracial peers due to not being "enough" of one race to "count." In Kema's case, the rejection here came not from her peers, but from an adult in her school community. We can argue here that perhaps the adult did not see her as Black at all, which is another misperception because it is a mismatch with her self-perception. If this adult had first been able to slow down and sit in the *friction* of his discomfort that arises when a girl who doesn't immediately appear to him to be Black tells him that she identifies that way, then he might have been able to truly listen and provide space for her identification. Then the adult man and middle school girl might have had a drastically different conversation. Even if the man had said "This is a group for Black girls, is that you?," he would have created space for her to identify. There are many options he could have taken to allow Kema to identify for herself.

CHECKING THE BOX

Similar emotions of confusion and dismay emerge when mixed-race kids are asked to fill out questionnaires, forms, or surveys that require them to choose a singular race. Gaither's work found that when mixed-race folks fill out forms where with a single choice for racial identity, as so many routine forms do, they experience a drop in self-esteem (2015). In investigating such forced racial identity choice and the impact on the cognitive functioning of mixed-race students, Townsend et al. (2009) asked mixed-race undergraduates to complete some complicated cognitive tasks. The researchers prompted half of the group to identify themselves racially prior to a task by checking all the racial–ethnic labels that apply and the other half by checking only one. The findings were clear. Those who were forced to choose only one race reported lower self-esteem, lower motivation, and lower self-agency.

Failing to provide racialized choice to mixed-race youth creates a lack of power, lack of ability to affect their social environment, and ultimately an invalidation of self. Conversely, when mixed-race youth are given the opportunity to self-identify prior to a cognitive task, they experience multiple benefits such as demonstrations of increased agency, motivation, and self-esteem (Townsend et al., 2009). In a similar vein, Gaither (2015) finds increased cognitive flexibility, creativity, and even, perhaps, a protection from stereotype threat when multiracial people can self-identify.

As we can see, the issue of checking boxes has an impact on mixed-race children and youth. We must also locate box checking in both current and past historical moments and sociopolitical movements. The history of checking boxes comes from the history of the U.S. Census, which has taken place every year since 1790. The U.S. Census, for various troubling political purposes, maintained categories that, in a sense, articulate mixed-race heritage such as "mulatto," "octoroon," and "quadroon," although such terminology sprang from racist pseudoscientists—eugenicists—attempting to further hone their racist science. At various points, it gave multiracial people a single box to check—a singular option of Black, or white, and so on—up until the 2000 Census, which introduced the Mark One or More

(MOOM) category. As a result of the new category, political scientist Lauren Davenport (2016) reports, "Since 2000 the number of Americans identifying as White and Black has more than tripled" (2016, p. 52). The 2015 Pew study finds those who identify as Native American and white occupy the greatest share of those who claim a multiracial heritage at 50%, with those claiming Black–American Indian heritage coming in next at 12%, white–Black and multiracial Latinx both at 11%, white–Black–American Indian at 6%, and white–Asian at 4%, with the remaining 5% being some other combination (p. 32). Such a change in racial identification, Davenport writes, denotes a "discontinuity from the past and a rupture to racial norms" (p. 52). In this moment of rupture, for mixed-race people, race became two things: (1) "more of a conscious decision than an automatic label," and (2) "not a mutually exclusive concept."

However, the history of the MOOM category is far more complex than the numbers above suggest. The creation of the MOOM category, political scientist Kimberly Williams notes (2006), was driven not by multiracial people, but by white women leaders in the multiracial movement who were partnered with Black men. These white women sought to have their children classified under the singular option of "multiracial." One questions if their motivation might have been for their children to have simply no longer be classified as Black (Joseph, 2013, p. xvi; Williams, 2006, p. 12).

Kema, the same 12-year-old 7th-grader excluded from the My Sister's Keeper Club for Black girls, tells us of her creative approach to one school form that didn't provide spaces for her self-racialization. Kema clearly states throughout her interview, "I don't really think that I could identify as one thing [if forced to]. I wouldn't want to." She then explains, "In science yesterday, we had to take this survey and there was only like singular races, there wasn't even an 'other' box." She continues, "my teacher, she's a white lady and she was just like [in a high-pitched, 'teacher' voice] 'pick the one that you want the most.' That was kind of weird." Kema, however, defies the teacher's instructions and says, "so I made my own [box]." The term that she tells us she chose to put in her box was "mixed." The girl reports that the teacher "seemed kind of annoyed."

Sibling differences are once again interesting to note here, as they're a theme that runs throughout this book. The girl's 15-year-old high school sophomore brother Ty, who identifies as Black at school, also expresses strong feelings about box checking. He says, "I don't like when it's like a box and there's like check boxes and it's like Black, white, Asian, Hispanic, and all that. And there's the other box. It's like usually the only box." In saying, the "other box" is the "only box." Ty is simply saying it's *supposed to be* the preferred choice for mixed kids. However, he states emphatically, "I don't like checking the other box." Instead, he states, "I usually check Black instead of other." For him, this choice makes sense because "I feel like it's who most of my friends are and I feel like it's who I hang out with and I feel like that's who I am the most." It's interesting to note that Kema doesn't name friend groups in her sense of self-identity while Ty does. Both mixed-race siblings, however, have strong emotions that amount to their simply disliking box checking.

(SOMETIMES) CHOOSING WHITENESS: WHITE ADJACENCY

Self-identity and mixed-race kids' racial identification processes become particularly complicated propositions when they meet white privilege. Takuji, a 16-year-old 11th-grader, who early in the interview tells us that he is "Japanese American and white," says that he often describes his race to people at his large, predominantly white public high school as "half-white." When we push him to explain why, Takuji says, "I think honestly I say 'half-white' because I think being half-white you kind of get a leg up. That's not something I like going out and saying but that's kind of how I feel." He continues, further explaining how his choice functions at school: "I see a lot of the Asian students getting pushed towards like math and robotics and stuff like that and I think identifying as half-white I'm kind of opening up my opportunities to go into writing or something like that."

Takuji did not address how the "half-white" label might illustrate an interior versus exterior sense of self, meaning how he understands himself versus how he can position himself at school. For example, he does not explain why he told us earlier that he "is Japanese American and white" versus why he says at school that he is "half-white." Takuji doesn't discuss why he doesn't use an alternative phrasing, "half-Japanese or "half-Asian/American," or that in saying "half-white" the other half remains silent because it is evidently obvious: His other half, Asian Americanness, is readily visually readable so it doesn't need to be named. He does, however, talk about using his racialized labels strategically. His particular strategy is a form of what we call white adjacency, when a light-skinned or white-skinned person of color can claim white privilege. Although those reaching for white adjacency might not *be* exclusively white, their closeness to whiteness remains, by either passing in certain situations as white, or being considered "close enough" to white by folks for whom white remains a privileged status. It's important to note that to activate white adjacency one does not simply need to be able to pass as (close enough to) white, but must also have a desire to claim whiteness—if even just partially and largely symbolically. For example, we understood that Takuji isn't trying to "pass" as white; whiteness represents freedom in school path to him.

Schools are often places where whiteness is hypervalued and students of color are stereotyped. Students recognize that whiteness is privileged and even celebrated in classroom settings. Their choice of white adjacency capitalizes on this understanding. When Takuji says "being half-white you kind of get a leg up," he understands how whiteness is a tool for access to privilege, even as he feels chagrined admitting this, or as he puts it, "that's not something I like going out and saying." Furthermore, he claims whiteness happens as part of negotiating stereotypes of Asian/Americanness as math and robotics students (i.e., nerdiness to this boy). Whiteness means freedom, and in the case of school, freedom to study what he wants (writing) and to pursue his own academic interests without having racialized stereotypes placed on him.

This mechanism of claiming another identity in order to escape stereotypes about your own group is not exclusive to mixed-race individuals. Sociologist Mary Waters (1994) describes how Caribbean immigrants have performed what she deems "strategic ethnic distancing," a type of purposefully placing themselves apart from Black Americans (e.g., by playing up their Caribbean accents) in order to show that although they might *look like* Black Americans to white outsiders, they *aren't like them*. Political scientist Davenport suggests that Waters's theory can be applied to mixed-race people who are part white and do not want to identify with their minoritized background. Now this may or may not be Takuji. Or rather, it may be him sometimes and not other times. In the classroom it might feel right to claim white adjacency, but as this young athlete tells us, on the baseball field he proudly claims his Japanese heritage. As Takuji puts it, "I actually take pride in [my Japanese heritage]. Being from Seattle, that's where [Seattle Mariners baseball player] Ichiro did his thing. I enjoy carrying on the legacy."

Such racialized flexibility, scholars note, is more typical of mixed-race white–Asian people than mixed-race white–Black people. The research of political scientist Davenport (2016) is useful here again as she writes that even for very light skinned Black folks, "biracials' [whose] blackness can go undetected externally . . . [identifying as Black] typically remains a key component of internal political identity." Furthermore, mixed-race people of African descent "perceive an affective attachment to Blacks in light of the Black American community's struggles against racial oppression—a community to which biracials have always belonged." Thus, "socially, Whiteness remains largely a non-option for biracials of White-Black parentage" (Davenport, 2016, p. 64).

Returning back to our mixed-race Asian American Generation Mixed adolescent Takuji, we want to make clear from his story that he is not at fault for desiring white adjacency in the classroom. As he narrated story after story of racial bias in his schooling, his educational experience has illustrated that he will get rewarded for performing whiteness. In addition, we don't want to condemn teachers for the very practices that they were racialized to perform. However, we want to illuminate the harm that ultimately comes for the students of color, and indeed all of the students, when whiteness is held up as the norm and standard—the only pathway to success in school. Although we want to encourage identity flexibility, it should not be a vehicle for students to escape the stereotype of one group of color or for students to ingratiate themselves to whiteness.

We also want to contrast white adjacency with the old notion of "passing." Traditionally, passing means leaving one's family and one's community for an identity that will reap greater status and financial rewards, and greater physical safety. Typically, scholars focus on people who try to pass as white. White adjacency is not passing for—or being mistaken for—white—but rather being given proximal privileges to whiteness. It's about being close enough to reap some of the rewards of whiteness, especially when compared to darker-skinned students; white-adjacent students, however, are also reminded of their nonwhiteness in various ways, as, for example, Takuji pushing back against math and robotics precisely because he feels them being pushed toward him. We will further explore the politics of skin color, or colorism, in the next chapter.

As a historical phenomenon, passing, as literary scholar P. Gabrielle Foreman (2002) signifies with her phrase "passing through" whiteness, passing is a temporary phenomenon; sometimes, as critical race scholar Cheryl Harris (1993) writes, it was simply an economic necessity. Those mixed with white, sociologist Miri Song notes, move out of an identity as a person of color (not consciously passing as white per se, but not seeking out their community of color) at a certain tipping point. Song (2017) notes that this point "comes from a loss of meaning and identification or it can arise from the sense that multiracial ancestry is simply not consequential for either the parent or his or her children—though the latter does not necessarily mean that one's multiracial ancestry is entirely devoid of meaning." Song notes that such a moment more often happens when the multiracial, part-white person marries a white person, and when that multiracial person is Asian–white. At that tipping point, "One's multiracial ancestry becomes largely inconsequential, or purely symbolic" (p. 162). Our role, as radical listeners of mixed-race children and youth, is to hear these stories of white adjacency, and to illuminate the ways in which their stories reflect back privilege. Then, as we will explore in the next chapter, we can together explore the moments of discomfort, or the friction, that comes from challenging racially biased notions, and then work, together, to change them.

RADICALLY LISTENING TO MIXED-RACE IDENTIT*IES*

The mixed-race youth and children who shared their stories with us made it clear that their racial identities were constructed in interactions with their families and their friends, and in their own interior senses of self. They also developed their racialized identities through interactions with unfamiliar others. One interaction that many multiracial people document is being confronted by the question "what are you?" In both multiracial studies and Critical Mixed Race Studies, mixed-race people note that they have often felt this question as a direct invalidation of not only one's self-identification, but even one's humanity (Jones, 1994).

However, not all mixed-race kids feel the same about the "what are you?" question. Although her 15-year-old, 10th-grade brother Gray, who identifies at school as both mixed and Black and white notes, "I don't honestly like that question," his 13-year-old, ninth-grade sister Aiyana, who identifies the same as Gray, says, "it depends on like how it's asked." She posits, "Because if you were to walk up to me and say hey, what's your race . . . some people even have the nerve to say 'what are you?' If they ask me that, then it gets me in a different mood. If they asked, 'what's your racial identity?,' I might answer differently and in a more polite way." Aiyana also notes, "I know I don't get asked that question as much as you do, Gray, or as much as Dad does because they automatically assume [Mom: what do they assume?]. They assume that I'm white. And assumptions in race is a very risky game to play because it's, to me it's annoying."

As the conversation unfolds, while Aiyana talks about the question as being "risky" and "annoying," she also acknowledges that much of her thought around the question is hypothetical because it is rarely asked of her. Aiyana does say that when she discloses her chosen way of describing her racial background to people as "mixed," people tell her "[*raises voice an octave*], 'oh really, I thought you were white.'" This seems to be a hurtful reading to the girl as her ending statement on the matter is an open-ended one, "And I was like, like . . . [trails off]."

What Aiyana shares speaks to education scholar Sandra Winn Tutwiler's (2016) insight, "Young people accuse each other of acting White or acting Black. This indictment can be directed toward a person of any race, and the accuser can be of any race as well. However, when a Black peer states that another Black peer or a mixed-race peer is acting White, it is meant as an insult. It is a jab of sorts—and a charge that a peer's behaviors are not in keeping with what it means to be Black. This accusation can be very distressful to the young person on the receiving end of the condemnation" (2016, p. 143). For Aiyana and others whose identity is not heard as their chosen racial identity, the hurtful words register as beyond just accusations of, in Winn Tutwiler's words, "acting White"—to actually being *seen* or *mistaken* as white. Aiyana experiences such misrecognition of her identity, whether genuinely or as a way of simply provoking her, as pushing on a soft spot that was particularly tender for this young woman, as it was for Kema earlier in the chapter.

Nevertheless, not all mixed-race kids balk at being asked the "what are you?" question, particularly if the question is part of an exchange between multiracial kids who desire to connect around their mixedness. Twelve-year-old 7th-grader Lucy, who identifies at school as mixed and comes from a Black and white background, explains, "I know mixed kids and mixed people don't like the term 'what are you?' But it's hard in other ways to ask if you're genuinely curious, because I know with my friends I just say, yeah, I'm mixed, because that's just how I say it. It's like, it's just what I am. But, if they were curious, I think it's hard to ask without saying what are you? Or what is your race?" At the same time, Lucy, who attends a diverse, all-girls middle school that consciously attends to racial issues, acknowledges, "That could seem very objectifying and putting people into boxes." What Lucy is illustrating is that the agentic nature of identification, which she is able to shift and choose, is important. In Lucy's case we can see how for some mixed-race people, identifying themselves and both asking about and claiming their own multiraciality vis à vis the "what are you?" question happens in concert with defying others.

LISTENING TO RACIAL IDENTITY DEVELOPMENT

As we have heard in this chapter, multiracial children and youth undergo racial socialization in a variety of ways. So how do we, as educators and parents, best support mixed-race kids as they choose to stick with or change their teams? First, as this chapter has made clear, we radically listen to them, to their stories of the pushes and pulls of identity formation beyond monoracial identity development models. As we listen we can also be attentive to the research that shows that mixed-race kids change their racialization as they negotiate various gatherings in their lives, from teacher interrogations, to hallway friend group hangouts, to classroom small-group work, to lunchroom table socializing. Our listening to the literature and the children helps to both challenge and support current multiracial identity development to more fully accommodate children's flexibility, movement, context, and agency. This chapter has been a focus on that agency.

One way to immediately support mixed-race kids is to radically listen for and use the racial labels that they choose at any given moment. Follow an individual's cues: listen, be open, and do not rely on preconceived notions of "racial looks" when you feel the need to name their racialized identity(ies). For example, in our dialogues and conversations with mixed-race children and youth we listened carefully for their cues of racial self-identification and then used them following their lead. In other words, if a student would call themselves "mixed," we would follow that lead and call them "mixed," and if another student would refer to themselves as "Black," we would do the same. It is not our job to racialize or impose our choice of racial labels on students. Radical listening and then using the identity labels kids want to be called can be meaningful for them.

These children and youth are racially fluid in ways often unseen and misunderstood by adult members of their school communities. Due to stereotypical representations, or, more often, the lack of representations of mixed-race people, teachers and schools are unable to fully listen to the experience of mixed children. In school, mixed-race kids can experience what communication scholar George Gerbner (1972) describes as symbolic annihilation, or representational absence (1972, p. 44). Adult inability to listen to kids affects the discipline, expectations, and self-determination of students and their identity development, and ultimately it can make the difference between mixed-race children developing and thriving or shutting down and deteriorating in school settings. In the next chapter we investigate these specific experiences of mixed-race kids and implicit bias.

CHAPTER 3

"He Didn't Even Know My Name"

Singling Out Mixed-Race Kids Through the Forces of Implicit Bias

In Chapter 2 we focused on the agency of children and youth as they listen to and make sense of race, both constructing and choosing their own racial identities. In this chapter we move more into the land of racial ascription—or perhaps better put as external racialization. In other words, we are moving from kids choosing their own racial identity to others imposing racialization on them. For mixed-race people whose race is sometimes not easily read, racialization is about the multiple, complicated, and at times competing forces by which the self makes sense of race internally. It is also about how the "other" or the observer makes sense of their race; racialization marks the spot where the constructedness of race meets its intractability. Mixed-race children's agency is usurped through racialization in many forms.

In the previous chapter we examined one form of agency-theft-through-racialization: when multiracial kids are seen as a racial identity that does not fit with their own self-conception. In this chapter we examine a different form of agency-theft-through-racialization: when mixed-race kids experience racialized stereotyping because of others' implicit bias. This theft happens when observers are quick with their assumptions, or their racialized reading of a mixed-race child or adolescent. In particular, when observers interpret racial ambiguity, make racialized assumptions based on their read of that ambiguity, and act on their interpretations and assumptions, they are not slowing down to really listen to what the child or youth wants. Sometimes, this means that a person doesn't read a mixed-race child as their chosen identity, as we saw in Chapter 2; at other times, this means that a person does read a mixed-race child as their chosen identity, and simply sees that chosen identity as a stereotype. This was the case with Rue.

Rue, a 16-year-old 11th-grader, who early in our interview tells us that she identifies as Black at school, but will reveal herself to questioners to be Black and white if pressed, recounts such a moment from 8th grade. This was a time "at lunch and I was the only Black kid in the classroom. I was eating with a class full of white kids and of course out of all the people [a white teacher] asked me a question saying, 'do you know how [Black football player] Richard Sherman's dreadlocks work?'" Rue acquiesced to his questioning, not having the power or the language to say, "why are you asking me—of all the kids in the class—these questions?"

But this attention did not feel good to Rue. After having a back-and-forth interaction with the teacher about the workings of Black hair, she notes, "I just remember feeling very pointed out in that moment because everyone looked at me when he asked me that question. I just felt really on the spot, and I was a little bit embarrassed." Rue pauses and clarifies, "Not embarrassed, but the fact that he pointed me out in front of everybody wasn't the best experience." She makes sense of why she was the one singled out by saying that she was clearly asked because, "Well, I'm Black and so I must know what dreads are." She continues, putting herself in the position of the teacher, "Everyone knows who [Sherman] is but let me just ask the one Black person in the room who would know." Rue makes her interpretation of the teacher's chain of thoughts clear as she talks through how she makes sense of the interaction: "I must know what Richard Sherman's hair is, I must know what dreadlocks are. Because of the way my skin color is, I have to know." Rue finishes her story by describing how this teacher was not one of her classroom teachers, and that, even, at her small private school, he did not attempt to get to know her. In fact, "He didn't even know my name so he was just like, 'you.'"

In our interpretation of this story, first we must hear Rue's pain, and how this event, 4 years prior, remains a formative one for her. But next, if we try to understand the teacher's point of view, we might postulate that maybe the teacher thought that he was performing a positive action in this moment by making a connection with a student. More specifically, perhaps he even thought that he was engaging in antiracist action by making a connection with a Black student. We empathize with teachers who struggle to align their impact and intentions with students of color. However, in the student's perspective, which is the one we are radically listening to in this book, we have to highlight the fact that the teacher was marginalizing her as the sole (mixed-race) African American girl in her classroom. He was quickly assuming a lot about her; in these assumptions he did not make space to listen to who she really was. The "who she was" here includes all of the complexities of her racial background as a mixed-race African American girl who identifies as Black at school.

In addition, the pain of this story lies in being singled out as different. That perception of difference comes from a flatness, the teacher's one-way desire to consume a singular version of Blackness that is based on curiosity and little else. Without permission or dialogic engagement, the teacher uses Rue as a Black cultural informant, who is expected to share out the "secrets of her race" at his whim. She is not valued for herself, for her individuality. She isn't even respected enough for the teacher to know her name, or to ask her what her name is. The pain in this story thus also comes in the teacher's refusal to hear her voice in her own terms. In singling out Rue, the teacher also forces her to consider whether she belongs in that room, or which aspects of her are valued.

Social psychologists Gregory Walton and Shannon Brady (2017) note that three of the questions people ask themselves when ascertaining essential questions of belonging are "do I belong here?," "do I have anything in common with people here," and "can I be me here?" (p. 272). As we explored in the previous chapter, for some mixed-race kids such questions might, in an instant, put into question a setting that has previously felt safe—indeed, this might be the case for all kids whose internal and external senses of self, or how they see themselves and how they're read, don't always align. The "me" that Walton and Brady define as at the center of identity work is slippery when the external and internal grind against each other. Indeed, that racialized "me" might be situational. In this example, the external self that Rue comes to understand through the teacher's reading isn't her—it's a stereotype, not the way this budding filmmaker, artist, softball player, sister, daughter, and friend sees herself. Furthermore, such racialization is dictated in tandem with the racism of outside observers, in this case of Rue's teacher.

In the previous chapter we framed and talked about mixed-race kids who described sometimes being read as white or having the experience of occasionally being white-passing, regardless of desire. We also talked about multiple-minority kids who shifted in their identifications with different schools and life phases. We note here, as always, that race is in the eye of the beholder and that racialized readings are not transcendent, across all readers at all times (Saperstein, 2013). In addition, we call on the words of education scholar Sandra Winn Tutwiler (2016) who argues, "Reducing mixedness a priori to race reaffirms essentialist identities in a way that denies complex subjectivity and ignores the lived ways that people negotiate their multiple and shifting identifications" (2016, p. 59). In other words, race is important, but it's not everything. We are now going to examine the experiences of mixed-race children and adolescents like Rue whose phenotypes prompt observers to link them with racialized stereotypes. We look here at two particular categories of mixed-race kids, first, those who are largely read as monoracial people of color, some of whom report people being "shocked" or "surprised" that they aren't "just Black," for example; and second, those who are largely read as racially ambiguous people of color, including those who report being interrogated about their background *and* who experience clear marginalization as people of color that also ends up devolving to anti-Black bias. As always, we want to note that although we are making a distinction between kids who are read as monoracial people of color and those who are read as multiracial people of color, that distinction can easily shift situationally, geographically, and in all other ways. We are following the lead of the students who report to us how they are read.

We identify two central factors: *implicit bias* on the part of the observer, with the significant effects on the mixed-race child being disproportionate levels of disciplining, and negative health outcomes, among others; and reading of the mixed-race person as *ambiguous*, with the significant impacts being cognitive depletion (which we will shortly define), anxiety, and fear. These factors lead to social distancing of the mixed-race child from the person reading them and from their educational and social contexts. Furthermore, where in the last chapter children's stories of fighting racialization, choosing different paths, and self-actualization around race buoyed us, in this chapter, unfortunately, our kids meet the forces of racism, and largely anti-Black racism. For a variety of reasons, they do not report having the same ability to speak back to racism. This reality is simply harder for many to hear. In addition, in our small sample, and not coincidentally, all of the kids who reported teacher neglect, hostility, and disproportionate discipline are part Black. In this chapter we continue to rely on the data that the 2015 Pew survey provides, and which was borne out in the stories of our interviewees, that mixed-race people who are part Black, like Rue, experience life in ways that "are much more closely aligned with the black community." In contrast, those who are mixed race and of Asian descent who the Pew survey reports, statistically "feel more closely connected to whites than to Asians" (Parker et al., 2015). Although our own mixed-race Asian American participants describe experiencing being misread in a wide variety of ways, they did not share similar stories of experiencing implicit bias and racism in their schools. We will explore what *singling out* means for mixed-race kids in this chapter. First, we review the literature on implicit bias. Then we connect to perceptual ambiguity, cognitive depletion, and mixed-race kids. As always, the stories of our participants weave their way throughout our literature. But before we go any further, here's an exercise.

ASSESSING YOUR OWN IMPLICIT BIAS:
A RADICAL LISTENING EXERCISE

In order to prepare for this chapter, please take the Implicit Association Test (IAT) at https://implicit.harvard.edu/implicit. Afterward, please set yourself up to listen to and share your results with your critical friend in a radical listening session, just like in the previous chapters. Set your timer for 2 minutes, and have speaker one go first as the critical friend partner listens intently for the speaker's intended message (attempting to not hear through the filter of their opinion). Switch after 2 minutes, and then at the end of the exercise share your impressions of each other's responses. You can talk about what you were expecting before you took the test. What surprised you? After you have read this chapter, come back to your answers. Have any of your answers shifted? Have any of your answers resonated with what you read?

The Kirwan Institute (2017) defines implicit bias as "the attitudes or stereotypes that affect our understanding, actions, and decisions in an unconscious manner." These biases, which encompass both favorable and unfavorable assessments, are "activated involuntarily and without an individual's awareness or intentional control" (2017, p. 10). One's implicit bias can be assessed through the IAT (Greenwald et al., 1998), a measure widely used to assess a range of issues. Where there is a stereotype, there is an ability to test for it with the IAT. In the case of race, there is a large body of data about implicit biases toward African Americans and the impact of those biases. We will cover some of that research below. But first, to understand what is being measured you must understand the test. In effect, in order to assess a person's implicit bias about Black people, the test asks participants to pair negative or positive words with brief images of Black or white faces by clicking left or right on the computer.

The research finds consistently that it's much easier for a person to pair negative words with Black faces and positive words with white faces—or rather, we are much faster at such pairing. Allison remembers sharing this research with an audience and a woman speaking up. She said, "I've taken this test before and I don't like it. I knew they were trying to get me to put negative with Black faces, and every time I saw that I'd say 'no' and then click." This intuitive audience member highlighted an important point: Yes, we can and do act in antiracist, nonstereotyped ways. We can consciously choose to move against bias. However, pausing, saying no, and then clicking takes much more time, far more energy, and greater cognitive reserves than simply going with our automatic assumption. Working against bias, against our automatic assumptions, takes time, effort, practice, and deep cognitive training. Our brains are far better suited to not work so hard,

A question that often comes up is "so what?" What does a high-bias score on this test really mean? Allison once gave the IAT as an assignment to her social psychology class. Students were asked to respond, much like you were. A number of students happily reported that they had "passed" the test. However, this is not the type of test that you pass. Nonetheless, many folks feel like their character, or more precisely, whether they are "racist" is determined by this test. But let's be clear: This is not some litmus test for whether a person is good or racist. Rather, the IAT is a simple test of speed and how much a person has been affected by, and how much their brain has taken in, stereotypical messages about groups of people. This is, however, not a way to let folks off the hook. Implicit biases are impactful, profoundly so. We often like to think about ourselves in the driver's seat of our decisionmaking. We like to see ourselves as always conscious, always making rational decisions. But we aren't. We are powered by an amazing brain that is often working outside our awareness and, in the case of implicit bias, outside our control. Some circumstances push us to work based on our biases, or rather, that facilitate our reliance on implicit bias: when we are busy, have to make multiple decisions, are under time pressure, or have reached a cognitive overload. Do those scenarios sound familiar? Do they remind you of a workday, or driving, or a medical visit? They should also remind you of a busy, active classroom.

Our educational system has created a context where teachers are often placed in classrooms where they have to be overburdened, are under time pressure, make multiple decisions, and thus experience a cognitive overload. We want to emphasize that we are not blaming teachers, but rather highlighting the context in which we have put teachers. What if we didn't have high-stakes testing that both ate up valuable classroom instruction time, and dictated where school resources were allocated? What if we didn't have classrooms packed with more than 30 children? What if our norm was team-teaching, where teachers could learn from each other in a critical friend model, checking each other on their implicit bias? What if race and equity training were simply a standard part of teacher education programs, of teacher in-service days, of weekly faculty meetings? Perhaps we'd have a context that wouldn't demand that teachers operate off of their "gut," which means, as we now know, off of their implicit biases. But this is not the educational system we have. We will explore some of these "what ifs" in Chapter 4 when we imagine better options for teachers, administrators, and school communities.

CHOKING ON THE SMOG OF IMPLICIT BIAS

Again we face a "so what" moment. Perhaps these biases live safely within our heads. Maybe we are able to override their automaticity with our intentionality. Not surprisingly, the stakes of implicit bias are incredibly high. In fact, they can be life or death. Scholars have robustly examined the impact of implicit bias and found it to be wide-reaching, affecting decisionmaking, hiring, firing, and medical care (The Kirwan Institute, 2017, p. 39). Implicit bias has been implicated in the school-to-prison pipeline through its effects on student engagement, achievement, and discipline (The Kirwan Institute, 2017, p. 27; Okonofua et al., 2016a, 2016b). This means that how children view themselves, while of central importance, is not the only factor in deciding how they are doing or how they are being perceived in school; how teachers and administrators view and treat children is incredibly important as well. We will spend time understanding what implicit bias is and how it affects mixed-race children.

For this conversation on implicit bias we will rely heavily on the work of psychologist Jennifer Eberhardt (2019). She states, "Implicit bias is a kind of distorting lens that's a product of both the architecture of our brain and the disparities in our society" (2019, p. 6). Our brains interact with an overwhelming amount of information each day, each second, in fact. In their sophistication and efficiency our brains rely on creating patterns, associations, and speed in order to process and make sense of the world. These patterns and associations are often the foundation for preference, which then, because of the ways in which preference is racialized in our world, lead to bias. Then, preference, instantiated in bias, when combined with action, becomes prejudice. So, you might ask, are our brains hardwired to make associations (even when false) that are fundamentally racist? Our answer to that, guided by Eberhardt's above statement, is no. Our brains are not hardwired to see particular associations, or to make particular biased interpretations. Rather, our brains create certain interpretations with the limited information available to them.

A more elegant way of describing the ways in which bias works comes from another psychologist. In a PBS interview a few years back, Beverly Tatum, a renowned psychologist and former president of Spelman College, explained that messages about race are like a smog, filling the environment with obscuring particles of stereotypes, of bias, about who is good, who counts as a person, who is to be feared, and who is revered (2003). These caustic materials often enter into our brains from the media, which we will discuss in the next section, but they also seep into our interpersonal exchanges as well as in how we observe people interacting. The smog oozes out of the pollution of our history and our institutions such as our schools. All of us, including young children and adolescents, breathe this smog and learn very quickly about who belongs and who doesn't. We need to remember that young children and adolescents are breathing the smog with their developing brains. Even as bright, sophisticated, and smart as all of our children are, they are still learning about race in the context of what their immature brains can understand. They're still learning how to categorize—who belongs in what group—and what counts for membership.

This smog analogy is particularly powerful and helpful if we take it a step further. Tatum calls us to think of the smog as poisonous messages that are ubiquitous in the air we breathe: What if we are asthmatics who still must survive in the smog? Although those of us without breathing issues might feel some discomfort with smog in our lungs, those with asthma will have an increasing number of asthma attacks and in the worst-case scenarios, a shortened life span. In fact, this is how a smog of oppression works. For example, the American Psychological Association (2013) has come out to say that racism affects health, and the American Pediatric Association (APA) has said that racism is affecting *children's* health in particular and therefore is a public health issue (Trent et al., 2019). We have consistent evidence that people who report experiencing racism have higher rates of heart disease, obesity, and diabetes—in short, diseases linked to life stressors (2019). Here, at the writing of this text, we are watching a pandemic unfold with clear disproportionate impact on Black, Latinx, and indigenous people due to profound intersections of racism, economic realities, and the higher rates of the aforementioned preexisting conditions. The science indicates that the chronic daily stressors associated with racism, and the larger stressors and barriers associated with systems of oppression, add up to fewer years of life. In other words, when you are on the downside of power along race lines, you are the asthmatic in the smog of racial oppression. But let's remember—smog isn't good for anybody.

When children are in this feeling, they are surrounded by a smog of racial oppression. This means that they are able to learn who is on the up and downside of racial power quickly, because these messages are, as psychologist Claude Steele writes, "a threat in the air" (1997). They are the stereotypes that are reinforced by who they see in positions of power, who they see positively portrayed in media representations, and who they see in their everyday interactions in the world around them. Children are also seeing who is more likely to be homeless, who is more likely to be working particular jobs, and who are more likely to be killed by police. This piece on how children see people interacting with others based on race was particularly important to our mixed-race students who reported being read more readily as African American. Children read as Black reported that they were disproportionately disciplined, singled out, and neglected in classroom spaces.

Mara, a 12-year-old 7th-grader who identifies as African American and participated in the session with her white mother Emily, initially shrugs off Emily's questions about being treated differently at school. Eventually, Emily wears her down: After Emily comes up with example after example of Mara experiencing racism at school, she begins to agree that yes, she is treated differently. Emily prompts Mara to tell us about her interactions with her math teacher, a man her mother says, "is disliked" (although she doesn't specify by whom), and in Emily's words, "made a racist comment about a mixed-race Asian student using chopsticks instead of a fork." This comment goes undiscussed by Mara, but it serves as the gateway for her to finally do what her mother has been asking for: to share her own experience of unfair treatment in her classroom.

Mara tells us, "If I ask [my math teacher] a question, he won't really answer or he'll say that I'm already supposed to know that like a different teacher should have already taught me this. He doesn't really listen to me. . . . A few times I've asked him a question and then another student has come up and asked him a different question and he's just gone and helped them." As soon as Mara begins telling her story, her words rush out and she no longer claims that she has nothing to share. When we ask her how her experience with her math teacher makes her feel, she responds, "Well, it's pretty bad. Because then I have to take all my work home and do it at home with her [*gestures towards her mother*] helping me." It's also important to note here that Mara is the only student of African descent in her classroom.

Ty, a 15-year-old 10th-grader who identifies at school as Black and discloses his whole racialized background to us as Black, white, and Indian, shares an eerily similar story about his own middle school math experience at a different school, and with a different math teacher. He explains, "Well, a few years ago in one of my classes, my math teacher he treated me differently, I felt like he treated me differently. He'd single me out a lot. And if I didn't know something, I would almost get shamed for it, more than, in comparison to other students." After this statement, Ty repeats for emphasis, "in comparison to other students," and adds that in contrast to his classmates' treatment by this teacher, "I would get like the worst of it probably." Like Mara, Ty was doing something ostensibly "good" students are supposed to do: They were asking questions when they didn't understand the material. In response their white male teachers summarily dismissed both children. Ty uses the words "get shamed" to describe his teacher's behavior toward him, and Mara describes behavior that sounds precisely like shaming (refusing to answer, saying that she should already know the material, ignoring her). Like Mara, Ty was the only Black student in the class.

Mara and Ty, the students experiencing differential treatment in their classrooms, are the asthmatics who are breathing the smog. Later on, Ty describes doing poorly in this math class for the first time in his schooling, and elects to retake the class the next year since he felt like he simply could not learn from this teacher. Mara struggled her way through her class but felt the extra burden of having to take her schoolwork home: Her family experienced the additional weight of the teacher's refusal to properly help her. The rest of the students in the class also breathed in the smog of these two teachers' implicit bias instantiated in differential treatment. They saw how the teachers shamed these two Black-identified mixed-race students—the only students of African descent in their classes. They saw how Blackness was demeaned in their classrooms, how Black children were designated as unworthy of help, and how, in direct comparison, other children were invested in with greater patience and greater resources. They learned that Blackness was simply less than.

Ty's sister Kema told a story about observing how whiteness was valued in her middle school, the same school where Ty was in class with the shaming math teacher, and of a moment where she learned that all students didn't deserve to breathe the same fresh air. "In the halls, our principal, she was more strict on the dress code with the Black kids. 'Cause there's this girl in our grade that . . . dresses older. [She wears] crop tops and stuff. She said that the principal once complimented her on her outfit even though it's against the dress code. She's white. [pause] And blonde." Kema says, in essence, that the principal complimented a white girl for the exact clothing for which she would discipline Black girls; she applied the official dress code differentially. What Kema observes is borne out in research. Morris (2005) writes that not just the behaviors but the dress of white and Asian American youth are rated by school administrators and teachers as "harmless" and "well-mannered" (Morris, 2005, p. 43). This is a moment in which white and Asian American youth are provided with gas masks, while Black, Latinx, and Native American youth are given polluted air to breathe.

Are there places with no smog? The simple answer is no. Each city, each school district, even each classroom has its own variation of smog. We have yet to encounter, or learn through research about an institution such as a school where someone isn't on the up, or downside of power, a place where stereotypes about a group do not exist at all. And yet, this is not the same as saying that we are doomed to systems of oppression or racism. Mara and Ty's experience does not have to be—and should not be—typical of a mixed-race African American—or any child's experience in the classroom. Listening to these children's differential experiences should serve here as an impetus for schools to acknowledge the disparate educations children are facing inside their classrooms, and to take steps to clear the air.

MEDIA AND THE SMOG

Why might Ty and Mara's teachers have thought them to be less deserving of math instruction? To think more about this smog, let's move from interpersonal instantiations of implicit bias to the role of media. Communication scholar Travis Dixon (2019) has done extensive work on how media paints the racial picture of what we perceive reality to be. Drawing on decades of how media effects scholarship, Dixon posits that exposure to race-based stimuli in media affects social perception and social cognition (2019). In fact, media effects scholars like Dixon draw on the classic work of George Gerbner and Larry Gross (1976) to understand *cultivation theory*, which posits that the more time we spend consuming media, the more we believe that our lived reality is actually akin to our televisual or media-constructed one (p. 76). Heavy users of media are also subject to something Gerbner et al. (1980) deemed "Mean World Syndrome": As they ingest more portrayals of violence, they believe quite simply that the world is a mean place. But the world doesn't look like what television shows, and, as Dixon shows, the news is often showing stereotypical representations of minoritized people, in particular, not documenting them accurately.

Dixon and his team examine three stereotypes of African Americans in the news: (1) as criminally involved, (2) as absent fathers, and (3) as poor. He found that African Americans make up 27% of those who are poor in the United States but 59% of those represented as impoverished in news and opinion media. Conversely, white families comprise 66% of the population who are poor, yet they make up only 17% of those represented as poor in the news. In addition, the news overrepresents the criminal involvement of

Blacks by 11%: While Blacks make up 26% of those who are arrested for criminal activity, they make up 37% of those shown in news and opinion media. By contrast, the news underrepresents the criminal involvement of whites by 49%: Although white people make up 77% of the people who are arrested for criminal activity, they are only shown in media and opinion news as being criminally involved 28% of the time (Dixon, 2017; Dixon & Williams, 2015).

Lastly, the news media has dramatically overestimated—to rates that are statistically significant—the unavailability or "absenteeism" of Black fathers. When commentators and journalists describe the lack of available fathers, they mention Black fathers 60% of time and white fathers only 20% of the time. However, according to multiple reports, including the CDC, Black fathers are actually involved in parenting at rates that match or exceed other racial groups' involvement. In one study, for example, only 20% of white fathers took their children to school or extracurricular activities while 27% of Black fathers did so (Dixon, 2017; Dixon & Williams, 2015). Again, according to the cultivation hypothesis, what we see is what we believe. These messages add up, in the quantitative ways Dixon describes, to our altered perceptions about who is good or bad, criminal or innocent, poor or middle class, or an involved or absentee parent. All of these messages contribute to the smog, the very real and palpable smog that inhibits our ability to see clearly, and that directly affects our health, our opportunities, and the ways in which we think, including the ways in which we parent and teach. Perhaps worse, while the media is a large "smoke stack" that emits this smog, we need to be aware that it's not only media that adds to the pollution. Our children are learning not just from media, but from what they observe in real life. And their observations are racialized.

Children note who they see in positions of power and who they see working menial jobs, and the races of those positioned as "powerful" and "weak" among us. Our children observe how we interact with strangers and loved ones, and indeed, the ways in which our interactions with both strangers and loved ones are racialized. They notice who we invite to our homes and how we treat each other. They note the race and gender of their doctors, their dentists, their babysitters, their teachers, and their principals. As parents we have control over some of these smoke stacks and none at all over others; as teachers we have perhaps even less control. And there are countless other smoke stacks, all of which contribute to the ubiquitous smog in our lungs.

Just as was the case with much of the psychological literature we examined in Chapters 1 and 2, Dixon's work investigates this issue in Black and white, which leads us to ask about the role of mixed-race kids and the media. What is clear from our radical listening sessions is that when mixed-race kids are racialized as Black (both with their self-identities and their racialization by their teachers), they are experiencing anti-Blackness at school—as Rue, Mara, and Ty all note. In addition, regardless of racialized identity, all of our children learn the lessons of anti-Blackness very well.

This analogy of the smog is a central piece of how we understand what happens in schools, and how mixed-race kids negotiate their place in their school environments. This piece is particularly important for families and teachers who cling to spurious notions of color blindness, which fail to prepare children and youth for the realities of implicit bias, as we will see in Chapter 5. We need to give all of our children gas masks even if we hate the smog. Hating the smog—or pretending it's not present—will not make it go away.

SMOG KILLS

We are going to pivot in this section to a topic that might, at first, not seem like it fits in a book on mixed-race children. What we are focused on here is implicit bias as it directly impacts Black people, and not exclusively those who are mixed race. As this book is explicitly antiracist in focus, issues of anti-Black racism—how to fully understand and therefore how to fully combat it—should be at the forefront.

As we have indicated thus far in this chapter, the smog is dangerous and can lead to health outcomes and death. As we are completing this book during a surge of racial uprisings due to the murders of Black people at the hands of police, we would be remiss if we didn't discuss what is at stake and how implicit bias seeps in, how it obscures our ability to see the people and children we care about. We need to take an important detour into the research on the dire consequences of implicit bias. Psychologists Jennifer Eberhardt and Phil Goff showed an image of a blurred out/pixelated gun to a number of people. The majority of folks who saw the initial image could not readily identify it as a gun. Eberhardt and Goff took an initial image of a gun and degraded it down to a fuzzy image. They then produced 41 images from completely out of focus to a sharp image of a gun. Next, they showed people these images and timed how many images the respondents had to see before they could identify the object as an actual gun.

In their study, Eberhardt and Goff provided three conditions (three small experiments within the larger experiment). In the first condition, they subliminally primed people with an image of a Black face, meaning that they showed people an image so quickly that if we asked them if they saw an image they'd say, "what image"? In the second condition, people were shown no face at all. In the third condition people were subliminally primed with a white face. What the researchers discovered was that those people who were subliminally primed with an image of a Black face were faster at identifying the image as a gun than those who saw no face at all. In other words, people experiencing the first condition saw *fewer* pictures before identifying the image as a gun than those who saw no face at all. Those people who saw the white face were *slower* in identifying the image as a gun than both those who saw a Black face and no face at all. Those primed with a white face took more slides to actually see the image as a gun. Goff and Eberhardt hypothesize that this means that "Black" and "criminal" are so closely associated that when people are primed to think about Blackness, it's easier to see ambiguous objects as criminal objects, in this case, guns. Conversely, in the context of whiteness, because white and criminal are *not* associated, it's harder to see an ambiguous object as crime related.

Goff and Eberhardt took this data to police officers, who found it compelling. This meant when officers are in a predominantly African American neighborhood, or when they are told a suspect is Black, or when they actually see a Black person, that due to implicit bias they might be more likely to see a wallet as a gun. Or conversely, when primed with whiteness, or seeing a suspect who is white, they might assume that an ambiguous object is harmless, rather than a gun. We must pause here and invoke the officers who shot Amadou Diallo 19 times in Brooklyn, New York, in 1999 when he was reaching for his wallet, and the officer who shot 12-year-old Tamir Rice in Cleveland, Ohio, when he was playing with a toy gun in 2014, only two of the more public and notorious stories of police misrecognizing Black people as dangerous.

Implicit bias does not just sit within our brains—it manifests in our interactions—sometimes with impacts of hurt feelings or exclusion, and sometimes with life and death consequences. We can also think of how this implicit bias may show up when someone views a mixed-race child and racializes them in the way that is most associated with their hair, skin, facial features, or perhaps even clothing, choice of sport, or musical taste. In other words, when mixed-race kids are read as Black, they may be subject to implicit biases held about Black folks. It may not matter that a mixed-race Black and white boy understands his identity as mixed when he is pulled over by a police officer, if a police officer reads him as Black.

Another example of these dire consequences of implicit bias comes from Eberhardt's research on death row sentencing: "In cases involving White victims, the more "stereotypically Black" the defendant is perceived to be, the more likely [he is] to get the death penalty." More specifically, the research team gave participants in an experiment pictures of death-sentence–eligible defendants. They were asked to rate those pictures as more or less "stereotypically Black." They were told they could use any features to help them decide, including skin color, facial features, and hair texture. They found that those men who "looked more Black" had been more than twice as likely to be sentenced to death than those who "looked less Black." This was the case even after controlling for significant contributing factors such as the severity of the crime, class, and attractiveness of the pictures. Eberhardt summarizes the impact of these findings by stating:

> It's not just group membership that influences perceptions; it's whether an individual's physical appearance triggers the sort of pernicious stereotypes that suggest that blacks are inherently so dangerous that they deserve extermination. . . . That's a sign that our perspectives, our criminal justice process and our institutions are still fueled by primitive racial imagery. (2019, p. 130)

This data is another way of speaking to the issue that it isn't only how mixed kids identify that determines how they are treated—how they are *identified* by others matters a lot. Although the data is mixed on how preconceived ideas about phenotype are related to how children self-identify, we can take these and many more studies together in order to postulate a similar effect: Those who have darker skin and with more stereotypically Black phenotypes experience more negative outcomes. Phenotype does matter with regard to how others categorize mixed-race children and adolescents, and we need to be aware of whether a child's physical appearance "triggers pernicious stereotypes."

IMPLICIT BIAS AND MIXED-RACE KIDS

There is very little psychological research about how mixed-race children are perceived in terms of implicit bias and subsequently how implicit bias affects mixed-race kids in particular. We want to be clear here that our referring to the perception of "mixed-race kids" does not amount to a particular racialization: Some mixed-race kids who are actually part white, as in the examples of Rue, Mara, and Ty thus far in this chapter, describe identifying and being read monoracially as their group of color. But some part-white kids might be read as white. Others who are of two groups of color might be read as neither or one of the groups. And again, situationally, all of this might change over the course of their days, weeks, or lifetimes. There are signs in the literature, though, about how implicit bias might (and most likely probably does) affect mixed-race children whose racialization is not easily readable, or who are "racially ambiguous." Eberhardt states, "Speed and *ambiguity* [emphasis added] are two of the strongest triggers of bias. When we are forced to make quick decisions using subjective criteria, the potential for bias is great" (Eberhardt, 2019, p. 285). Eberhardt also points the way to how we can address these biases: by causing friction—the concept we begin to address in the Introduction and will talk more about below.

Our previous examples of implicit bias research highlights the high stakes and consequences of implicit bias in terms of the justice system and life or death consequences. We turn now to the high stakes of the classroom as we hone in on what might be happening to mixed kids in the classroom. The Yale Child Study Center has produced several studies that indicate even in preschool and early childhood settings that Black children are seen by their teachers as guilty and scary. Furthermore, when researchers directed teachers to "look for trouble," they looked at a great number of times and for longer durations of times at Black children (Brown, 2016). This data should be considered in concert with other studies that show that when shown images of Black and white boys' faces, raters consistently overestimate the age of Black boys by 4 years; in effect, raters see Black boys as men far more quickly than white boys (Goff et al., 2014). Thus, while arguably all mixed-race kids, as kids of color, experience implicit bias, those who experience implicit bias in the form of disproportionate discipline at school (and result in the school-to-prison pipeline) are, to put it plainly, the children who look Black to their teachers, administrators, and other members of their school communities.

We can take one particular, compelling example of how implicit bias manifests within the classroom to understand how implicit bias affects discipline. Psychologist Jason Okonofua, a former graduate student of Eberhardt, did a set of studies about the role of implicit bias in discipline. Okonofua used a common methodology in social psychology, creating a consistent stimulus and only altering tiny bits of information. In this case he created a fictional referral (another word for a teacher's note indicating what the child did wrong) for discipline for a child in class. The child's first transgression was repeatedly getting up to get a tissue. Later that same child committed a second infraction of sitting in class with his head down. For the experiment, the researchers sent this referral to teachers across the nation, including Black teachers, white teachers, teachers in predominantly Black schools, and in predominantly white schools, in order to ask them how they would discipline the child. Although seeking to control for obvious variables, the tiny bit of information that Okonofua altered was the name on the referral. Half of the teachers received a referral with the name "Jake" and the other with the name "Darnell." Okonofua found that "Darnell" was more likely to receive a stiffer form of discipline and a steeper escalation of discipline on the second infraction than "Jake"; this recommendation of stiffer discipline came across the board from white teachers, Black teachers, and teachers of both diverse and homogenous school communities. The suggested punishments include "Darnell" being removed from the class.

Such removal punishes the child not only socially but academically, as he will not receive the benefit of classroom instruction for the time he misses, and when he returns to class, he will be behind the other students. Furthermore, the research of Christle, Jolivette, and Nelson (2007) have demonstrated that removing Black and Latinx students from the classroom doesn't actually change their behaviors. Remember, the only way to account for the difference in how the student was treated was through their racialized names. When the teachers were asked why they disciplined "Darnell" in the ways they did, they were more likely to use the term "troublemaker" to describe him. In effect, this study found that merely seeing the more commonly associated Black–American name Darnell on a paper scenario was enough to move teachers' biases to action. Education scholars Anyon et al. (2018b) note that we need to comprehend that from many school communities' points of view, "misconduct is understood as an indicator of students' cognitive or developmental deficits." However, they point out, "Some scholars have argued these youth-focused approaches are a form of social control that largely obscure the actions of school staff, discount institutional context, and ignore structural inequality" (2018b, p. 2).

Our mixed-race African American participants shared a number of stories that echoed such teacher bias. For example, Man Man, an 11-year-old 6th-grader, told a story of teacher bias with his 12-year-old, 8th-grade sister Velma. Both of the children describe themselves as identifying as African American at school, and attending a predominantly Black Catholic school that has predominantly white teachers. These two siblings' closeness was evident throughout their interview, with them easily finishing each other's sentences, and Man Man often asking his big sister Velma to explain a story for him, then piping in to help finish the story. This was the case for this story. Velma prompts Man Man, "Can you tell them about your detention?" In response, Man Man says, "No, you can go." Velma continues, "So he got a detention from her [his teacher] for supposedly for yelling at her, which I don't know if this is true or not." Here Man Man interrupts his sister saying, "It's not true." Velma, not acknowledging him, keeps going, saying, "but to handle this she had told another teacher, which was a Black teacher, the only Black teacher in the whole school." At this point Man Man jumps in again, saying, "Well, she didn't tell me I had detention, she told the other teacher." Velma continues, "And this teacher's a Black male right?" She continues for emphasis, "He's African American. He's like the only guy and African American and I don't know why [the white teacher] told [the Black teacher]."

Here Velma pauses. "It could have been race. [The white teacher] could have been scared to tell him [Man Man]." Velma continues, "Anyways, we go outside for this after-school recess or whatever it is, and she had told the guy [the Black teacher] to tell him [Man Man] that he had detention. So I'm wondering, why she wouldn't tell him herself?" Velma answers her own question without pause, stating emphatically, "I don't think she could handle telling [Man Man] he had detention." We share, here, some repetition in Velma's narration of the story because it illustrates both how she was making sense of it for herself and her brother, and what she was emphasizing in the story. Furthermore, Velma explains that Man Man isn't alone in his issues with this teacher as she notes this same white teacher, "couldn't handle another [Black male] student in his class." After Velma's narration ends, we ask Man Man directly, "Do you get the feeling that your teachers are afraid of you?" Man Man says, "I mean, I guess so." Velma agrees with her brother's sentiment, but also expresses how outrageous it is that grown-ups would be scared of an 11-year-old, gesturing to him and saying, "They can be afraid of that guy."

Both of us were so disturbed—and yet not surprised—by this story that we had to ask for the details again. We had to hear these children narrate how an 11-year-old 6th-grader's white female teacher was so "scared" of a less than 5 feet tall, less than 100-pound boy that not only could she not tell him that he had gotten a detention (which, he states to us that he did not deserve), but that she had to find not only another teacher, but a Black male teacher, to deliver the news of the punishment to him. This story also stands out because it is not an anomaly: It is a version of so many others happening in classrooms around the country. For example, in Seattle, Washington, in the spring of 2019, a couple of months after Velma and Man Man shared their story with us, a white female teacher called the police on her Black male 5th-grade student after "feeling threatened" by him (Bazzaz, 2019).

But what if we shift the lens on understanding "Darnell" and Man Man's "misconduct"? We wonder if there was friction here, if the outcome could have been different. What might have happened if the teacher was truly supported in slowing down, pausing in her discomfort? What would her actions have been, had the teacher thought, "Why am I scared of this boy and what does that mean?" What if that teacher had then been able to share these very uncomfortable thoughts with a critical friend teacher–partner to help her work through her biases? If the teacher had support to think about those uncomfortable feelings and been able to listen to, and really get to know Man Man, or "Darnell" for that matter, would that teacher still be afraid? What about if the teacher had invited Man Man in to her classroom, not for detention, but to get to know him, to help foster a sense of belonging with him, to radically listen to his stories, so that she wouldn't be afraid of a 10-year-old?

There is another story being told here with Velma and Man Man: Velma truly hears and understands Man Man's story. The two mixed-race siblings are co-constructing this story, finishing each other's sentences, and demonstrating their shared understanding. What we see Velma doing here is narrating "his" story—one that is too painful for him to even tell. This tight bond and racial literacy hasn't been forged accidentally. Throughout their interview the two describe how their white mother, who is parenting the two of them alone, carefully instills a racial consciousness in them, and fights hard for them to be heard in every setting, especially in their school. This radical listening, at home with Mom and between siblings, is what mixed-race children need to successfully negotiate school. At least here, in their own family, they celebrate their understanding of what happened.

They point out racism where it is at play and refuse to blame Man Man, the victim of racism. This, we hypothesize, allows them to tell the story with a combination of matter-of-fact, light-heartedness tinged with disappointment, as opposed to tears, fear, and sorrow. Velma slows the story down. It's a story she has heard, and, we suspect perhaps even told before, and it's clear that she really listens to her brother. Man Man and Velma's place of understanding becomes the locus of solace and belonging that so many of the kids we interviewed were asking for.

PERCEPTUAL AMBIGUITY, COGNITIVE DEPLETION, AND MIXED-RACE KIDS

As we listen to mixed kids talk about their experiences of racism, we have used the research on implicit bias to understand what might be happening. Here we move to what might be happening for the "listener"—the person who is trying to make sense of and listen to the mixed-race child. We have heard through the stories our participants shared with us and the previous body of empirical work that the identities of many mixed-race people can be fluid. This dynamic identity movement serves as both challenge and opportunity for a child's agency, but it also poses a test for the listener. How do we truly hear youth if their answer keeps changing? If race is a salient lens by which to understand a person, then an adult interacting with a mixed-race child may be pressed to categorize and understand that child. Consciously and as we will see, unconsciously, the listener is asking "Who is this person? How do I make sense of them? Where do they belong?" In this chapter we have turned to the role of the observer and away from the overt, "Oh I thought you were this?" questioning, to the implicit perceptions that actually drive much of our interactions, especially those interactions in a school community. These unconscious factors include both implicit bias and also cognitive depletion due to perceptual ambiguity.

Perceptual ambiguity is simply the inability for an observer to "clearly" identify the race of the mixed-race child. This kind of ambiguity turns out to be pretty distressing for observers. Research has found that racially ambiguous people "complicate social perception" (Gaither et al., 2018, p. 260). Further research found that people take longer to categorize racially ambiguous faces than unambiguous monoracial faces (Gaither et al., 2018). In the cases of racially ambiguous faces, people must look for other contextual cues to help them resolve this perceptual conundrum. Freeman et al. (2011) found, for example, that when subjects were presented with an image of a racially ambiguous man of Black–white descent, the person was more likely to be categorized as Black when he was wearing a janitorial outfit than when he was wearing a business suit. In other words—according to Gaither's interpretation—"perceivers will seek out additional information until they find an end point that resolves that ambiguity even if those cues are unconsciously applied" and racially biased (Gaither et al., 2018, p. 260).

The drive to "resolve" ambiguity is shown in the above study. As with implicit bias, this unconscious process is not inconsequential. It has been linked to another psychological process of cognitive depletion. Here is one way to think about cognitive depletion: We often think of our brainpower as being unlimited, an immeasurable ocean of ability and cognition. A more accurate analogy is that our brain is a "reservoir" that can be tapped and drained, and leads to a reduction in the ability to think. There is a limit on our ability to think. There are many factors that drain this reservoir: needing to make many decisions, being hungry, tired, overwhelmed, and also ambiguity. When this reservoir is drained, we are more likely to make mistakes and have a harder time thinking. The simple tests done to assess cognitive depletion are often cognitive performance tasks—when "cognitively depleted" people perform worse on those tasks.

Cognitive depletion is an important factor in the context of race-based discussions. On the one hand, research has found that raising the issue of race and discrimination explicitly in a conversation cannot only lead to an increase in open-mindedness for whites, but may actually encourage them to act more fairly, especially when they are given time to think about their decisions (Eberhardt, 2019). On the other hand, these conversations have also proven difficult for white people. Research has also found that when talking about racial issues, white people report and indicate higher levels of stress. They are often worried about making a mistake, causing offense, or being accused of racism. This translates into bodily distress, with studies finding that when white subjects are prompted to talk about race and/or asked to talk with a person of a different race that their heart rates increase and blood vessels constrict; in effect, their bodies are preparing for fight or flight. They also show signs of cognitive depletion (Eberhardt, 2019). Other work finds that this increased anxiety and cognitive depletion leads to reduced social interactions (Gaither et al., 2018, p. 18; Plaut, 2010).

A study conducted by Gaither et al. (2018) brought this research on cognitive depletion to bear on mixed-race people's experiences. She paired white study participants with "racially ambiguous" study participants who were of a Black and white racial mix. Indeed, white people who interacted with "racially ambiguous" mixed-race people (whose race was not identified) had high rates of cognitive depletion (lower performance on cognitive tests), in line with previous research. In effect, "when participants did not know their partner's racial background their interactions were more taxing and the biracial confederate [the mixed-race people who were "in on" the study] also perceived more negativity." In other words, the white people felt more negatively toward the mixed-race people who they couldn't categorize.

This is the science behind the "what are you?" question that animated multiracial studies so many decades ago. The students we interviewed often encountered the cognitive depletion of outside viewers, combined with implicit bias. We have personally experienced this frequently as well. One faculty evaluation for a large lecture class that Ralina received early in her career stated something to the effect, "if you just told us what you *were* I could pay attention in class better." That student was suffering from cognitive depletion and in this case was unable to see her professor as a purveyor of knowledge because she was so stuck on not being able to categorize her racially ambiguous looks.

Let's apply this study to Ty, the Black-identified 15-year-old high school sophomore who earlier in this chapter explained his middle school math teacher's shaming him for asking questions. Ty, and later his parents, shared another story of differential treatment by another teacher in his middle school, this time his language arts teacher. Over the course of a 6-week, end-of-the-year project, students researched a topic and turned in weekly assignments: from the first step of a topic statement on an index card, to the scaffolded pieces of the project including research sources, a rough draft, a final draft, and finally a PowerPoint presentation. Although Ty diligently turned in all of his assignments on time, his teacher, it turned out, never read any of them over the course of the 6 weeks, and so did not catch the mistake Ty made in step one: choosing a fictional event instead of a nonfiction one. It wasn't until Ty's final presentation that his teacher pulled him, the only Black boy in the class, out into the hallway to tell him that he failed the assignment because he chose his topic incorrectly. Ty came home in tears. And so his parents met with the older, white female teacher.

During the meeting, at which Ty was not present but was told about by his parents, the teacher refused to acknowledge her mistake or talk about the work that Ty had completed in the class, asserting instead, in Ty's words, "that I shouldn't be in the [gifted] program." Furthermore, she talked about Ty's probably wanting to "focus . . . more on basketball." Ty said, "My parents got pretty mad about that." The teacher made this statement, Ty said, despite the fact that he had never spoken to her about playing basketball. In processing this situation with us, Ty said that at the time, "I didn't really understand it until these last few years. I've been starting to realize, like exactly what she was talking about." In other words, Ty says that as a 6th-grader he didn't decode his teacher's racial coding that inferred that Black boys should play basketball and not be in honors classes, a phrase summed up by conservative talk show host Laura Ingram's "shut up and dribble" comments to LeBron James. When he was in 6th grade, Ty says, "I don't know, I was the only kid who was Black in that entire class, and it seemed like she just singled me out just because of that, 'cause there was no other reason for her to say that [I shouldn't be in the gifted program]. I feel that there was no other reason to say that. I had been getting an A or B in her class and I'd been trying, so there was no other reason for her to say that."

At first read this story appears to be cleanly and clearly about implicit bias. But on second read, this story could also be about implicit bias *and* cognitive depletion in the vein of Gaither's work. After all, many might read Ty as racially ambiguous: light-brown-skinned, curly-haired, mixed-featured, tall and athletically built. Perhaps she had questions about his racialization, or his racial ambiguity, and she racialized him as Black through basketball and also lowered her expectations of him in the process. This young, mixed-race African American student wasn't wearing a janitorial outfit or a business suit, but instead was in class metaphorically wearing a basketball uniform instead of a polo shirt in the eyes of his teacher.

From the combination of research and anecdotal stories offered here we believe that cognitive depletion is a factor in school for many mixed-race children. We draw upon the research to suggest that if a mixed-race child is racially ambiguous or seen as a racial minority, they are more likely to suffer the negative impacts of implicit bias. Just like implicit bias, cognitive depletion affects behavior in relationships. Thus, for many mixed-race African American kids, in particular, their teachers' cognitive depletion and implicit bias structure their school environments.

A CLOSING DILEMMA, AND A CAVEAT

While putting together this chapter we faced a dilemma that indeed we face throughout this book: When psychological literature all but ignores the experience of mixed-race children, how do we relate it to their experiences? Not only is the literature limited with regard to mixed-race kids, but it continues to reify the Black–white dichotomy and divide. As you will have noticed, we were not able to present a lot of data on how people of color besides Black folks fare with implicit bias. There is spare research that does speak about this, examining the impact of implicit bias on Latinx, Asian Americans, and Muslims, for example (The Kirwan Institute, 2017). The story pretty much ends the same, though: Where there is smog or a negative stereotype, there is implicit bias. The impact of implicit bias is overarching anti-POC-ness. Just as children aren't color-blind, neither are their educational environments. We also did not hear that their "ambiguity" necessarily allowed them to be heard more than Black students. In fact, teachers' implicit bias combined with cognitive depletion in the face of racial ambiguity can make situations more difficult for mixed-race kids.

In addition, as we did in the previous chapter in the section on white adjacency, we also want to note the very real light-skinned privilege of colorism that many mixed-race children who are part white experience. Critical race scholar Angela P. Harris describes racism as "discrimination against persons based on their racial identity, which in turn is traditionally designated through a complex mix of self-identification and other-identification through appearance (including color) and ancestry." She distinguishes racism from colorism, which she defines as "discrimination against persons based on their physiognomy, regardless of their perceived racial identity." Harris notes, "The hierarchy employed in colorism, however, is usually the same one that governs racism: light skin is prized over dark skin, and European facial features and body shapes are prized over African features and body shapes" (Harris, 2008, p. 54). As we have alluded to in this chapter, lighter-skinned African Americans fare better than darker-skinned African Americans in criminal sentencing, stereotyping, educational attainment, and family income, to name just a handful of factors (Blair et al., 2002; Keith, 2009; Keith & Herring, 1991). To give the example of one study, being dark-skinned and of African descent, legal scholar Taunya Banks (2000) notes, decreases a man's chances of being employed by 52% (2000, p. 1721). Mixed-race children and youth who benefit from light-skinned privilege (which is most definitely not all mixed-race kids, but many who are part white) need to understand this privilege as well.

Just as in the last chapter we warned that the lure of white adjacency could ultimately play into a courting of white privilege and a problematic utilization of privilege, we warn here against claiming mixedness in the face of implicit bias. We don't want to give you the impression that the solution to implicit bias is for adults to push children to seek white adjacency, passing or even claiming mixedness. Mixedness is not some escape hatch to the impact of racism. What we hear is story after story of how race and bias affect mixed-race kids. We can hold empathy for any parent, or teacher, who grasps on to hope that being mixed-race amounts to transcending race. However, we need to listen to these voices, voices of today's youth who say that their mixed-race identities have not shielded and protected them from racism or implicit bias. In the previous chapter we heard youth speaking to their agency, their ability to push back and define themselves. Here we have listened to them talk about when their agency is robbed and their experiences are invalidated. However, as in the story between Man Man and Velma, we have also heard that talking, listening, and validating each other can help make sense of these moments. In short, radically listening makes a difference.

Thus far we have established a foundation of how children and young people make sense of race and can agentically construct their identities. We have also addressed the push and pulls of contextual factors on self-identification and the impactful role of how mixed kids are perceived vis à vis implicit bias. This foundation has highlighted the pitfalls, and at times harrowing consequences of misperception, failed racial ascription and, to put it bluntly, racism. But as we will see, mixed-race kids' experiences of (at times lack of) self-identification and others' implicit bias also point the way toward solutions that can be implemented in the classroom and at home. As we listen to the young people, the theories, and the empirical evidence, important stories emerge. We will listen to stories in the next chapter of how teachers can foster meaningful relationships with mixed-race kids.

CHAPTER 4

"Relationship Is Key"

How Teachers Are Radically Listening to Mixed-Race Kids in Schools

We asked our mixed-race student participants which teachers made them feel the most like they belong at school. Ty, the 15-year-old 10th-grader who comes from a Black, white, and Indian background and identifies as Black at school named his history teacher Mr. Day as being just that person. So we interviewed him. Mr. Day teaches at a large, racially diverse urban high school. In an interview with us, Mr. Day notes that for him, "relationship is key." His teaching philosophy comes from a Maya Angelou quote that is, in his words, "People will forget what you said, but they'll always remember how you made them feel." Although Mr. Day notes, "All the content that I do is important and it'll be beneficial for students in their educational career and maybe their professional career," what actually makes him "consider myself the most successful" is "if my students come to my space and they feel like they felt seen, they felt validated and they felt like they were treated as more than just a person who was supposed to be graded."

In other words, Mr. Day upholds relationships with his students above all else. If that foundation is there, "especially for a lot of students of color, if you have that established relationship, you can be talking about how paint dries and students are more likely to roll with you. They may not roll with the content . . . naturally because they're interested in it [but] because you're talking about it they're going to follow you and they're going to do work with you because they appreciate you." Mr. Day provides a solution for how to radically listen in a school community in such a way that benefits all children. In this chapter we will listen to the voices of successful teachers, such as Mr. Day, in tandem with the words of our student respondents who give voice to the ways in which they were (and also were not), in Mr. Day's words, "seen," "validated" and "treated as more than just a . . . grade."

The children we interviewed told us that problematic racial ascription, misreading, and racism in the classroom deeply affects their relationships with teachers. Put another way, these relationships affect their ability to learn, to feel seen, heard, and to trust their teachers (Anyon et al., 2016; Stevenson, 2008). Consistent research shows not only gaps between kids of color and white children in terms of academic achievement and disciplinary outcome, but also in student engagement, climate, and relationships. In short, children of color report having fewer positive relationships with school adults (Anyon et al., 2016; Cook et al., 2018; Gregory et al., 2018; Okonofua et al., 2016a; Skiba et al., 2014; Stevenson, 2008; Yeager et al., 2014). The bulk of the research on these gaps has focused on establishing that these differences exist, and on Black versus white children to the exclusion of other racialized groups (Bottiani et al., 2018). More recently, however, the research has turned slowly but deliberately from documentation to remediation of academic achievement, engagement, and disciplinary gaps (see, e.g., the 2018 *School Psychology Review*, Volume 47, issue 2). That research targeted a root cause of these disparities: failed student–teacher relationships (Anyon et al., 2016; Bottiani et al., 2018; Bradshaw et al., 2018; Cook et al., 2018; Cornell et al., 2018; Gregory et al., 2018; Larson et al., 2018; Okonofua et al., 2016b; Voight et al., 2015). In the words of Anyon et al., "Policies and practices which aim to improve racial equity in education need to attend to relationship dynamics in schools and develop school staff members' skills in connecting with youth of color" (2016, p. 350).

The children and youth we interviewed clearly detail the difficulties that come with being mixed race in school. In fact, what we heard from them the most were the challenges, so much so that we had to set out on a second round of data collection in order to hear solutions. Indeed, even after this second round very few of our students responded positively to our question "Who makes you feel like you belong in school?" Most students simply could not identify any teacher who played that role of fostering belonging for them: The teachers like Mr. Day that we highlight here stand out as all too rare. The psychological literature, too, focuses on the problems experienced by mixed-race children in educational environments. But what we know from our lived experiences and from the voices of the children and teachers we interviewed, we are more than the sum of our challenges; we are more than our trauma. What also emerges from our children's stories is their healing, resilience, and generative capacity to be healthy, to do well, and to even thrive.

The solutions are right here, available to us if we listen. The children have told us what they want. In the words of Kai, a 10-year-old Black, white, and Mexican 4th-grader, who identifies as Black and Latino at school, "Don't just call on one person pretty much the whole time. If you see different people that raise their hands up or like they don't really answer the question, pick on them so they can get a little more comfortable raising their hands or answering the question." Kai's advice came after sharing how his teachers silenced him while he noticed they encouraged his classmates, often girls, to speak; he is telling us that he simply wants his teacher to value his voice in class. Furthermore, in the words of Jessica, a 12-year-old Asian American, Native American, and white 7th-grader who identifies as Asian at school, teachers simply need to "stand up for [kids of color who are being targeted], like you know, use your privilege, and like stand up for other people." This means, in a very basic way, "I mean, like, talk to the children who are being racist to other kids." Jessica's advice came after she iterated a heartbreaking experience of racism on a school trip; she simply wants her teacher, who heard about the comments and chose not to say anything, to intervene when she hears about her students experiencing racism, and not to pretend that she simply doesn't hear.

The psychological literature, despite its focus on the negative, also shows us that there is evidence about what works, and that there are real ways to follow Mr. Day's, Kai's, and Jessica's suggestions that amount to simple, tangible, trainable ways to foster radical listening. Plain and simple, we are called to hear their stories as the children and youth tell us; to refuse their objectification; to protect them from being overwhelmed; and to listen in new ways to their humanity. The fallacy of a hierarchy of humans is replicated through systemic, institutional, historic racism. It also circulates through interpersonal racism, the pervasive smog of implicit bias that tricks our brain into seeing "the other" as deficit. These various racisms cause the misreading, the invisibility, and ultimately the hierarchy that our children feel. The solution, the means by which we can heal, and ensure our children are heard, is through relationships. In this chapter we map out the ways in which schools can foster such relationships from improving school climate to creating spaces of racial listening that affirm the humanity of all children.

SCHOOL CLIMATE

Schools can foster positive relationships with students of color by intentionally working to create a climate that affirms the most minoritized students in the building. School climate is a way we can understand how students get along with each other, staff, and teachers. Voight et al. (2015) state that "climate refers to experiences of safety, connectedness to school, opportunities for meaningful participation and the quality of relationships between students, [and] staff." "These factors," Voight continues, "are related to both student achievement and behavior." School climate predicts outcomes such as achievement levels, suspensions, and expulsions. Climate is also linked to how middle schoolers actually view themselves, their rates of depression, and behavioral problems. In effect, when middle schoolers rate their school climates more favorably, or as being more safe, their outcomes—behavior, mental health, academic achievement, and disciplinary outcomes—improve (Voight et al., 2015).

Voight et al.'s 2015 study examines student and teacher survey data from more than 400 California middle schools. Their findings indicate that Black and Latinx students reported experiencing less favorable school climate. To be more specific, Black and Latinx students rated their schools lower in terms of safety, feelings of connectedness, positive relationships with school adults, and opportunities for participation. We also want to highlight another finding from this research: Climate—*while experienced differently by children of color*—affects *all* children. *All* students have a more positive assessment of school climate when there are clear and strong norms of cultural diversity being respected and active efforts focused on closing the opportunity gap. Schools with a value placed on multicultural-ism, made real by training and a diverse curriculum, also have students who feel more positively about school climate.

And yet, multiculturalism as it currently exists in many schools might not actually meet the needs of all mixed-race students. Indeed, multiculturalism can be so ubiquitous in U.S. schools that Suárez-Orozco and Suárez-Orozco (2001) note that "entry into American identities today is via the culture of multiculturalism" (2001, p. 357). But this multiculturalism is often a monoracial-specific version, which does not necessarily allow for mixed-race students to share all of their stories. Mica Pollock writes, a "racial regime" can be a challenge because traditional multiculturalism happens "one at a time" (2004, p. 42). As there is no room for multiple forms of mixture, this can be particularly hard for multiple-minority multiracial kids. The question remains, as Cauce et al. write, "How does one recognize ethnic differences and support ethnicity as an important dimension of self-definition without paradoxically encouraging group divisions and intergroup tensions that of-ten result when ethnic categories are emphasized?" (1992, pp. 140–141). The challenge for mixed-race kids doesn't always come in color-blind spaces, which education scholar Sandra Winn Tutwiler notes, "disappear mixed-race students," but also from multicultural ones that fail to see all of the shifting, changing, and dynamic identities that mixed-race students bring to school (2016, p. 206). One way to listen to a variety of student stories for all minoritized students is by creating affinity groups in schools.

AFFINITY GROUPS: FORGING MIXED-RACE KINSHIP IN SCHOOL

Bringing groups of minoritized students together to share their stories en-ables a school to create, in the words of Voight et al. (2015), "a positive school climate . . . that makes students feel emotionally, physically safe, part of the school community, that adults in the school respect them, care about them and have high expectations for their wellbeing and success, and they have opportunities to provide input in how things work at the school." As a matter of fact, the participants in our study also talked about the cen-trality of their peer relationships. As children become older, their peers have more and more influence on them. As we mentioned in Chapter 1 in our discussion of racialization and children's choice of friends, many of our participants chose to be around other mixed-race kids, noting, as Black and white 12-year-old 7th-grader Lucy, who identifies as "mixed" at school, does, "a lot of my close friends are mixed, like, a lot." This, in essence, creates a de facto affinity group.

In a more official capacity, school affinity groups are one way that schools can foster connections for minoritized children. Rosetta Eun Ryong Lee, outreach specialist at Seattle Girls School (SGS) in Seattle, Washington, and nationwide leader in diversity and inclusion efforts, leads independent schools in creating their own affinity groups (Lee, n.d.). Lee describes how affinity groups are one of the many pieces that must be in place in order for a school to be antibias. Indeed, SGS proudly proclaims its anti-bias mission, and the affinity groups fit firmly into that mission (Lee, n.d.). Some of the salient features that Lee lays out in the creation of affinity groups are: faculty and staff hold annual discussions around affinity groups "to gain or reattain [sic] shared understanding"; affinity group meetings are not held concurrently so that students with multiple identities do not have to "choose" which of those identities to honor, and the head of school sends home communication about the affinity groups early in the school year so buy-in comes from the top.

Several of the participants spoke about the amazing and supportive impact of their school affinity groups, and so we interviewed Diana Kwon, a school leader whose work supports affinity groups at one of the schools a number of the student participants attend, and whom a number of our participants at that school named as the person who helped make them feel as though they belong at school. Ms. Kwon works at a small, independent school that is known for being both progressive and racially diverse. She created affinity groups at her school after students from her own minoritized background repeatedly congregated around her in the lunchroom; soon after this experience she attended an affinity group meeting at the National Association of Independent Schools People of Color Conference (PoCC). She describes reporting back to the students about affinity groups as a space to "get together based on our racial identity and cultural background and . . . talk about stuff that was real to us, important to us. Things that we wanted to vent about, talk about, connect about. And you can talk about whatever you want about being" a member of that group. She said that the students jumped at the opportunity. From both student and faculty demand, what began as one affinity group grew organically to a variety of groups for different school populations that included minoritized students in terms of race and ethnicity, sexuality, and even neurodiversity. Kwon notes that having the multiracial affinity group means that there is a place for "a kid [who] would be living in two different spaces . . . And [instead of] . . . feel[ing] for the kids like I have to pick one aspect of myself . . . I can show up fully as this mix. . . . It's like sometimes I don't feel that sense of full belonging in either half of my affinity spaces. But when I show up to the mixed-race space, even though we're all different mixes of different things, there's something that just feels really shared."

Kwon also describes affinity groups as spaces that embrace a diversity of experiences within any given group identity. Giving the example of the Black affinity group, she notes, "This is not a group for all the kids who think about Blackness the way you do. It is really about setting up a space where various experiences of Blackness and that sense of belonging and worthiness or not, within the group and outside of the group can be openly talked about." Affinity groups aren't student-led clubs, but rather adult-facilitated spaces where, Kwon shares, the adult in charge, who ideally shares the same identity as the students, is careful to acknowledge that "this is not about me rehashing my childhood. This is not about me working out my own stuff. This is about me being an adult who mirrors them, the adult who's most likely to say, 'I know what you mean.'" In addition, "If there are things that bubble up from that group, you're the adult responsible for advocating to make sure that gets addressed somehow, whether it's amplifying and talking to a teacher directly or amplifying it to a grade level conversation or an administration conversation."

Kwon gives the example of when, in the Asian/Pacific Islander affinity group, a group of students shared their feelings that their teachers' expectations for them were higher than other students in a particular math class. Kwon encapsulates the students' concerns as "that somehow non-Asian kids would get a [math] problem and they would get affirmed in ways, that when they got it right, it was like, of course you did. And so they felt there were different criteria." The students were identifying a moment of implicit bias on the part of their teacher which dictated that all Asian American kids were supposed to be good at math. These different expectations make it hard for them to ask for help, or to have their efforts fully appreciated. After the affinity group meeting, Kwon followed up with the teacher and said, "I'm not saying you're doing this, but I'm saying the kids feel this. So something to think about is, please do think about how do you respond to various students. Because true or not, the feeling came up multiple times for multiple kids." Kwon notes, as Jessica did in the start of this chapter, that if students are bringing up incidents, that as adults in a school community, "we have a responsibility to do something about it. That's one of the responsibilities as far as I'm concerned of an adult facilitator" of an affinity group. Kwon radically listened to her students and used her power to lean into an uncomfortable moment with her colleague. She engaged in friction in this moment, and in doing so helped him listen better. Following the tenets of radical listening, (1) she deeply listened to her students and in the process heard about power inequities they were experiencing in the classroom; (2) pursued an uncomfortable conversation full of potential conflict with her colleague, centering their students' concerns; and (3) provided him with guidance for action to change his behavior.

We can see how the affinity group, and having an adult able to radically listen within that group helped to address the kids' concerns. While perhaps not all students in school communities are using the words "affinity groups," students are asking for spaces to be heard, and affinity groups are easy ways for schools to do just this. But, as Kwon notes, they are more than simply student clubs. Affinity groups are a way for schools to support minoritized populations, and they are also a mechanism to support intergroup dialogue, or difficult conversations between majority and minoritized populations (Tauriac et al., 2013).

Although the psychological literature provides little research on the empirical impact of affinity groups, publications in independent school trade journals speak to the history, how tos, FAQs, and pitfalls of affinity groups (Denevi & Richards, 2018). There are a handful of articles that address affinity groups for teachers—meaning groups where teachers can come together according to shared identity (Mosely, 2018; Pour-Khorshid, 2018). This work gives us the opportunity to hear that teachers themselves benefit from affinity spaces where they feel supported, as in the critical friend model. If this helps teachers, then might it work for students? Furthermore, as Kwon bluntly puts it, "If the overall school population isn't welcoming and the parents are welcoming, sometimes affinity spaces are the one time during the entire school day, like 24/7, that they feel like they belong. So how dare we not provide a space like that?"

We also want to note that not all children are able to attend schools with affinity groups. In fact, one of our participants, 16-year-old Rue who identifies as Black, and has Black and white heritage, told a story of being shut down at her own small, private, majority white school when she and other Black students approached the administration about beginning what one can think of as a Black affinity group, a Black Student Union (although a BSU doesn't traditionally have the adult facilitation that Kwon describes as the basis of her affinity groups). Rue recalls that a white female student heard of the Black students' request and complained that she would be left out if the school were to begin a BSU. Instead of supporting and listening to the needs of the Black students, the administration supported and listened to the white student's fragility and denied the Black students the right to create their own group.

Although majority students might raise such concerns, schools have the responsibility to provide a sense of belonging for all students, which means articulating why, for example, "segregation," is permissible in certain educational environments. Rosetta Lee, the school leader we cited earlier, has produced a useful guide (see Appendix C) that schools can use to address concerns around a variety of things including, for example, segregation. Lee writes, "Restrooms, sports teams, churches and synagogues, and school clubs are all ways we self-segregate based on interests, beliefs, sex, etc. Affinity groups are just another form of that optional self-segregation" (see

Appendix C). Put another way, school leader Kwon stated that she responds
to parents who object with the explanation, "this is a temporary space, a
very miniscule space that your [child] doesn't get to go into. You're ok with
[a girl child] not going to the men's bathroom. You're ok with her not going
to the teacher's lounge. You're ok with her not showing up to another grade
level's classes. There are so many ways that your [child] is not supposed to
be in certain spaces." She continues, encouraging folks to think more, "Why
is this space so problematic? Because I'm trying to get them to think about
what is unacknowledged fear around assembly? Or unacknowledged privilege." Students are asking for their protected spaces to connect with each
other, share stories, and hear each other. In essence, minoritized students
are asking to gain a greater foothold in order to feel like they belong more
at school. Affinity groups can provide these building blocks of belonging.

Radical Listening Activity: Affinity Group Time

For this activity you will enact a sample affinity group meeting for part one of
the activity; you will connect with your critical friend in part two of the
activity. Please gather a group of three to five folks who are like you in some
similar way: race, gender, class, sexuality, or an intersectional identity (i.e.,
women of color). Do not shy away from privileged identities (i.e., a group of
white, cisgender men). As you prepare yourself to read the conversation
prompts below, note that the conversation you will have is simple. The stories
that members tell might be sad, but they do not have to be stories of trauma.
They can be funny stories, stories of joy. Each person will go around and
answer three simple questions (inspired by those used by Rosetta Lee in the
Asian/Pacific Islander Affinity Group at Seattle Girls School).
    Please also note the important sample ground rules shared by Lee:

Sample Ground Rules
  1. What goes on in the group must stay in the group. When
     appropriate, leader(s) will act as advocates for the group to help
     bring about change for those in the group.
  2. Don't put down other groups.
  3. No side talking—respect the speaker.
  4. No interrupting.
  5. Be supportive.
  6. Respect those not in the room by not using names when talking
     about other people.
  7. Give everyone a chance to talk.
  8. Stay on topic of discussion.
  9. Don't put words in other people's mouths.
  10. In this safe space, every question is a good question (Lee, n.d.).

For a group of folks who gather around a mixed-race identity, the three starter questions would be:

1. "What's good?" (which gives the opportunity to begin a check-in on a positive note).
2. "What's mixed with you?" (which prompts the affinity group member to think about their personal minoritized identity that is being celebrated in that space).
3. "What's mixed in the world?" (which encourages the affinity group member to see their experience as existing beyond themselves and the gathered group of folks).

After experiencing the affinity group, please connect with your critical friend to unpack the experience. As in previous chapters, set up your 2-minute timers, and take turns in the serial testimony, radical listening manner. You can answer these prompts: What was it like to have the experience of an affinity group with your identity foregrounded? What did you notice? How did you feel?

CENTERING STUDENTS' VOICES IN THE CLASSROOM TO FOSTER POSITIVE RELATIONSHIPS

Affinity groups are about fostering belonging. But what about when belonging is shunted aside and conflict arises outside those groups? If affinity groups are when students can choose the people they want to be with, those who are "like them," educators need other approaches to address issues that come up when students can't simply choose the folks with whom they want to connect. Tatiana, an 8-year-old 2nd-grader of Black, white, and Latinx background who describes herself as Black and white at school, describes how one of her teachers centers and really listens to students' voices. She tells a story about what happened in her Spanish immersion public school classroom: "We were in English class [and] somebody said something that Black people were stuff, and white people were stuff, and mixed people were stuff. And it wasn't nice." When this type of negative talk happened, Tatiana told us that the students who observed the behavior "told the teacher and Maestra said that isn't nice. We have to have a talk about it." The talk comes in the form of "healing circles" where "we have like a bear or something like that. We pass it around and you get to talk. . . . The healing circles are where everyone goes into a circle around the rug. We talk about how people are being mean. You look around and see if anybody has a hand up. If their hand's up that means that they got hurt by you so you've got to say sorry for what you did. So you keep doing that in a circle." Tatiana finds that "[the Healing Circles] are really good because you can see if anyone is hurt because then you can apologize." Tatiana's public Spanish immersion school previously received a grant for restorative justice (in which teachers are moved not to go straight to punishment, but rather to seek solutions from those who have been harmed), and this particular teacher worked hard to enact some of the tenets in her classroom.

Another teacher at Tatiana's school, Maestra Catalina, shared the following story with us. One morning a couple of years before, in her 2nd-grade classroom, one of Maestra Catalina's students, Pedro, a lighter-skinned Mexican American boy, told Esperanza, who is African American and Latinx, that she was "too dark" to play with. Esperanza was very upset. Maestra Catalina quickly intervened: She went to Esperanza and [*standing next to her*] told all the children that it was not ok to exclude classmates because of their skin color. She then asked Esperanza what she'd like done about the situation. This question comes from both the empathic focus of the teacher and lessons learned from restorative justice. Esperanza said that she wanted to think about it and decide tomorrow. She came back the next day, having written a letter. Esperanza told the teacher that she wanted to read the letter to the class and to Pedro. She read the letter, in which she talked about how bad it felt to be excluded because of her skin color, how it wasn't right, and how she didn't want it to happen again. The other children, moved by what she said, agreed with her letter and then decided to come up with class rules about discrimination, that not allowing someone to play because of how they looked or their gender wasn't allowed. They did this all without shaming or harming Pedro, who made the comment, but rather by educating him and others in the class. After this was done, Maestra Catalina went back to Esperanza and asked her what she thought about this process. Esperanza responded, "I feel like I'm on the clouds." This story shows how centering the experiences of our children and really listening to them help them feel empowered to deal with bias. This teacher, in fact, organized a way that ensured that all students in the classroom really heard this child; the entire classroom listened to her hurt and listened to her request for solutions. It shows that the basics of radically listening to children can be used to not only address one wrong, but support all children in their learning.

DEEPENING RELATIONSHIPS IN THE CLASSROOM: EXPECTATIONS AND ACCOUNTABILITY IN RELATIONSHIPS

The example of affinity groups and restorative justice circles in schools demonstrate how school opportunities can deepen relationships between minoritized students and school adults, and make them more authentic. Now we will move to other moments in school that can provide—and shut down—opportunities for deepened listening and relationships, this time in the classroom. But while we will focus on opportunities for success, there is much research demonstrating that teachers are more likely to perceive Black students, in particular, as threatening, problematic, troublemakers (Gregory et al., 2018). A large body of literature has documented the biases of teachers toward Black and Latinx students, finding that teachers expect less in terms of not only behavior but also academic achievement from these children (Stevenson, 2008). Additionally, Tenenbaum and Ruck's (2007) meta-analysis of teacher expectations and behavior toward white, Black, and Latinx students found that teachers held more positive expectations of white students than students of color. Teachers' racialized expectations reduce the opportunities for children of color to participate and be heard in their classrooms in meaningful ways. This contributes to the robust findings that Black, Latinx, and indigenous children are more likely to be disciplined more harshly for misbehavior and are more likely to receive exclusionary sanctions for the same behavior as white children (Gregory et al., 2018).

When racial disparities in discipline are felt and seen by children in schools, such disproportionality contributes to lower feelings of care, connection, and respect for all children in that school (Anyon et al., 2016; Voight et al., 2015). By middle adolescence children of color have come to anticipate being treating differently by teachers; they are in fact, and unsurprisingly, aware of the low expectations and also the differential discipline described in the research. There is also evidence to indicate, as we will discuss later in this section, that in this context teachers often "overpraise" mediocre work, especially that of children of color. This research also rings true beyond middle school schooling experiences, as students' experiences of connectedness in both high school and even college are affected by whether a school is equitable or not. When those youth see racially inequitable discipline, it effects all students' connectedness at a school (Anyon et al., 2016; Voight et al., 2015).

WISE FEEDBACK

However, connectedness can be forged, particularly in the classroom context. One way in which such connectedness (a way of forging belonging for students) is created is through providing "wise" feedback. Walton and Wilson (2018) note that

'Wise' is borrowed from Erving Goffman (1963), who used it to describe straight people who saw beyond the homophobia of the 1950s to recognize the full humanity of gay people. Later Steele (1997) describes 'Wise schooling' as practices sensitive to the experiences of students who confront negative stereotypes in intellectual settings. . . . Wise does not mean 'good' or 'superior' or that other approaches are bad or unwise. (2018, p. 618)

Some educators seem to instinctively produce wise feedback. As Mr. Day stated in the opening of this chapter, children must be feel seen or heard by the adults around them; if they do not feel seen or heard, they begin to lose trust. In the educational endeavor, trust is essential: It is the foundation of the relationship and connectedness about which we are speaking. Other teachers who might not instinctively produce wise feedback can be taught to do just that. Yeager et al.'s (2014) work on feedback offers an elegant, simple means of reestablishing trust.

April Pak, a computer and language teacher at a large urban middle school, shared how she holds high expectations for her students of color. Ms. Pak is one of the teachers identified by one of our student participants as someone who made her feel like she belongs at school. In an interview with us, she gives the example of a conversation she has just had with a handful of Black female students who are succeeding in her class now, late in the quarter, but who had struggled earlier. She explains that she told them, "'I'm going to be real with you. . . . Here's the thing. You just finished this assignment. You did it well, and now you know how to submit it. The reason I was so hard on you two assignments ago when you didn't do it and you didn't hand it in is because I know you can do it. This is now proof that you can.' Being honest and reminding them to see the growth that they've made is so important. An affirmation that they are building those skills, that they can do it because you have seen them do it as you walk them through it." Ms. Pak's "being real with you" philosophy, which demonstrates true faith in the abilities of children of color to perform academically, stands in contrast to overpraising mediocre work of children of color, which has the opposite impact of what perhaps teachers who engage in such behaviors intend. Instead of that child being bolstered, what is actually conveyed is a teacher's low expectations, is a denigration of a child of color's intellect and capabilities. Teachers must provide critical feedback in the way Ms. Pak illustrates, a supportive, encouraging manner full of high expectations. Yaeger's team describes this as wise feedback where, students understand that they will neither be treated nor judged in light of a stereotype, but will instead be respected as an individual (2014, p. 805).

In one study, Yeager's team demonstrated that a very specific form of wise feedback was effective at increasing students' effort, engagement, and more specifically their likeliness to resubmit an essay. They worked with 44 7th-grade students in public middle schools. The team had the students write an essay. In a randomized control study half of the students received feedback as usual: "I'm giving you these comments so that you'll have feedback on your paper." The other half of the students received wise feedback that stated, "I'm giving you these comments because I have very high expectations and I know you can reach them." (It should be noted that in assessing the results, the issue of class was controlled so the power of the intervention was not affected by the profound and complicated issues of socioeconomic status.) There was a stark difference in the outcome of these simple statements. Those students who received the wise feedback that articulated high standards and belief that the student could achieve more were more likely to revise their papers and resubmit them. This was *especially true* for Black children in the sample, and even more so for Black children with low levels of trust (meaning they didn't feel like they could trust school adults). In other words, Black children who had lower levels of trust were more likely to revise and resubmit than the control group. This translated into not only better scores on the essays, but also better grades in the class and other core subjects overall. The authors remind us that:

> critical feedback must be conveyed as a reflection of the teachers' high standards and not their bias. The student must be assured that he or she has the potential to reach the high standards, lessening the possibility that they're being viewed as limited. Students must also be provided with the resources, such as substantive feedback to reach the standards demanded of them. (Yeager et al., 2014, p. 806)

The Yaeger et al. (2014) study demonstrates the power of feedback that conveys high expectations and the belief that a student can improve and achieve.

This is a very simple intervention: We are talking about the mere placing of notes on a paper without necessarily changing the actual behavior of the teacher. What would be the impact if we supported teachers in holding those expectations *and* changing their behavior? The next two studies demonstrate the amazing impact of what happens when we provide teachers with the support they need and for which they are asking.

EMPATHY

After establishing the dramatic impact of implicit bias on teacher's disciplinary actions (see the Jake and Darnell scenario we discussed in Chapter 3), Jason Okonofua's research has moved on to investigate what can be done to address the stark gap in how they discipline children with different racial identification. Okonofua worked to find something that would value teachers' expertise and humanity—to not treat them as if they were in need of remediation. The basic premise of the intervention was empathy and the foundational belief that "a teacher who makes his or her student feel heard, validated and respected shows them that school is fair and they can grow and succeed here." An empathic mindset encourages teachers to seek to understand the feelings and experiences of the student who may be the cause of misbehavior too. This mindset focuses on sustaining positive relationships and tries to foster trust as a means of creating positive behaviors. The

empathic mindset encourages teachers to view discipline as a chance to create shared understanding with students and an opportunity to support relationships. Ultimately, it is an approach where empathy, understanding, and
listening are at the center. It's important to note what this empathic mindset does not require. It does not ask that teachers avoid disciplining, agree
with their students, or ignore problematic behavior. Instead the readings
the teachers did as part of the study encouraged teachers to set limits and
provide consequences for problematic behavior. We understand empathic
mindset as a radical listening practice. The pathway to make a student feel
heard and validated—the sentiments, again, that Mr. Day opened this chapter with—is empathy.

In order to address the disparities in teachers' disciplining of children of
color versus white children, Okonofua et al. (2016a) and his team worked
with 1,682 middle school students in five diverse schools. Interestingly,
20% of the participants reported a race/ethnicity that did not fall into one
of the research categories. In other words, they either did not indicate a race
at all or indicated that they were multiracial. Teachers at these schools were
provided with brief online training in an empathic mindset. Teachers were
asked to participate in one 45-minute and one 25-minute online reading
followed by a guided writing exercise. These readings and exercises encouraged the empathic mindset. In the writing exercise, teachers were told that
what they wrote would be used to create a teacher-training curriculum so
that teachers could benefit from "your experiences and insights."

The findings of Okonofua's empathy intervention were remarkable.
Teachers who received the empathic mindset intervention were *half* as likely
to suspend students over the school year. This was true even when controlling for students' race, gender, and previous suspensions. The students who
had teachers who received this intervention reported that their relationships
with the teachers improved; this was especially true for those students who
had actually been suspended in the prior year. The students indicated that
they felt more respected by the teachers in the intervention. Okonufua et al.
(2016b) concluded, "Simply understanding, feeling understood may be
enough to initiate a better teacher student relationship" (2016b, p. 5523).
Mr. Day, who is dedicated to the success of his students of color and laments
what he sees as the daily disproportionate treatment of students of color,
expresses a desire for his colleagues to learn this basic empathy. His advice
for his colleagues who have not tapped into their empathy, or who treat
kids of color disparately, is to "encourage [them] to do personal development because PD [Professional Development] is not going to teach you how
to be a decent human being to your kids and see your kids as human beings. . . . If you didn't like being treated like a number [as a student], don't
treat your kids like a number." Day sees the work of personal development
being that of empathy: seeing kids of color as just like you. This means of
seeing and hearing teachers is essential and a lesson that should be lifted

up from this work. All our work should treat teachers as the experts they are, as the people who hold great capacity for care and change as opposed to treating them as deficit-based, lacking in skills, and as perpetrators. This demonstrated empathy for *teachers*, their work, and their insights may have helped to facilitate their capacity for empathy.

STUDENT CONNECTEDNESS

Empathy is key in facilitating adult–student relationships, or the measure known among researchers as student connectedness, what the Centers for Disease Control and Prevention define as "the belief by students that adults in the school care about their learning as well as about them as individuals" (2009, p. 3). The criteria often used to assess school connectedness are simple and compelling:

(a) "Most of the adults who work at the school treat me with respect"; (b) "If I have a problem or concern there is at least one adult in the school I feel comfortable talking to"; (c) "Most of my teachers care about how I am doing in their class"; (d) "Most of my teachers encourage me to do my best"; and, (e) "If I felt my safety or the safety of others was threatened, there is at least one adult in the school I could go to". (Anyon et al., 2016, p. 346)

These questions address basic, foundational human needs for connection. Theorists and researchers point to the lack of connectedness between students of color and teachers as one of the root causes for the stark and painful racial inequities in schooling, which is to say academic and disciplinary racial gaps (Bottiani et al., 2018; Stevenson, 2008; Voight et al., 2015). As we can imagine, school connectedness is related to a host of outcomes and is evident not only in differential discipline and suspension rates, but also GPA, college attendance, and high school dropout rates (Crosnoe et al., 2004; Durlak et al., 2011; Murray & Greenberg, 2000; Woolley et al., 2009).

Here we find consistent research that shows that children of color report fewer connections with school adults (Anyon et al., 2016; Bottiani et al., 2018; Okonofua et al., 2016b; Stevenson, 2008; Voight et al., 2015; Yeager et al., 2014). Black, Latinx, and Native American students report feeling less likely to "feel cared about by an adult at school" (Gregory et al., 2018). Children of color consistently report lower rates of support, encouragement, and care from school adults (Anyon et al., 2016; Bottiani et al., 2014; Bottiani et al., 2018; Voight et al., 2015). For example, Bottiani et al. (2014) examined 20,000 high schoolers living in the eastern United States found that Black students reported lower rates of experiencing caring from their teachers than white students (2014, p. 16). Anyon et al. (2016) examined survey data from a large school district including close to 30,000 6th- to

12th-graders. This study stands out as one in which the researchers pay attention to those who identify as mixed race. The findings here were consistent with those mentioned previously: multiracial, Black, Native American, Latinx, and Asian American children reported less connectedness with school adults than their white peers did. In summary, we have robust and consistent evidence that children and youth of color are likely to experience poorer school climate, fewer opportunities for engagement, and less connectedness at school than their white peers. The limited empirical data we have about mixed-race children is that they suffer the same experiences of disconnection at school. Our participants told us the same things. Indeed, in our small sample, our participants shared so few positive and meaningful connections with adults in school settings that we needed to set out on a second round of data collection in order to seek out those data. Fifteen-year-old 10th-grader Olu, who identifies as Black and Asian at school and describes his ethnic background as Nigerian and Asian, sums up the sentiments of many of the participants: "Not a lot of [moments of connection] came from my teachers, now that I think about it. The only things that I notice is that when little [racist] comments were made they didn't know how to address them."

AN EXAMPLE THAT WORKS: GREET-STOP-PROMPT

In order for Olu to feel connected in school, it's most likely not enough to simply give him a high five on the way into school. High fives, or literally greeting students at the school door, are something that started the school year at Ms. Pak's school, but in the absence of other substantive systemic changes to address the significant issues of student of color disproportionality, they felt like an empty gesture to her. One personal intervention Ms. Pak makes, although she doesn't use this phrase, is teaching students of color to code switch. Linguist Carol Myers-Scotton describes code switching as a tool that individuals use to signify group membership (1993). For minoritized people in particular, code switching enables one to know when it's safe and appropriate to speak a "home language" and when to transition into language of power for access to privilege. Ms. Pak makes this vital and complicated process transparent for her students by telling them, "Here are the two modes of communication you will have to learn to survive in. Let me provide you structure and a construct to understand what it means to be in this one context and this in another context because you have to be told that to understand it. No one ever told me that." Ms. Pak said, "I feel like the sugarcoating, acknowledgment, the high fives are nice, but the deep engagement [such as on code switching] is, I acknowledge that you're frustrated. I acknowledge that this is hard for you, but I know that we can change this, if you do this other thing that's going to help you come back to the work and get started faster."

To address school connectedness, positive discipline/engagement, and implicit bias, Cook et al. (2018) created a program that focused on three components: (1) increasing teacher empathy, (2) self-regulation skills for teachers to be able to manage difficult behaviors, and (3) strategies to enhance positive classroom management. This program—called GREET-STOP-PROMPT—was found to successfully address the gaps in school connectedness, specifically for Black boys (Cook et al., 2018, see Table 2). In creating their intervention, they were informed by previously supported models and previous research that indicated that teachers often get limited, insufficient support and training on classroom management strategies. One model they relied on was Gregory et al.'s (2016) "My Teaching Partner," which provides coaching, developmental guidance, and video-based instruction for new teachers from experienced teachers. She did a yearlong study with a school, in which she provided teachers with comprehensive training on implicit bias and education. The teachers loved it and they showed great post-test changes in their understanding. However, at the end of that year there were still no differences in the academic achievement gap. Gregory went back the next year and did the same training, this time adding senior mentor teachers for the classroom teachers. Those mentor teachers provided support on how the teachers could improve their relationships with their students (all of their students, not just the students of color). They even videotaped interactions between the teachers and their students and the teachers received coaching from senior mentors on how to strengthen relationships. At the end of that year, not only did the academic gap disappear, but so did the discipline gap. Further testing has shown that this model eliminates both disciplinary and achievement gaps for kids of color through its focus on supporting positive relationships between children and their teachers. The challenge, however, was feasibility, cost, and scale.

Cook's team created a combined intervention at three elementary schools that were under federal and state oversight for their racial disproportionality in discipline and negative academic outcomes. They addressed preventing problem behavior through classroom management, reducing the impact of implicit bias, and positive strategies for addressing problem behavior.

They incorporated wise feedback and focused on empathy and coaching as in Okonufua's plan. In addition, the staff at school buildings were simultaneously undergoing training in a districtwide positive behavioral intervention. Cook's team focused on creating a highly feasible and replicable intervention.

In these schools Black males were 2.5 times more likely to be referred to the office for disciplinary issues than their white peers. Cook's team employed a community-based participatory action research method with the schools, and worked to create both the intervention and the research with teachers, administrators, and the school community. Through this

collaboration they were able to base the intervention not only in the aforementioned research, but in what the teachers and school saw as the root
causes of the problems—a lack of teacher training and support on disciplinary strategies, and implicit bias.

Cook's model provided two, 3-hour-long training sessions and weekly
coaching to teachers, administrators, and support staff. The training and
coaching focused on three actions: (1) GREET: in which teachers enact proactive classroom management to prevent problem behavior; (2) STOP: in
which teachers focus on regulation and recognition techniques to combat
their own implicit biases; and (3) PROMPT: in which teachers respond to
problematic student behavior with empathy and consistency (see table in
Appendix D). Their work resulted in an extraordinary *two-thirds* drop in
office referrals for Black boys following this intervention. Those youth also
reported statistically significantly improved school connectedness and belonging after the intervention. This intervention proved to be low cost and
high yield. Teachers rated the program as feasible and acceptable. This is an
important step in the ability to replicate this study.

Although simply stated here, it is important to note that this is one of a
handful of experimental studies on how to intervene to reduce disciplinary
and relational gaps. Its findings are impressive and again elucidate processes
that can be used to effect change. At the foundation of this study, as in all
aspects of relationship building, is what the three teachers we interviewed
describe as simply listening to the full humanity of their students of color.

SHARING WHO WE ARE WITH OUR STUDENTS

All three of the teachers describe the importance of sharing who they are
with their students as part of the reciprocal process of affirmation. And it's
no accident that the three teachers our participants reported as making them
feel like they belong at school are people of color. The teachers' stories help
illustrate these connections. Ms. Pak, who describes herself as coming from
a Korean, Japanese, and Chinese background, explains, "I think a huge part
of why I'm successful with my kids who are minoritized or mixed race is
because I was that kid in a very white town, white school, that experienced
a lot of isolation because I was culturally different and had different cultural
context, which put me in a situation where I was always odd. . . . I think
because of that, as I've gotten older, I've recognized how much that trauma-
tized me, how much that has influenced who I've become as an adult, and
how much I wish that there had just been even one teacher who acknowl-
edged the full range and breadth of who I am as a human instead of this
idea of what it is to be a good student." Ms. Pak doesn't hide these aspects
of herself from her students but rather "embrac[es] fully who I am and just
show[s] up and . . . [says], 'This is who I am. Who are you? Be proud of

that. Just embrace who you are, no matter who you are.'" This makes a difference, Pak says, because, "I feel like if there were maybe more teachers who were comfortable with being that open and that vulnerable, I think the kids would then feel comfortable being more open and vulnerable."

Eleven-year-old 6th-grader Mariah, who identifies as mixed or white at school, and her 14-year-old, 9th-grade sister Mia, who identifies as white and Black or mixed at school, describe the characteristics of Mr. Charlie, a teacher who made them feel connected in school, versus the rest of their teachers who don't. Both of the girls come from a Black and white background, and are together describing their experiences at their small, predominantly white private school. Mariah notes that Mr. Charlie "felt like a little more open than the other teachers would be with us . . . with Mr. Charlie, it would be a lot more open and I think the way he treated us felt almost . . . [like] equals instead of students pretty much. . . . Less like students and more just like people he's talking to. I never really feel like I'm being talked down to necessarily, but it feels more like he's just talking to us, which was really nice. He would just talk about today's issues and other things which was pretty refreshing. I also learned a bunch of different things. I think more teachers like that would [take the same approach]. . . . I would definitely like that a lot more and I think other people would too." With other teachers, in contrast, "It almost felt like. . . . I mean it doesn't feel exactly like this but sometimes it almost feels like they're reading from a script because they're teaching lessons from a book, or there's specific things that they planned out." This makes them feel like "robots," Mariah complains. Mia further explains, "If teachers can master that [act of treating students like equals] or really execute that well, they become the most popular, well-liked teachers, because students like their class because they feel less . . . not necessarily demeaned but more happy, and they feel like they can express themselves a little bit more."

Mr. Day describes following a similar philosophy with his students, as he details in his story. Mr. Day exposes his own vulnerability to his students with hopes of fostering shared vulnerability. Mr. Day says, "I bring in my personal story when I start my classes every year about my personal educational journey as a mixed-race Black–white person, person of color and not having any teachers of color in school, and what that meant for me and being raised by a single white mom. . . . I treat my students like full human beings and I have authentic conversations. I don't shy away from the personal while also not crossing the boundary professionally." In the 45-minute-long conversation during one of Mr. Day's free periods in his classroom, there were no less than five students of color who popped their heads into the classroom at various moments to just say hi. Ralina asked Mr. Day if this happens frequently, and he affirmed that indeed it does, all day, every day. In fact, even when he's teaching, students will pop their heads in for a quick hello. Mr. Day says that he goes out of his way to get to know both names and faces of students of color who he doesn't teach as well, so that he can say hi by name to those students in the hallway.

Although we were not able to observe Ms. Kwon in a classroom as we met in the teachers' lounge during her break time, by the rapt attention that the volunteer student workers gave her and their pleased smiles to be in the presence of her beaming smile, she plays a similar role at her school. Ms. Kwon describes how like Ms. Pak and Mr. Day she also shares aspects of her own life with her students, down to the food that she eats. Part of the affinity groups is a "lunchbox moment," in which Kwon notes, "I'll usually bring some sort of dish, just because I feel like one of the classic microaggressions around Asian identity is the lunch box moment. Where our foods are often [disparaged]. . . . And for me, it's bringing particularly the foods that haven't hit the mainstream yet. Just so that we can have our own lunchbox moments where we're like affirming and curious and that smells like home and not something awful." Kwon connects this "lunchbox moment" to the role she plays as an educator, of her mission in which, "I want to have a kind of different conversations [about race with my students] that I wish my parents had with me. And so, for . . . some of the kids where there's an absence of even pride-socialization of 'you are beautiful' or 'you are smart' and 'you belong' and 'you're worthy' . . . I want to make sure that they get that from somebody."

All three of these teachers are careful to share elements of themselves with their students so that their students experienced hearing their stories valued, as well as the stories of similarly minoritized people. Pak's success with her minoritized students comes about because of the hard work that she does with them inside of the classroom, but also because of the relationship that she fosters throughout their time in middle school. This experience is starkly contrasted by the experience of being tokenized in the classroom. This experience is not unique to mixed-race kids, but is emblematic of the experience of many minoritized youth at school. Thirteen-year-old 8th-grader Hiro and 16-year-old 11th-grader Takuji, who identify at school as Japanese (Hiro) and half Japanese, half white (Takuji), and describe their racial background as Okinawan and white, describe how the attention gets laser focused on them when issues having to do with Asians emerge in class. They lament that they are too enthusiastically encouraged to speak. Takuji notes that he sees the teacher's true rationale as, "I think that they're getting me to speak about [race] to educate everyone else but I'm trying to learn too." Instead of taking such an approach, Hiro says he wishes that the teacher should instead "maybe like spread out the attention," and Takuji adds that the teacher should "maybe only let us speak if we want to speak, don't just expect us to have something to say about it." What this ultimately amounts to, Hiro comments, is that "I feel like I'm sometimes used as an anchor. I'm sometimes used to start the conversation. But it is unenjoyable. Especially if I don't have an opinion and I have to talk."

In this conversation both of the boys are also clear about their own relative privilege in the classroom space as Hiro notes, "At least we kind of look white so we may be able to pass." Hiro and Takuji's comments here can be contrasted with those of 10-year-old 4th-grader Kai, who identifies as Black and Latino at school, and whose voice opens up the chapter. Kai tells us that he is not experiencing being tokenized in class—instead he is never called on. Kai simply wants to have his voice heard. Regardless of their experiences, Takuji, Hiro, and Kai are not experiencing the moments of teacher connectedness that Mr. Day and Ms. Pak describe as emerging when teachers genuinely share of themselves and create the trust that asks students to equitably add their voices to the classroom space.

INTERRUPTING RACISM FOR POSITIVE RELATIONSHIPS

On a very basic level, our participants were asking that teachers simply intervene when they witness racism. Xiomari, a 10-year-old 4th-grader who identifies at school as Otomi, an indigenous group from Mexico, and comes from an Otomi and white background, says that she felt very supported by her teacher when her teacher stood up for her desire to claim her Otomi identity when that identity did not seem evident to her classmate. Xiomari describes getting into an argument about her self-identity with the classmate she describes as a white girl. She explains, "I tell them that I was born in Texas and whenever I say that I'm Otomi they're like, 'no, you were born in Texas. You're Texan.' And they tell me that I'm something that I don't identify as." But instead of her teacher ignoring the discussion, Xiomari says that the teacher chose "to pull me and a girl out of the class. And he only asked me what she did, and I said that she was just saying that I am something that I'm not. And he explained to her that you can be something and something else at the same time." Furthermore, Xiomari notes that "every single time she says a racist comment he'll pull her out and he'll talk to her. And he doesn't let it slip like the teachers at my old school." It's important to note that Xiomari's experiences of racism at the old school that she references here were impactful enough that her parents pulled her out of school to home school her for 2 years. In fact, while statistically white children are home schooled for religious reasons, children of color are home schooled because of racial ones (Mazama & Lundy, 2012).

In this case, the new school was succeeding at fostering a positive relationship with Xiomari and her family, and making them feel as though they belonged at the school. This was due, in large part, to the teacher's actions. He clearly interrupted racism in Xiomari's classroom—resulting in Xiomari's feeling supported in her identity and heard. The teacher lifted up Xiomari's multiple identities, and supported her in articulating an identity that was "invisible" to a classmate, thus demonstrating how to radically listen in the midst of conflict. Critical education scholar Mica Pollock notes that "the act of making the in'visible' visible, and the un'heard' heard, is often the first step toward the development of transformative, equity-oriented educators" (Pollock, 2004, p. 885).

A different type of intervention needs to happen for students who need special advocacy in less-structured or nonpedagogical spaces such as the playground. Eleven-year-old 6th-grader Hugo, who identifies as African American at school and comes from a Cape Colored South African and white background, talked about how his teacher Mr. Mount facilitated difficult spaces for him. After having been home schooled for a number of years, Hugo had just begun attending a midsize K–8 public school. Hugo said that Mr. Mount eased the transition for him by "mak[ing] sure on the playground and stuff, everybody is included, and there isn't like, oh here's a group, here's a group, here's a group. No, just make one group. Make sure everybody gets a chance to be included." Hugo was clear to say that this wasn't a one-off, or as he put it, "not team-building, because it helps temporarily," but a more long-lasting form of investment that enabled "friendships [to get] started between the groups." What Mr. Mount did, Hugo explained, was to figure out, "Say there's a leader of this group and a leader of that group. Make them become friends, because then the groups are more inclined to be come together. And then have a leader of those, and let those two become friends and then it's one group." Hugo pointed out that this was a racialized process as Mr. Mount, who is Black, "did really good at getting the minorities of my class to become a majority, because they bridged the gaps between, 'Oh, you're a minority, you go over there. We're a majority, we stay over here.'" For kids like Hugo who felt as if they were left out, or as he put it, "There's a no-man's land," Mr. Mount said, in Hugo's words, "'No, there's a bridge. You go through it.'" Hugo explained how Mr. Mount got the kids from different groups "to talk, watch movies and then hav[e] us only able to sit in one square, and so the groups had to be interconnected." All of these activities illustrate how to help mixed-race kids feel like they belong and are heard in their request for belonging.

Although Mr. Mount's process is thorough, thoughtful, and long term, sometimes the interruption process is simply the teacher's interrupting their own racism and implicit bias. After sharing the story about differential treatment in his math class (Chapter 3), 15-year-old 10th-grader Ty, who identifies as Black at school and comes from a Black, white, and Indian background, answers our question "What do you wish would've happened differently?" as simply, "that I was just treated the same or that it just didn't happen at all, if I wasn't treated like everyone else." The implication was that instead of the teacher instantly and implicitly reading him as "one of those basketball players" that instead she had slowed down and gotten a chance to see him in his complexity.

The scholarship on the impact of implicit bias on students in school environments leads educational researchers such as Anyon et al. to note that that while some recommendations emphasize "the need for teachers and other school adults to improve their relationships with students of color in order to create a positive school climate" (2018b, p. 392), for true change to occur schools need four factors: "cooperation between groups, equal status, common goals, and support from authority figures in the institutions within which [the negative] interaction occurs" (p. 393). We fundamentally believe that radical listening is the bedrock for these four factors to come together in order to create substantive change. And, in addition, larger system change is needed in tandem with interpersonal change. Thus, we need both improved relationships, institutions, and structures in order to change the experiences for students of color.

"TEACHERS, I WANT YOU TO KNOW . . . I THINK IT STARTS WITH EDUCATION"

Oyin, a 19-year-old college sophomore who identifies as Blasian at school and lists her ethnic heritage as Filipino, Nigerian, and Malaysian, provides one answer for teachers on how to best teach mixed-race students. Oyin notes, "Teachers, I want you to know. . . . I think it starts with education. . . . Maybe as a white teacher, I don't know if this is how they feel, but if you come across something that you don't know if it's right or wrong for a student to have said, I think it wouldn't be bad of you to go to a teacher of color and ask, or a person of color. Even go up to the student, because there's nothing wrong with asking." What Oyin is talking about is not tokenizing a student in the way in which Hiro and Takuji balked, and instead entering into a dialogue of coequals in which teachers become radical listeners.

Oyin continues, "Like if a teacher came up to me and asked me [about a racial issue] I would be like honored to tell you why that made me feel that way. I genuinely don't think that teachers do that to be racist. They genuinely, I feel like they genuinely do not know. If you don't know like ask a question." Pointing out a particular hypocrisy, Oyin asserts, "Teachers preach that all the time, if you don't know ask a question. So why don't you ask too?" This can feel risky, Oyin notes, or "Maybe they think it's a waste of time, maybe they think oh I just want to teach these kids and get out." But the risk is worth it as "if you make more of a connection with your students of color then they won't feel as ostracized when they're in class, they'll trust the teachers more. Then there'll be a whole ring of respect. I'm going to tell you teachers to ask questions too. That's what I would say. Yeah."

The interventions and strategies both from successful teachers and successful research projects are not radical or outside of our ability as educators, administrators, parents, and those who support teachers. If we give teachers enough time, support, and training to focus on the relational needs, then we are able to make the disparities significantly diminish. The research shows that focusing on teacher strengths, teachers as experts and teachers as people who want to connect helps to achieve this precise goal. We also know from the literature and from hearing from children themselves that these negative outcomes occur sometimes despite not only good intentions on the part of teachers, but *because* of their efforts. The stories we have shared from teachers and students have been shown in psychological research as well. The research states that what it takes to make an impact on children of color's experience in schools is to strengthen relationships, to remove the smog of implicit bias, and to help teachers truly see their students. In the next and final chapter we discuss how families can take similar meaningful and worthwhile risks at home.

CHAPTER 5

"We Were Taught"

Family Practices of Radical Listening, Positive Friction, and Talking Race

What we have learned from the research, but most importantly from listening to families, is that supporting mixed-race children through radical listening takes work and skill. Radical listening is manifested through self-reflection, humility, and bravery; these three skills take practice. Such skills, as the previous chapter illustrates, teachers can practice at school, but parents too must practice at home. Throughout this book we have seen examples of parents practicing the skills of supporting their mixed-race children with self-reflection, humility, and bravery. In Chapter 1, Linda, who is Vietnamese American and white, recounted a story full of forgiveness and joy in which she told her 5-year-old son, Caleb, who has a Vietnamese American, Japanese American, and white background, "we need to work on this a little more," when he "failed" to greet his preschool class with the correct saying for the Vietnamese New Year. Linda's unguarded, nonjudgmental attitude paves the way for Caleb to explore all of his racialized identities with family support, both at the young age of 5, and in the future.

Families, and in particular, multiracial families in which parents' racializations don't always match the races or racial identities of their children, must often work hard to practice open and honest race talk. One pair of siblings, 12-year-old 7th-grader Lucy, and her 14-year-old, 9th-grade sister Gia, both of whom identify as "mixed" at school and both of whom come from a Black and white background, described to us how race talk is a constant and integral piece of their home lives. As Lucy explained, they learn about race not by accident but because "we were taught." Lucy went on to clarify, "In our family, race is really important, because we have two different. . . . We have two parents of different races, so it's like, it was important to learn about the significance of each race, and hardships and stuff. So we were taught pretty early on about our identity, and how we should embrace it and stuff." What's interesting here is that having a multiracial family background is the very reason to embrace race talk, as opposed to the very reason to ignore it because of a color-blind fallacy that "we are all the same," or that mixing races somehow makes them disappear. In fact, Gia and Lucy's household was necessarily color conscious in refutation to the whiteness of their elementary school; as Gia explained, "I think I knew I was mixed, and knew the impactfulness of race before a lot of people in my elementary school did. They . . . most of the people at my elementary school were white. So it was like they didn't really know what was going on. I was like, I'm mixed, so yeah. That's how it is." And the "that's how it is" translated in Lucy and Gia's household to commonplace, everyday, and thoughtful conversations about race; "that's how it is" meant that race is always a topic of conversation.

Throughout this book we have shown that mixed-race children know race (Chapter 1); that they also know their own multiplicity of identities even when others don't (Chapter 2); that they are limited by racialized stereotyping (Chapter 3); and are bolstered when supported by school adults in their identity development (Chapter 4). Thus, what becomes clear throughout each of these chapters is that self-conscious race talking—which in turn normalizes conversations around race as routine—is the route that provides mixed-race children with the most positive way to explore their racialization. As the work on racial socialization suggests, proactive, positive discussions of race can help support children of color, and in fact all children, in preparing to engage with the racialized world around them (Bowman & Cleopatra Howard, 1985; Hughes & Johnson, 2004). In addition, racial socialization has been found to correlate positively with general measures of children's well-being and identity (Anderson & Stevenson, 2019; Hughes et al., 2006). In addition, this type of race talk has been shown to serve as a protective factor against racially biased/discriminatory experiences (Spencer et al., 1997). Gia and Lucy's conversation with each other flowed fluidly as they discussed a variety of topics around race and mixed race, including a long riff in which they asked each other to comment on how they think their facial features or parts of their body have been racialized (which parts were "Black" or "white"), from their noses to their legs, to their eye color, lip shape, and hair texture. One of their parents confirmed that this particular "racializing body part" conversation that they shared with us was one that they frequently have at home as well.

However, not all families who raise mixed-race children choose to embrace race talk in the ways in which Caleb's, Gia's, and Lucy's parents do. We had the privilege of listening to many parents who were wrestling with how to engage in any race talk with their children, or with how to speak to their children about their identity(ies) at all. We heard stories in which these types of conversations were not only uncomfortable, but painful and fraught. They were often layered with fear for their children, a hope for color blindness, or what sounded to us like a desire for their child to achieve some proximity to whiteness. But ultimately, at the heart of these fraught dialogues was *the failure to radically listen to their mixed-race children*: a failure to hear and uplift their desires for their racialized identities, even, and perhaps especially, when their racial choices didn't match up with their parents. In this chapter we will explore what happens within families when race talk is suppressed, what happens when it's encouraged, and most of all, what happens when it is rooted in radically listening to mixed-race kids. We will end this last chapter with a guiding exercise that all families can undertake to radically listen to their children and to construct a way to have race talk in their lives: create a family mission statement.

FRICTION WITHOUT POSITIVITY: REFUTING A CHILD'S RACIALIZED IDENTITY

Twenty years ago sociologists Miri Song and David Parker began their 2001 book by stating a fact that has been true for centuries, and remains true to this day: "The topic of mixed race can bring out the worst in people" (2001, p. 19). Mixed race, like other "controversial" topics, Song and Parker write, "tended to elicit polarized views, so that while some regarded mixed people and 'mixing' as hugely problematic, others saw it as the answer to many of our social ills" (p. 19). They articulate the dilemma that many parents of mixed-race children have to face every day in their parenting: How do they face the attitudes of family, friends, and even their children's schools that they are parenting not just children, but little people whose being remains for some, highly symbolic? To rephrase Song and Parker, how do they radically listen to their own children's experience while silencing the controlling narratives of multiraciality as a symbol of racial transcendence, or a symbol of pathology? And, moreover, how do they parent a child toward a healthy racialized identity when their child's racialized identity might be entirely different from their own?

As we discussed in Chapter 1, racial socialization is often cast as what parents and caregivers say to our children, or in other words, what messages we impart. However, as we have discussed, this narrow view ignores what our children bring to us to help us further our families' understandings of our own identities; what they ask us to enrich our families' conversations around identity; how children fight with us about our own readings of their identities; and how they negotiate their own identities time and time again with and without us. Our previous chapters highlight the myriad ways in which mixed-race children's identities change: over time, in context, and in relationship. Much like we heard from the teachers in Chapter 4, parents and caregivers too have to make space for an authentic engagement that hears all of the registers of these changes. Part of the particular work of radically listening to our mixed-race children and youth comes in the inherent complexity of raising a child who is (in most cases) racially different than their parents. We will also see in this chapter that radical listening work arises even if a parent is of a similar multiracial mix to a child (in other words, if the child is multiracial and the parent is multiracial as well). Even if a multiracial individual shares a similar identification as mixed race, Song and Parker note, there is "little evidence of a shared sense of commonality: Only about one third of those surveyed believed they had a lot in common with other multiracials of the same racial mix as they, while even less (17%) felt a sense of commonality with other multiracials of different racial backgrounds" (2001, pp. 141–142). This work can become especially challenging if the child might choose a different racial identification than the parent.

There are few hard and fast rules around mixed-race identification, outside of the fact that mixed-race people's identification changes in multiple ways, across an individual's life span, and within a family generationally. Sociologist Jennifer Bratter (2007) describes how generationally the labels that mixed-race people use might change. She demonstrates that "families where parents are of two different single-race backgrounds," for example, with one parent who identifies as monoracially white and a second who identifies as monoracially Asian American, are likely to classify their children as multiracial. But take that same case, and substitute the Asian American parent for a Black parent, and you'll find that those children are both more likely to both be labeled and more likely to label themselves as Black, as we explored in Chapter 2 (Brunsma, 2005; Rockquemore & Brunsma, 2002). Those children and adults are *less* likely to choose a multiracial label (Matsuoka, 2008). Adding to the complexity, Bratter and other scholars demonstrate that mixed-race parents are actually less likely to categorize their children as "multiracial" and more likely to categorize them as of a single race (Bratter, 2007, p. 821; Qian, 2004; Qian & Lichter, 2007).

How then do multiracial kids of multiracial parents identify? What happens when different racialized identifications within the same mix occur even within the same family? Indeed, this particular multiple-multiracial family formation isn't unique: as of the 2000 Census 53% of children with multiple races were living with one or more parents with multiple races (Tafoya et al., 2004). Illustrating this demographic trend, we had a number of multiracial parents participate in our research with their mixed-race children. Miri Song notes, "One common convention for first-generation mixed people (individuals with two distinct single-race parents, such as Black and White, or East Asian and White), has been to employ the language of fractions to say that they are half X and half Y. But if one parent is multiracial (or if both are), the question of how his, her (or their) own children should be seen becomes far from straightforward because there are no established conventions for how second-generation mixed people should be identified" (p. 37). One of these participant pairs of second-generation mixed-race people was 13-year-old 8th-grader Percy, who as we discussed in Chapter 2, gave us the rich metaphor "stick with your team," when it came to his identifying as Filipino, always and in all circumstances, even when he isn't read as Filipino. Percy participated in his dialogue with his mother Zita. Zita explains, "So we're both Filipino and white. So my dad's Filipino, my mom is white, of French descent. His [Percy's] dad is half Filipino and half Irish descent. So he's half, from both sides." However, Zita insightfully states, "but . . . yeah, identifying with one or the other I think is not the same as what you are." She never describes her racialization as one or more particular identities, instead narrating racialization by proximity:

> And me growing up, it was hard because I lived with my Filipino grandpa and my dad who's Filipino. And my parents were split up, so I'd go between living with my mom, who's white, and then my dad, who's Filipino, and my grandpa. And I always felt a strong pull towards my Filipino culture, but because I'm mixed, that's complicated, right? So I don't fit in either place. Filipino people are like, you're not really Filipino. White people are like, you're not really white. And even though my mom is white, her partner, ex, whatever, all the guys that she was with and married other than my dad were African American. And so I wasn't like white, either. It was like, oh my other siblings are half Black, half white. And so it gets pretty complicated to be mixed.

Throughout this narration Zita never claims her own racialized identity. Instead she talks about the races of the different family members with whom she lived, leaving herself blank. Although Zita notes, "I always felt a strong pull towards my Filipino culture," she also asserts that she was pushed away from that culture, as well as from whites, by twice saying that being mixed is "complicated" and that she failed to "fit in." The "complications" of being mixed in Zita's narrations are about being excluded from both of her home cultures, and not being able to claim a singular racialized identity.

In the interview itself, after she narrates her exclusion from communities as a result of being mixed race, Zita looks over at her son and says, "So I don't know how he identifies as . . . and I try to instill in him that he has some kind of culture and difference, but I don't know how it affects him, because we live in a majority white area, and his school is mostly white." Taking the opportunity of the interview she asks him, "So how does it affect you?" Percy responds, "It really doesn't affect me, 'cause when I think about what I identify as, I think about what I want, not what other people call me. So I really like the Filipino culture, and I think it's great, versus . . . I know I live the white style sort of, but if I had a choice, I would live in the Philippines rather than here." What's interesting is that Percy's identification as Filipino doesn't come about through his physicality, or how others might racialize him, but through him "liv[ing] the white style," a statement on the demographics of his neighborhood or school, or perhaps even his white stepfather.

Throughout the conversation Percy continually reaffirms his commitment to his racial identity as Filipino, while his mother continues to test that identity, stopping him during each of his assertions to ask if he really, legitimately, and authentically identifies that way. We assume her questioning comes from love, comes from the desire to protect and connect, and also from her curiosity about how his socialization is so different than her own. However, Zita's constant questioning of Percy's racial identity choice causes him to tear up in frustration. What Percy did not receive from his mother are the radical listening qualities we heard our Generation Mixed participants asking for: deep engagement and curiosity, matched with affirmation.

Some scholars note that the one-drop rule of hypodescent—the idea that mixed-race individuals, and in particular mixed-race African American individuals, will always identify with their racial minority (or Black) background—is waning in popularity, and that mixed-race Asian American–white folks, in particular, are less likely to identify as Asian (Parker et al., 2015). But Percy's response demonstrates otherwise (Bratter, 2007; Roth, 2005). Furthermore, as we have listened to stories throughout this book we might also understand Percy's assertion as a snapshot of his racial identity that indeed might change as he moves into high school, college, work life, adulthood, parenthood, and beyond.

LISTEN TO YOUR CHILD EVEN WHEN YOU DON'T THINK THEY "LOOK" LIKE HOW THEY IDENTIFY

Although she did not express it outright, Zita's frustration with Percy might have been because they shared the same racial identification, but he chose to identify differently than she. When a child is a *different* race from a parent, the process of separating a child's racial choice from our own can feel even more difficult. Thus, while it might be uncomfortable for us, we need to understand that a child's different racial identification choice from ours is not necessarily a rejection of us as a parent, or our identit(ies). In addition, a child's similar identification is not necessarily a sign of embracing us or our identit(ies). Citing a swatch of interdisciplinary scholarship, education scholar Mica Pollock (2004) writes, "Youth is an important time for such paradoxical reproductions of race: much literature on youth culture has examined how young people actively redraw received lines of racialized difference even as they erase and blur them" (Pollock, 2004, p. 33). Ms. Kwon, the educator from the previous chapter, articulates the particular challenge that she sees multiracial children having to experience as well: "The reality is multiracial kids are typically born to monoracial parents who may or may not understand that experience. Gay kids and trans kids are (often) born to straight and cisgender parents who not only may not understand [the] experience or may actually have hostile attitudes toward that identity." She points to this difference in identity as a place that requires parents to pause and reflect.

We listened to another conversation in which another mother, Elena, was struggling to radically listen to her child's mixed-race experience and support his racial identity choice. Elena was different from Zita in that she didn't share a racial identity with her son. Elena is white, and her son, an 11-year-old, 6th-grade boy, Hugo, identifies at school as Black. Hugo's father is Black and South African, and as Elena explained in detail, multigenerationally multiracial as Cape Colored. The family has lived all over the world, including in London, Malawai, and the United States. In our space together, Elena begins her conversation with Hugo by asking him "What was it like when you lived in Malawi, the first five years of your life, and you were considered the *muzungu*, or the white kid." Hugo retorts, "They didn't really call me *muzungu*, but I fit in more than you, because you're white and I'm at least partly dark-ish." Hugo follows up with, his voice rising in pitch, "It wasn't like in Malawi they shunned me. They were just like, 'who are you? I don't recognize you.' And then a few weeks later, they're like 'oh, hey.'" The conversation develops like this: While Elena introduces Hugo's racialization as one of others' exclusion, he reframes it immediately as others' curiosity on the way to belonging.

From this conversation Elena switches immediately to Hugo's chosen identification as African American. Elena asks Hugo, "When you say African American, actually this has been something I've been curious about. How is your African Americanness, I'm going to make an assumption here, different from her [*gestures towards Allison*] African Americanness?" It should be noted that Allison in this interview wore a floral head wrap and large dangling earrings. Although she is often read as mixed race because of her light skin, people see her clearly as Black. In this moment, Elena's gesture revealed that she read Allison as authentically "African American." At this Hugo diplomatically says, "I would suspect it's different? But I don't know how, since I don't know where you're from and stuff." What Hugo invites is an opportunity to listen. He does not make assumptions about Allison's "African Americanness." Perhaps he reads her skin color, or facial features, or perhaps he reads her head wrap and earrings; regardless, he makes space to hear a story of her African Americanness that he doesn't yet know.

The conversation continues: Hugo doubles down on his identification as either "African American" or "Black," responding to us that his racial identification doesn't change when he travels, when he attends different schools, or when he fills out forms. Her son's explanation isn't sufficient, however, for Elena, and she says, "As an American, when I think 'African American' I think your [*gestures again towards Allison*] look. I look at him and go 'African American?' Huh, this is interesting." In Elena's slippage between "American" and "white" she again erases and refuses to hear Hugo's identification; Elena is also avoiding saying the word "white." This is an example of a failure to enact radical listening, a failure to believe what her mixed-race child is saying. Failing to listen has an impact on Hugo. As Elena balks at her son's identification as Black in multiple forms throughout the interview, her son ends up not just tearing up as Percy did, but with tears welling up, spilling over, and crying. We pause the dialogue to let Hugo wipe his tears, drink some water, and take a breath, and in that moment are surprised to see that Elena does not comfort her son in the midst of his tears.

Later on in the interview Elena recounts how Hugo was running around their neighborhood with, in her words, a "pack of feral boys" who were playing the common childhood game of "ding dong ditch" (ringing a doorbell and running away before the person can answer the door). Elena repeatedly refers to a Black boy in the group of boys (who is not her own son). She describes how one of the parents reacted after the game ended. The mother of the other Black boy in the group, who also happens to be white, reached out to the parents of the other children to talk about the risks for her son of racism that come from him being perceived as a threat. This mother was terrified that he would be left behind in this "innocent game." She sent out an article that detailed the bias and risks for Black boys. Elena recounted this story with disbelief and became overwhelmed by her emotions, explaining,

> [I] think as a mother, I've never thought about what it's like raising a child who's a target. It's like, he's a kid, how can you target a child? And how can you target an adult, either? But as a mother, that whole mama bear thing. And it was the first time. . . . But I read the article, and then she and I have had conversations about it, and it's just, how could you, regardless of skin color, how can you target a child? Especially knowing [the other boy], he's a great kid. It's just sad to me that that's even a reality, that's even a conversation that needs to happen. But it does.

As Elena speaks, her voice wells up with emotions. She feels the weight of racism for Hugo's friend, whom she sees and understands as a Black boy (perhaps after some education by that child's mother). However, in this entire interaction, what Elena does not comment on is her own child's safety. She does not see, in fact, how her own brown-skinned son, who sees himself as Black, is also statistically a "target," in the word she chose. She does not see how her own son is also Black.

Furthermore, in making sense of this painful session, and as scholars, dialogue facilitators, and mothers sharing the dialogic space between Hugo and Elena, we can't help but note what just happened moments before and in this moment: We observed a stark discrepancy between the empathy Elena conjures for another child she racializes as "Black" here, versus the disconnect she seemed to have from her own child she refuses to see as

"Black" moments earlier. Perhaps it's here that we can see that her refusal to listen to Hugo's description of himself as Black is in the hopes to keep him protected from being "that kind of Black person." What she is grappling with is that his proximity to her whiteness, his mixedness, is not a protective shield. Color blindness is not a salvation here. Most importantly, as we radically listen to Hugo's voice, we note that he does not want the shield of color blindness.

Elena is not alone in racializing her child in a manner that is discordant with his own racialization. Miri Song (2017) notes that "spousal ethnicity and the physical appearance of children, along with other key factors such as generational distance/remove, *shaped, but did not determine* the ways in which parents identified their children" (2017, p. 62). Indeed, we can understand how, in a racist society where people of color are so visibly and frequently mistreated, why proximity to whiteness is appealing; we can understand how the urge to protect and shield is so compelling. We can understand how ignoring a child's Blackness might feel like a viable way of living for certain parents. And yet, for our children, and for Hugo here, this strategy is unsuccessful. We argue, and what we have heard from many, is that as parents and caretakers our job is not only to protect but to prepare. Elena shows us how parents can spend too much time engaging in fantasies or hopes of color blindness. Ignoring race and ignoring racism does not mean that their children will escape the impact of racism due to their proximity to whiteness; it simply leaves children unable to cope when very real moments when race and racism emerge. Radical listening is about hearing our children and understanding their identification even if it makes you uncomfortable because it is not your own. We need to listen to children like Hugo, who repeatedly, in the face of his mother's denial, tells her that he identifies as Black.

In addition, while this miscategorization is happening at home, it echoes what happens outside of home. Research has shown that how mixed-race folks (like Latinx people) racially and ethnically identify themselves often does not correspond with how others categorize them (Brunsma, 2006; Herman, 2010; Itzigsohn, 2009; Roth, 2012). In one study by Herman almost 50% of respondents who identified as multiracial were classified as monoracial; in Herman's (2010) study, its noteworthy that the part-Black respondents were most likely classified as Black by observers. Observers use racial signifiers such as hair, nose, lips, and skin color to classify people as Black (Alejandro-Wright, 2013; Blair & Judd, 2011; Brown et al., 1998). Furthermore, children categorize others by skin color the most (Alejandro-Wright, 2013). In light of this research, sociologist Cynthia Feliciano (2015) makes the argument that instead of the one-drop rule maintaining importance today, we should have the "dark-skinned rule" (Feliciano, 2015). A quick peek into these research findings demonstrates that others racialize multiracial children without their permission. The home front can be a space that counters such experiences.

Radical listening can help provide that space. Or as the experience of Hugo and Elena illustrate, the failure of a parent to radically listen can mean that the home front fails to counter such experiences.

PERFORMING COLOR BLINDNESS: ON NOT LISTENING TO RACE TALK

What we see in the two previous examples are the barriers to listening: fear, parents' own sense of and demand for their child's identity, and perhaps a hope for color blindness. Here is another, complicated example of the ways in which color blindness can play out. Eleven-year-old 6th-grader Mariah, who identifies at school as either mixed or white, and her 14-year-old, 9th-grade sister Mia, who identifies at school as mixed, stood out among all of our sibling pairs as having the most silent, or rather avoidant conversation about race. Both girls, who have a white mother and Black father and attend predominantly white private schools, tripped over their words when discussing issues of race, and used awkward, uncommon aphorisms such as students "of diversity" when referring to students of color. Sociologist Eduardo Bonilla-Silva (2002) describes such uncomfortable race talk as a type of "rhetorical incoherence" that "avoids direct racial language" (2002, p. 41). Mariah also stood out as the only participant who described herself as identifying at school as "white" (as a stand-alone racialized identification) in addition to "mixed." Both girls responded that prior to us asking them, they had not talked very much about questions pertaining to race and their own racialized background.

When their parents, Karen and Darrell, joined us in the interview, the family shared a story that made it clear that explicit race talk was verboten in their immediate family, notably quite different from the practices of the children's grandparents, and in particular the girls' Black grandmother. Sociologist Miri Song posits that some mixed-race youth and their parents are exhibiting a type of "generational 'tipping point' at which minority heritage is regarded as of little or no significance" (2017, p. 40); this generational tipping point rubs against the ways in which the older generation experiences and talks about race. In this case, the girls' grandmother understands and wants to verbally process race, much to the dismay of the younger generations.

When her Black mother-in-law came to live with them, Mia and Mariah's white mother Karen notes, "She would just blurt things out that were on her mind. . . . She would say lots of things about race, or people's race." For example, the 2014 remake of the movie *Annie* came out with a Black cast, and Karen, Darrell, and girls would get upset when, in Karen's words, Darrell's mom would "call it Black *Annie*." Karen continued, explaining that her immediate family was upset that instead of simply saying the movie was called *Annie*, her mother-in-law would casually say, "Like 'oh the Black *Annie*?'" This wasn't the only racially tinged form of talk that made Karen and the rest of the family uncomfortable. Karen continues, "And she would really reference race a ton in just her everyday conversation." To our prodding about what these race conversations sounded like, Karen said, "Now that you asked [*about race coming up*], I felt like it came up a lot more around the dinner table, because [*to Darrell*] your mom would just blurt out stuff that we would just go 'oooh, that wasn't put in a very sensitive way." Mia extrapolates on her mother's sentiment of what feels more natural for their immediate family and explains to us, "We don't necessarily, like you [*Karen*] said, have these intentional discussions as a whole group about it, because I think it could make us uncomfortable. . . . Maybe it kind of was when our grandmother lived with us. But not now."

Darrell, Mariah, and Mia's father agree with the sentiment of avoiding explicit discussions about race and promotes using color-blind language instead, saying, "The best way to something is usually not to go right to whatever thing is you're trying to get to." Instead, Darrell says, his philosophy regarding race is, "we're available and they [the girls] often know what our opinions are on things based on overhearing our conversations and the things that are important to us." In this statement we hear that their family's philosophy is that explicitly talking about race is wrong. When thinking about his daughters growing up, Darrell avoids discussing our prompts about race and instead says, "I don't have a sense of where I want them to land. . . . I think all kids are developing, and developing their sense of themselves, their identity. In the schools, I would love for that to still just be the focus. Like, 'Hey, we're all sort of figuring out our personalities, our family backgrounds, our preferences, who we are, how others see us, how we want to be seen.' And that's just morphing and evolving over the years. I don't want to box them into an end goal of where I want them to land at the end. I just hope that they'll be in environments that are supportive in a positive way, and affirming about their strengths and characteristics unique to them." Race isn't explicitly a part of Darrell's imagined "end goal" for his daughters.

In fact, all four members of the family discussed race in a decidedly sideways fashion even when we asked overt questions about race. For these very light-skinned girls who attend predominantly white private schools and, who might, to many, pass as white, perhaps this level of talk might be inconsequential, at least at the ages of 11 and 14. But such downplaying of race is consequential for the brown-skinned boy Hugo, who attended a predominantly Black public elementary school, and was currently attending a racially mixed middle school. It might become consequential for Mia and Mariah as they move through adolescence to adulthood. Mia and Mariah's story is also one in which their very loving parents are not preparing them for the realities of a racialized world. And they aren't preparing them—by having constant, explicit, and forthright conversations about race, privilege, and racialization—to not be drawn into the seductions of white adjacency. Another way of framing the family's avoidance of race talk is that they are enacting a reactive as opposed to proactive means of socialization. What we hear is that in addition to their stated openness about discussing all topics, their silence illustrates that they maintain an unease and discomfort around discussing race.

Research indicates that indeed many parents respond to racial incidents "after the fact," partly by finally having "the talk," a forthright conversation about the realities and consequences of racism that often includes practical, step-by-step rules for the behavior of children of color around police officers and other authority figures (Thomas & Blackmon, 2015; White-Johnson et al., 2010). However, scholars are providing emerging evidence that proactively anticipating, preparing children and opening up lines of dialogue provide more buffering against racial bias (Derlan & Umaña-Taylor, 2015; Thomas et al., 2009). The work of Howard C. Stevenson has been focused on how to proactively prepare children to deal with racism. He is an education scholar and clinical psychologist who has extensively researched racial socialization and what parents can to do prepare their children to deal with racism (Adams-Bass, 2014; Anderson et al., 2018; Anderson & Stevenson, 2019; R. E. Anderson et. al., 2019; Baker et al., 2018; Bentley et al., 2009; Bentley-Edwards & Stevenson, 2016; Coard et al., 2004; Davis & Stevenson, 2006; Hughes et al., 2006; Stevenson, 1994a; Stevenson, 1994b; Stevenson, 1995; Stevenson, 1998; Stevenson, 2008; Stevenson, 2017; Stevenson & Arrington, 2009; Stevenson et al., 2002; Stevenson et al., 1996; Stevenson et al., 1997; Stevenson et al., 2005). In particular, Stevenson has created a model focused on empowering kids of color to talk about race—specifically to agentically engage with, defend against, and change their appraisals of (how they make meaning of) racial discrimination through the Racial Encounter Coping Appraisal Socialization Theory (RECAST) model.

Like our work, this model moves away from construing children as passive recipients of their parents and caregivers' racial socialization, and toward envisioning them as engaged participants in this process. Such a move makes room for the possibility of teaching "racial literacy" to children, which Stevenson (2014) defines as "the ability to read, recast, and resolve racially stressful social interactions." Stevenson puts it plainly: "The teaching of racial literacy skills protects students from the threat of internalizing negative stereotypes that undermine academic critical thinking, engagement, identity, and achievement" (2014, p. 4). RECAST allows us to conceptualize that what children need from their parents is not merely a lecture, but actual skill, reflection, and preparation to engage with difficult conversations. Anderson and Stevenson put forth the idea that the confidence, efficacy, and proficiency of the parent and caregiver can mediate the impact of external racial socialization.

They also acknowledge that talking about race is hard work. They remind us that there may be stress, discomfort, and even trauma in our discussions of race. In order to combat the resultant anxiety and to create the skill needed, Stevenson states, we need practice and self-reflection (Stevenson, 2014). We, as parents and caregivers, in partnership with teachers, have to do the difficult labor to think about how we understand race, and what we want to teach our children about race. As we saw in Chapter 1, Linda shows us that she had to do her own work. She describes how she has had to understand her own experiences of abandonment and separation, yet seek out affiliation and connection. As she put it, "I need to understand my Vietnamese heritage for the sake of [Caleb]." We will listen below to the work that many parents like Linda devote themselves to, despite their discomfort and fear.

BEING VULNERABLE WITH YOUR CHILDREN

We have heard from the parents in the first half of this chapter that forthright conversations about race can be scary because they lay us vulnerable: We can feel as though we have little power over institutional or interpersonal racism in our lives, and for our children, in particular, such lack of power can feel especially scary. As Anderson and Stevenson (2019) would argue, our ability to approach this fear and talk about it will make the topic less scary for both us and our children. Most of us work on understanding race and our own racialization throughout the course of our lives. It's not a "one and done" phenomenon. What radical listening provides us with is a way to showcase the processing of our own racialization in tandem with their own. Sally, the white mother of teenagers Aiyana and Grayson, both of whom identify as either mixed or Black and white at school, speaks to her complicated feelings and the need to prepare and defend herself and her children against perceptions of others. She begins by addressing us and then pivots to addressing her children:

> Some people have guessed to me, which is another whole weird thing like if they see the kids, they'll say, 'is your husband Hispanic?' You know so, [*addressing the kids*] you guys are both in a situation where you'll both . . . [*doesn't finish thought*] I've never been in that space. Or at least I don't perceive myself to be in that space ever. And that's something that makes me feel, [*slows down pace of speaking in order to be very deliberate*]. . . . It makes me feel **sad**. It makes me feel **frustrated**. [*begins addressing us again*] And sometimes I feel like we've put them in a [difficult] position by having mixed-race kids. And I was saying earlier, I feel **guilty**. Sometimes I feel guilty because [of] my racial contribution to the equation. But realizing too, just as an

emotional matter, as a parent you want to have your kids be in the best possible position. It's an unwinnable proposition though. . . . My biggest concern is that I don't want them to feel shame. I don't want them to feel that the need that other people have to sort of put them in their place is a reflection of anything other than that person's need.

This conversation reveals Sally's vulnerability around her own racialization, and her honest and open processing about and around her teenage children. Sally joined us after Aiyana and Grayson had spoken with us together for about half an hour. Both of the children and Sally say that they often discuss race; reflecting this, Sally immediately dove into a candid reflection of her experiences as a white mother of mixed-race African American children, how her children's racialization is so different from her own, or as she puts it, "I've never been in that place." She also frankly grappled with her own emotions, her sadness, frustration, and guilt. She explained that she has to move beyond negative affect and move into action by articulating what she actually wants for her children: to not feel shame, the very emotion she narrates herself as feeling. Instead, she wants her children to be able to claim their identities, identify themselves, and ultimately have pride and agency in their identities.

This agency develops from conversations not just with Sally, but with their African American father who was unable to attend the interview due to a work trip, but attended later listening sessions in support of his children's participation in the Generation Mixed project. For example, Aiyana shared with us a discussion she had with their father about how he understands the openness of Blackness, and how he hopes she will thusly understand her Blackness. She recalls, "I actually had a conversation with my dad about being Black and how he said Black could be whatever you want it to be. Black could be literally anything. And the thing about people saying 'that's so white' [to me], it's like, what makes it so white? What is white about it? What I do is what I do." Thus, this young mixed-race African American girl was learning through dialogues with her father that her mixed-race Blackness should not be delimited by an outside gaze. Aiyana's recounting her conversation with her father was one of many conversations, not just "the talk" but rather an elaborated dialogic form of listening and sharing that supported Aiyana's racial identification.

PROVIDING ROLE MODELS FOR MIXED-RACE CHILDREN

The majority of the Generation Mixed families we listened to were from monoracial parents/caregivers with mixed-race children. When parents and caregivers' racialization is divergent from a child's racialization, the parents and caregivers' additional work becomes providing access for children to hear *their* stories told in the world around them. If this can't happen within the home, then families are faced with not having access to representations that are similar to their own identity at all, having to look to community/neighborhood for representation, and/or trying to find that representation in their school. For example, in the words of one white father of Chinese American and white twin 8-year-old boys, "My approach has been one, find a place where about one-third of the families are like mine and two, live in it." The "like mine" for this father meant, specifically, interracial families. This particular means of racial socialization requires the parent or caregiver to acknowledge their own identity, or put another way, the difference between their child's and their own experience. Rather than minimizing this difference, ignoring it, or hoping that it doesn't matter, parents and caregivers can work to provide models of racial socialization for their children even when the models don't come from them.

One Generation Mixed participant family modeled how to provide a multiracial role model for their child when both parents are monoracial. The family unit who arrives at our interview consisted of Ann, a Japanese American/Hawaiian mother; Eliot, a mixed-race Japanese American/white/Hawaiian cousin in her thirties; and Yuriko, the mother's 7-year-old, 1st-grader, mixed-race Japanese American/white daughter. As we discussed in Chapter 1, in the interview Yuriko told her mom and cousin, "I like being different so everybody's not like the same. Everybody's not the same hair color, not the same voice." For the little girl, being different was valuable: "I like to be different because I like to be unique in my own way." Yuriko's nonracialized and age-appropriate language lay the foundation for her later more explicit conversation about race with her cousin Eliot. When Yuriko was prompted to ask Eliot a question, she did so in such a straightforward and casual manner that it seemed like it was already a topic of conversation in their family: "What was it like when people think you're white?" Eliot responds, speaking slowly and thoughtfully to her little cousin: "You know, it's really confusing because depending on where I am in the world people will see me as a different thing. So when I was in Hawaii and people thought I was white and they treated me like I was a *haole* I felt like an outcast, like I didn't belong in the space where I was born and raised."

This cousin concludes her thoughts with a quick, "Yeah it's weird," and continues, "and then in Seattle people think I'm white." But then Eliot stops herself and doubles back, saying, "They don't really think I'm white [in Seattle]. So I feel more Asian here than I do back home." Eliot's response illuminates her own recursiveness on the topic of race, speaking multiple answers in a way that illuminates the multiple forms of mixed-race racialization. After answering Yuriko's questions, Eliot pivots her questions back to her little cousin, asking, "Do you feel like your racial identity changes depending on where you're traveling?" Yuriko responds, just like the first time, saying, "No I think I always am who I am." But this time she adds,

"But maybe when I get older, I'll realize it." Clearly, Yuriko can imagine that her racial identity might change because she is listening to the experiences that her cousin Eliot is describing. Yuriko has a potential charted pathway, when many children without this proximal representation do not. Ann made a clearly conscious choice to bring in Eliot to this interview. Ann's actions highlight the importance of providing Yuriko with a mixed-race role model.

THE WORK: PARENTS BRINGING RADICAL LISTENING INTO SCHOOL

Even though the work can often feel painstaking, caregivers and parents must also bring racial socialization into their children's classrooms when those classrooms don't represent the racialized experiences of their children. And we heard that families are doing just this by forging radical listening spaces within schools. We understand that schools are the crucible in which children are affected by and enact their racialized identities. Furthermore, racial identities dictate the distribution of opportunities as Pollock notes, "Schools are institutions where people encounter, struggle with, and re-produce many such received systems of difference and inequality" (2004, p. 32). As such, schools become the place into which parental racial socialization can extend and where many parents are trying to continue to cultivate validating spaces for their children.

Emily, a white mother of biracial Black–white children, participated in the Generation Mixed project with her 12-year-old, 7th-grade daughter Mara, who identifies as Black at school. Because of her difficulties navigating racist classroom spaces on Mara's behalf in her predominantly white K–8 public school, Emily wants to do things differently with her younger child, who at the time of our project is 5 and just entering kindergarten. Emily explains that she was "naïve" and wanted to deny the racism that was happening to Mara for so many years, particularly early in elementary school. However, now her eyes are wide open after radically listening to Mara's many years of inequitable treatment. Thus, she takes a different approach when her son begins school.

Emily explained, "My 5-year-old started kindergarten . . . this year and specifically in classroom placement I wanted him to be placed with any other students of color if at all possible, which is hard because it's such a white school." She has found, through her own reflection and radical listening to her older mixed-race child, that advocating for placement with other children of color is of central importance. Emily continues, "And I addressed that issue with the new vice principal who is an Asian American lady, and it was the very first time in our 8 years there that I felt heard, addressed, all in one in 24 hours. And then she even came up to me afterwards and I think because of who she is. Now she's in a leadership role." Emily also asserts that this new leader "gets it," she believes, because she is a woman of color, and thus moves quickly to address her concerns, instead of resisting Emily's advocacy for her child.

We also heard, though, about schools that were not so receptive to parents entering into school communities and advocating for their children. In fact, we heard many stories about the barriers to entering schools, many of which remain unspoken. For example, Conzuelo, a Mexican American mother of two Mexican–white elementary-aged children, told a story that detailed the tremendous labor involved in getting her children's school to radically listen to her two children. As she sat with us, she scaffolds a conversation for her children that allowed them to talk about their understanding of their racial identity. The children, 5-year-old kindergartener Peter, and 7-year-old 2nd-grader Nola, colored and examined the sound equipment in the room while they talked about how they understood how melanin works, how they are "caramel colored," and how "we are," in Peter's words, "Mexican, Florida, and Louisiana." Here, Consuelo introduced both laughter and a sense of playfulness into their conversations about race, ethnicity, geography, and their family histories. What unfolds in the conversation is Conzuelo's conscientious efforts to racially socialize her children. She begins first by articulating the challenging choices she must make in order for her kids to be radically listened to at school. We heard parent after parent detail this same conflict.

Consuelo, who is parenting her children without a partner, told us, "[You have to choose] either good schools, or a diverse neighborhood, and diverse school [or a white neighborhood]." Consuelo chose the highly ranked, academically rigorous, and yet predominantly white school for her children, as well as a safe neighborhood, which was also predominantly white; this also meant she didn't choose the school or neighborhood that was more diverse, where there were more children like her own. She balanced out these choices with her own work at home: "There's not a day that doesn't go by that I have to talk to them about [race]. Maybe it might be too much, but if I don't drill it into them, the schools that they go to are not going to do it. Their surroundings are not going to do it. Their teachers are not going to do it." Thus, Consuelo ensured that time outside of school, including, "the play dates that we have," were with children of color, and that "the stores where we go" were run by merchants of color, and especially Latinx communities. She went on to explain, "If I don't do it, then [school's] not going do it. I am super adamant about them knowing, and just hearing [Spanish]. We have TV time on the weekends. Part of that TV time, you want to watch TV, it's going to be in Spanish, or it's going to be in another language. It's a constant drill." Consuelo admits that this form of racial socialization isn't easy: "Yeah, but it's a constant battle." What's made it easier, she states, is family support, and in particular, "now that my mom and my sister have been here it's actually been really super helpful, because now I have that extra added support of somebody who speaks the language all the time. My mom is not going to speak English. It's always Spanish."

Because Consuelo and her family live in a predominantly white area, and her children attend a predominantly white elementary school, she very consciously connected her kids to their culture and to issues of race. In fact, Consuelo learned about our Generation Mixed project through her involvement with Families of Color Seattle (FOCS), an organization, she noted, that also connected her with events and playdates with other families of color (Latinx and others) all around the Seattle area. Consuelo described how she took the kids out each weekend to more diverse parts of town, and how she sought out cultural events; she found some of these events by scanning Mexican market kiosks for community fliers. She explained, "I make an effort every weekend to go down to [diverse neighborhoods with larger Latinx communities such as] White Center or South Park, or just get out, or got to, just I get out of the city, and my area, and explore other neighborhoods. This past weekend it was Independence Day, and it was so great just celebrating, and being around people that I know, that I can understand, that you can relate both socially, and economic, and all these statuses, it was just. . . . I'm always talking to them about what race is, and what ethnicities and backgrounds . . . where I come from, how I was raised, our family, our traditions, why we do certain things, and why it's so important that we speak another language." Being with Latinx people and other people of color help make Consuelo's constant lessons "real" to Peter and Nola.

In addition to working so hard at home at her children's racial socialization, Consuelo worked hard at her children's school. She describes her attempts at engaging the school at noticing that during Open House the lineup of teachers included only one person of color, and that the room included no visible families of color. Such demographic homogeneity is underscored by the lack of investment in the school's diversity committee. She recounts: "I've been to at least three curriculum nights already, and they make all these announcements . . . [and then they announce] 'oh, by the way we have a diversity committee.' 'Oh, by the way,' as opposed to, again, bringing that to the forefront, putting that up first. 'Oh, by the way we have a' . . . . It just strikes me each and every time." Diversity, in other words, is an afterthought at her kids' school, which makes Consuelo feel as though she and her children are also an afterthought. Consuelo continues, "It's bothersome in another way, because they have these diversity committee meetings at 9:00 in the morning. If you really think about it, who's going to make a 9:00 a.m. meeting, especially if you're a person of color? Not everybody's blessed with having the opportunity to get away from work. . . . How can we become creative enough to not have 9:00 committee meetings, or having more evening events, or reaching out to them somehow through the PTAs?"

The "oh, by the way" nature of the meetings, and the apparent thoughtlessness of engagement with families of color and families with working parents feel like the aforementioned high five in Chapter 4—a symbolic, even empty gesture without commensurate levels of engagement, authenticity, or frankly, work to make spaces available at the school. Consuelo then goes on to detail how she is trying to arrange her schedule to come to these meetings, and to also attend Friday morning singing sessions for the school community. Consuelo was also working to find other Latinx community members to sing at the school assembly in Spanish. The amount of labor Consuelo details is overwhelming to the two of us dialoguing with her in the studio. Yet when we reflect back appreciation (and blink back tears) for her efforts and acknowledgment of her hard work, she pauses and states that she hadn't really noticed; this is just simply what she does.

We must radically listen to Consuelo, Nola, and Peter's story to highlight what active, deliberate, and determined racial socialization in tandem with radical listening can entail. It gives us a chance to see how even well-meaning, "liberal," school spaces still provide real challenges to listening to both mixed-race students and their families. In radically listening to these parents we see, in real life, what RECAST entails. A parent can make a choice to reflect, understand themselves, and commit to work of preparing and supporting their children in navigating a fundamentally racist landscape.

We began this book by articulating what it means to radically listen to mixed race children. At the end of this book we hope that we have shared what our radical listening has heard. We have been diligent about articulating the problems, but we have also heard about the agency, resilience, and joy that families also experience. We heard that the demands for engagement, relationship building, and listening within school contexts are the same demands that children are asking of their parents. They are asking for their parents to really listen to them. We have just heard how hard this can be from the perspective of parents, and they have also, as Consuelo has done, helped us to think about solutions. We move to a close in this chapter by offering up a mission statement exercise that can help families center their racial socialization work around radically listening.

Radical Listening Exercise:
Race, Listening, and Family Mission Statements

We have spent countless hours listening to parents and working to support them with "how to talk to children about race." We are frequently asked these questions of racial socialization: "What do we say? How do we talk to them about race? What about mixed-race kids?" We have heard their stories of guilt, sadness, rage, and also of joy. In our effort to support families in their radical listening, and to support proactive racial socialization, we recommend that they create a family mission statement. Bruce Feiler (2013), who examined happy families, discovered that families with a mission statement found more joy in their lives. These families had a shared goals to come back to each other in the midst of distress, and for parents and caregivers to draw on the strengths of the children to help them navigated the complexities of parenting. Many families balk when we invite them to create a mission statement, imagining a complicated and disingenuous process. But writing a mission statement isn't hard, and, in fact, is often already implicitly embedded in many family's conversations. There are several guiding questions that you can use to help you write one that integrates both race and listening.

For this final radical listening exercise, we would like for you to first do this exercise with your family, and then share out what you've learned with your critical friend through the radical listening exercises you've practiced throughout this book. First, ask yourselves and your families the following:

Who are we as a family?
- What do we stand for?
- What are we like?
- Who do we want to be in the world and to each other?

What is our family motto?
- Even little kids can be encouraged to draw this, or, for example, to create a family crest.
- How would we know if we are living this motto? What would we be doing? How would we be treating ourselves, each other, and those outside our family?

What is our vision of racial justice? What would that look like? How would we know if we are living that dream?
- How do we live racial justice each and every day, in our classrooms, our home lives, our work spaces?

How do we listen to each other? How do we talk to each other?
- When conflict arises, how do we decide who speaks? Who listens? How do we come to a resolution?

Think about it this way: What are the things you tell your family over and over again? What are the statements that you use to encourage, soothe, or even discipline? What are the statements that begin with "we are . . ."? Then again, this process often makes explicit what is often implicit. The purpose of the exercise is to bring families together in shared conversation about values and to serve as a grounding, organizing, and shared means of dealing with all matter of issues, including racial identity. We can hear Sally and many others struggling with where to go and what to communicate. This is a positive, opening moment because Sally wants to talk and learn from and with her children. We also hear Elena and Athena struggling in such a way that resists learning from their children.

We work to remind parents that they already have goals, already have ideas of who they want their children to be. A conversation about racial identity isn't necessarily new, ancillary, or separate, but should be part of the larger conversation about who your family is, your family mission statement. For example, if a family has a family mission that is focused on kindness with the guiding statement being, "we are kind," then families would work to remind themselves to address questions or racial dilemmas with kindness. In other words, family members might remind each other, "we don't discriminate because that is not kind" in the same way they might say, "we don't tease our sister about her hair because that is not kind," or "we are going to meet with that teacher because the way he talked to you isn't kind." In the case of Sally's statement above, we hear her saying that she wants her children to be proud of who they are. Thus, her family's mission statement might be manifested in lessons of pride, and with actions and behaviors that show she is proud of them.

Mission statements don't just guide parents—they guide schools and other institutions. In Chapter 4 we can see that some schools have explicit, mission-driven commitments to racial justice. We find that those schools are often more equipped to address issues of race and have a more clear commitment to engaging in this work. These lessons are present here too for parental and caregiver racial socialization. As we have done throughout the book, we want to focus on not just the talking but the listening. Many of these exercises become places for parents and caregivers to tell, instruct, and direct. Instead, we encourage you to listen to each other. What does your child think your family stands for? Is that different than what you think? Why? You could do something simple like have a list of values, and have each family member identify which values mean the most to them, and which are the values they are working on. The invitation here, discussed throughout the chapter and the book, is that adult caregivers of children need to do the long, hard work of examining themselves, and getting ready to radically listen to what our children have to say.

"I Just Raise My Hand All the Time"

Keep Listening and Talking with and for Generation Mixed

As we concluded the writing of this book in the summer of 2020, we were undergoing yet another national racial reckoning. In Kenosha, Wisconsin, police officers shot 29-year-old Black father Jacob Blake on August 23, 2020. As Blake walked around his family SUV from passenger to driver side, the police shot him seven times. In the back. At point blank range. With his car door open. And with his three children, ages 3, 5, and 8, inside. They watched him get shot, and reports state that they were screaming and crying.

As they have done many times already, our children will witness the traumatic replays of this attempted murder. They will see this on the screens held in their hands or they will peer over our shoulders at the news footage. Our children will understand that a man, who might look like their father, their uncle, their cousin, their big brother, maybe even them in a few short years, is disposable in the eyes of the law. They will understand not only that their caretakers are unworthy of a base level of protection, but that they themselves are targets. Black children like the Gilliams, ages 6, 12, 14, and 17, are snatched out of their car and held at gunpoint in a mistaken case of car theft in Aurora, Colorado. Black boys like 12-year-old Tamir Rice, while playing with a toy gun in Cleveland, Ohio, are murdered by a white police officer. Replays of such instances are how institutional racism is solidified and codified: Black lives don't matter.

What is it like for a child to see their parent shot, attempted to be murdered by the people who are supposed to protect them? What about their trauma? What reckoning does that child have to go through to ever feel safe again? When they try to murder us, we know they don't see us as human. When they try to murder us in front of our children, we know they don't see our children as human either. The failure to humanize, to see a child as a person, is the core expression of racism and bias. To kill us is the extreme dehumanization, but to never listen to us is the mundane form.

And we, as educators and families, must fight such dehumanization by radically listening to our children, by having dialogues with them full of uncomfortable friction, and by moving to antiracist action that is spurred on by their wants and desires. Many of our families described this chain of events.

For example, 16-year-old, 11th-grader Rue, who identifies at school as Black, and her 10½-year-old sister Via, who identifies at school as mixed, share stories with us about how their family works through uncomfortable discussions of race daily, from negotiations on the teenager's use of "the n-word" to the ways in which racialized stereotyping will affect both girls. Rue explains that instead of pretending that their family is either color-blind or immune to race issues, they explore race together because of the logic: "When we're out in public I have a Black dad and a white mom, and some people don't like interracial marriage." Rue says, "They taught us how to deal with things that are out in the public and out in school. Even before school taught us about Dr. King, I learned it from my family." Rue and Via's family provides them with a space to understand race, to anticipate how it might cut them; they also underscore that that they have a place of refuge at home.

Via chimes in that their family race talk means to her that she's prepared for the situation when "maybe sometimes teachers will put people on the spot because maybe they'll pick someone [white] over you even if you're smart. They'll probably think, 'Black people aren't smart because they're dumb, and white people are always smart so I should call on this person.' Then they never get your opinions about something that you might actually have a really good opinion on something." Via has been taught to anticipate racism. This is her way of girding herself, as a 10-year-old. Hearing this comment we follow up with the question "Has that happened to you in class before?" She responds happily, "No, I usually get picked a lot, because I just raise my hand all the time." Her response shows her resilience—a resilience that her family has helped stoke through radically listening and engaging Via and Rue in conversations around race. The idea that she "just" raises her hand—as if it is easy—contrasts with her awareness that she needs to raise her hand—again and again. She is wise and has a lesson for us during these times: She needs to speak out to be heard, again and again. And we need to create the spaces for her to speak and more importantly, to be heard.

Although we and the literature have often come back to anti-Blackness, the children in this book pull us into nuance and into the depths of how racism impacts them. These young people are asking us to listen to them, to their movement, their agency, their decisions, and the ways in which they push on the very idea of race. It is not that they do not know who they are—it is that the world will not let them be. Our need to quickly categorize, neatly fit, and to sort betrays our ability to slow down, to sit in discomfort and to really listen.

And we understand how deeply difficult, and how truly exhausting it can be, to constantly engage in race talk, to, in Via's words, raise one's hand again and again. As the two of us are negotiating through our own race conversations with our children, we also continue to facilitate spaces for all different kinds of people, including teachers and parents. During the week Jacob Blake was shot, Ralina was facilitating a racial dialogue session for mothers wanting to learn how to talk more effectively about race with their children. A white woman expressed what so many of us are feeling around having conversations around race right now: She said she was exhausted. In response, a BIPOC participant respectfully sighed, "I'm tired too, but I don't have the luxury to lie down." In a second session Ralina facilitated that week, another participant added to this wisdom, saying, "When you're tired, rest. Don't give up."

We understand that in asking you to radically listen to your children that you are asking to listen to racialized hurt, to talk about racialized violence, to share in on experiences of racialized pain. We are asking you to sit in discomfort, that process of friction. In the summer of 2020 as we finished this book, all families have witnessed when individual actions (white police officers shooting Black people) continue to mimic institutional and structural action (government officials and police forces that refuse to acknowledge the humanity of Blackness including mixed-race Blackness). These are the moments our energy to engage in race talk drains away. What greater articulation of individual racism emanating from structural racism is there than shooting a man in the back as his three children watch from the backseat? The sentiment is clear: Black men's lives do not matter, and Black children's lives do not matter either.

The fatigue comes to the fore. We sit in our fatigue because we mourn the loss of so many lives due to racialized violence; we celebrate Black life holding on despite being shot seven times. But we can't stay stuck in this fatigue because we know that radical listening, racial dialoguing, talking, intervening together, does create change. Protesting creates change. We have seen this happen over the course of U.S. history. We also know that we can't sit in the despair because losing hope means losing the desire to fight. And that, to us, means losing our humanity.

We are all tired. Indeed, we understand the fatigue. But, please, let's stay in the work together, as radical listeners. For Jacob Blake and his children. For the Gilliam children. For Tamir Rice. For all of our children and all of us. Let's garner strength from Sweet Honey in the Rock's celebration of the mother of civil rights Ella Baker:

> Struggling myself don't mean a whole lot, I've come to realize that teaching others to stand up and fight is the only way my struggle survives.

Radical listening is struggling together, standing up and fighting together, surviving together. We can't afford not to.

We have one final exercise for you. We have encouraged you to practice skills of listening, to reflect on your own identities and take stock of your own biases. But now we ask in your final exercise with your critical friend. Spend 2 minutes speaking to the prompt: Have you radically listened to the voices of the mixed-race young people in your life? Have you experienced and invoked friction as they have told you stories that are uncomfortable or dissonant with your own experiences? Have you slowed down and persisted in that discomfort? Are you really listening? How will you continue to listen for them?

Generation Mixed Dialogue Questions

Your Racial Identity

1. What is your racial identity?
2. How did you learn about that identity?
   a. Who taught you about this identity?
3. Does your racial identity ever change?
   a. When does it change?
   b. Why does it change?
4. What have your parents taught you about race and your racial identity?
5. What have your teachers taught you about race and your racial identity?
6. How do you think your teachers identify your race?
   a. What do you think your teachers think your racial identity is?
7. At school, if someone asks you what your race or ethnicity is, what do you say?
8. What do you think other people think about your racial identity?
   a. How do you know?

Teachers and Race

1. Do your teachers know how you identify?
   a. Do you think they treat you differently because of this?
      i. If yes, how?
2. What do you wish your teachers knew about what it's like to be your race/identity?
3. Have teachers or people at school done anything to help support your identity?
   a. Like what?
4. Have teachers or people at school done anything that makes it hard to be you?
   a. What do you wish they would do differently?

5. Can you describe a time when you saw people treated differently because of race at school?
     a. What happened?
     b. What was that like for you and the people involved?
     c. What do you think should have happened, and what would you have liked to see happen?
6. Are there resources—like clubs, groups, or teachers at your school—to support your identity?
     a. What are they?
     b. What resources do you wish you had?
7. When do you get a chance to talk about your racial identity at school?
     a. What are these spaces like, and how does the conversation go?
     b. Do conversations about race happen in the classroom?
8. If you could tell teachers and schools anything about what it's like to be you (your race), what would you tell them? What do you want them to know?

Generation Mixed Participants

Participants are listed in the order in which we interviewed them. The sibling pairs all have the same last name initial. The fourth column lists the race the children and youth have chosen to identify as at school, which we culled from their self-identity in the dialogues, whereas the fifth is what they or their parents (for younger participants) filled out in the demographic forms they completed either pre- or postdialogue:

Pseudonym	Age	Grade	Race (self-identified)	Ethnic Background (as listed by them or parent)	Public/ Private School
Ty A.	15	10th	Black	Black, white, Indian	Public
Kema A.	12	7th	Mixed	Black, white, Indian	Public
Man Man B.	11	6th	Black	Unsure	Private
Velma B.	12	8th	African American	Brazil, Irish, African American	Private
Lucy C.	12	7th	Mixed; Black and white	Black, white	Private
Gia C.	14	9th	Mixed; white and Black	Black, white	Public
Hugo D.	11	6th	African American	American, African, Scottish, Swedish	Public
Takuji E.	16	11th	Half Japanese, Half white	Okinawan, Northern European	Public
Hiro E.	13	8th	Asian	Okinawan, white	Public
Rue F.	16	11th	Black	White, Black	Private
Via F.	10½	5th	Mixed	Black, white	Private
Percy G.	13	8th	Filipino	Filipino, French, Irish	Public
Mara H.	12	7th	African American	Zimbabwean, American	Public

Pseudonym	Age	Grade	Race (self-identified)	Ethnic Background (as listed by them or parent)	Public/ Private School
Mia I.	14	9th	Mixed	African, American, Caucasian	Public
Mariah I.	11	6th	Mixed or white	Caucasian, African American	Private
Aiyana J.	13	9th	White and Black or mixed	White, Black	Private
Grayson J.	15	10th	Mixed; Black and white	African American, white/European American, Native	Private
Jaylen K.	9	4th	Asian American	American, Korean, Filipino, Chinese	Private
Mila K.	10	5th	Asian	Korean, Filipino, Chinese	Public
Jessica L.	12	7th	Asian, Native American, and white	Asian, Native American, white	Private
Oyin M.	19	College sophomore	Nigerian and Filipino; Blasian	Filipino, Nigerian, Malaysian, Spaniard	Private
Olu M.	15	10th	African American, Asian	Nigerian, Asian	Private
Xiomari N.	10	4th	Indigenous	Otomi, white	Private
Nola O.	7	2nd	Mixed	Mexican, white	Public
Peter O.	5	K	"Louisiana, Florida, Mexico"	Mexican, white	Public
Yuriko P.	7	1st	"Hmm . . . the only Yuriko. That's me."	Japanese, English	Private
Kai Q.	10	4th	Black and white and Mexican	Black, white, and Mexican	Public
Tatiana Q.	8	2nd	Black and white	Black, white, and Mexican	Public
Caleb R.	5	K	Mixed (Asian and white)	Vietnamese, Japanese, white	Private

Sample Guide to Affinity Groups

We are excerpting a sample of the treasure-trove of information Rosetta Lee provides for school communities on the website, https://sites.google.com/a/sgs-wa.org/sgsprofessionaloutreach/affinity-group-resource-page.

Issues That May Arise

At SGS, affinity groups evolved out of the fact that we have an antibias mission and wanted to incorporate as many aspects of antibias work as possible. Almost all reaction has been positive, enthusiastic, and supportive. Negativity has traditionally arisen from three populations:

1. White adoptive parents of students of color who, at the base level, fear that we are somehow breeding resentment and they will "lose" their daughters. To offset this resistance, we reassure them about the nature of the affinity space (focus on self-pride rather than other resentment) and also share information and research about transracial adoptees that tell us that racial identity development is crucial. . . .
2. White students who feel "left out" or "excluded." The most powerful tool we have to offset this resistance is a white affinity group. Students who don't want to participate in this group and yet want admission into other affinity groups are guided in discussions about privilege and allyship.
3. White parents of white students who think that affinity groups are divisive and wonder "why can't we stress sameness instead of differences"? To offset this resistance, we share research and articles about the experiences of students of color in Independent Schools, as well as research on why color blindness and stressing similarities has no effect on racial attitudes. . . .

Language from Head of School

Sample letters for introducing affinity groups, responding to questions about the reasons for affinity groups, and responding to resistance to affinity groups.

The last two are no longer needed at SGS, as the full launch and training has addressed most questions and resistance. They are included here for ideas on how leadership can further support affinity groups if necessary.

Initial Introduction

As we get our schedules rolling here at school, the girls have been hearing about special lunch meetings called "Affinity Groups." During Affinity Group lunches, students of a certain affinity join together and eat apart from the rest of the school. Affinity Group lunches are designed for students to develop and strengthen their own racial/ethnic/group identity rather than as a time to learn about others. The qualitative difference between affinity group work and other aspects of school is that safety and trust must be fostered, expected, and assured by each member to explore shared racial/ethnic/group identity development (Borrowed from National Association of Independent Schools People of Color Conference)

The term *affinity group* is used as a bringing together of people who have an identifier in common, e.g., race, gender, religion, family status, etc. Affinity groups are for individuals who identify as members of the group and can speak to the experience of being a member of the group from the "I" perspective. This year we will have the Soul Sistas (African-American), the Asian Pacific Islanders, the Multi-Racial, the White, and the Latino/Latina Affinity Group meetings.

The term *alliance group* is used as a bringing together of people who have a common commitment to an identifier group, e.g., race, gender, religion, family status, etc. Alliance groups are for individuals who identify as members of the group and/or as people who support and stand in solidarity with that group. This year, we will have the Adoption Alliance and the Alphabet Alliance (LBGTQ people and their allies).

The term *interest group* is used as a bringing together of people who want to learn about, share, and engage in a special interest, e.g., hobby, skill, topic, etc. Interest groups are for individuals who want to gather to teach, learn, and share. Membership can be fluid and changing. SIGS are developed year to year. (Last year, we had Art SIG, Harry Potter SIG, Go SIG, Writing SIG, etc.) Students who are interested in starting a SIG can seek an adult sponsor, and that sponsor will find days and spaces for the group to meet.

Descriptions for all groups that meet at SGS are included in this letter. Please look over these and discuss with your girls whether they might be interested in participating. Announcements are made the week each group is meeting with details as to time and place. Your girls are welcome to join any of the groups to which they belong. However, these groups are completely optional, and students can decide on a week-by-week basis if they want to go or not.

Follow-Up After Questions Arose

In the next week, students will be able to participate in Affinity Group lunches (lunchtime meetings a couple of times a month for students who identify themselves a certain way). This practice began several years ago, initially as a request from some of our students of color, but it has since grown to include a number of groups. While initially it may seem counterintuitive at a school that stresses antibias work and inclusiveness, it is in reality an important piece of this work. We have found it is important to recognize that different groups within SGS may need room to find fellowship and kindred spirits to continue to fuel their drive to be a part of a truly diverse community. Diverse schools often offer "affinity groups" for families and students for these very reasons.

One way to commit to antibias work and to create a more multicultural environment is to permit people to feel safe and strong and reflected within their environment as they begin to do the hard and sometimes uncomfortable work of stepping out of their comfort zones and into the broader world. We have created groups in response to the requests we have heard from the students themselves and by ensuring that we have a leader from the faculty/staff who can reflect the named affinity and facilitate the group.

Attending an affinity group lunch is completely optional, and important that it is so. Our goal is for everyone to feel as though they have a safe and comfortable spot. Through continued education efforts at all levels, we will grow together as community in our understanding of each other and the work it takes to be a diverse and welcoming community.

But part of this journey is not developing "colorblindness." Difference matters. While many of us (especially those from more dominant cultures, or privileged backgrounds) try to see past the differences, the unintended effect of this is to deny others' experiences rather than acknowledge them, see them, and become an ally through understanding rather than ignorance. Students who attend the White Affinity Group have had conversations about becoming an ally, even when they have found themselves in situations where they may not be in the majority. It is a valuable discussion to have and continue having when your student is ready.

Some of this work is uncomfortable—no question. We will be working with all the students throughout the remainder of the year on developing skills and working with issues of oppression in a variety of forms. This is a journey and there is no quick, easy, or right resolution.

For parents, we hope to offer some ways to help you with your own journey—eventually we want to offer some programs here at school. We will also continue to send home flyers and announcements of wonderful opportunities for training here in the Seattle area as we become aware of them.

Table Describing GREET-STOP-PROMPT Practices

Note: The following table is adapted from Cook, Duong, McIntosh, Fiat, Larson, Pullmann, & McGinnis (2018), p. 141.

Table D.1. Linking Malleable Putative Root Causes to GREET-STOP-PROMPT Practices

Malleable Putative Root Cause	Purpose and Rationale for Solution	Specific Practices
Inadequate knowledge, skills, and self-efficacy with regard to proactive classroom management	Educators need to be equipped with the knowledge, skills, and confidence to proactively manage behavior so there are fewer behavior problems to address.	Specific evidence-based proactive classroom management techniques (GREET) • Greet students positively at the door • Reinforce students frequently, specifically, and contingently • Establish, review, and cue behavioral expectations • Engage students by providing opportunities to respond • Take time to voice high expectations and beliefs in the student (wise feedback)
Lack of recognition and regulation of implicit biases toward Black male students	Educators need to learn how to recognize and regulate their behavior in response to situations in which they are vulnerable to implicit biases that could negatively impact their decisions to engage in an exclusionary discipline action.	Mindful STOP techniques to increase self-regulation and effective decisionmaking • Stop and do not do anything immediately in reaction to the perceived problem behavior • Take a breath to regulate yourself • Observe your knee-jerk reactions • Proceed positively by doing what is most effective (not what you initially feel like saying or doing)
Insufficient training in progressive methods of responding to perceived or actual problem behavior as alternatives to exclusionary discipline practices	Educators must learn how to progressively respond to problem behavior in an emphatic, consistent, and appropriate manner in order to correct behavior, maintain the student in the learning environment, and preserve the relationship with the student.	A progressive system of responding effectively to perceived or actual problem behavior (PROMPT) • Proximity as the initial method to correct behavior • Redirection tactics to get the behavior back on track • Ongoing monitoring to shape behavior and capitalize on social learning (reinforcing peers) • Prompt the student privately with an effective command • Teach the student through a skillful communication if interaction (empathy statement, label the inappropriate behavior, label the appropriate behavior, give a rationale, outline the choices for the student to make, warn of a natural and logical consequence, give the student think time, and check back with the student)

References

Aboud, F. E. (1988). *Children and prejudice*. Blackwell Publishing.

Aboud, F. E. (2003). The formation of in-group favoritism and out-group prejudice in young children: Are they distinct attitudes? *Developmental Psychology, 39*(1), 48–60.

Aboud, F. E., & Doyle, A. B. (1996a). Does talk of race foster prejudice or tolerance in children? *Canadian Journal of Behavioural Science, 28*(3), 161–170. https://doi.org/10.1037/0008-400X.28.3.161

Aboud, F. E., & Doyle, A. B. (1996b). Parental and peer influences on children's racial attitudes. *International Journal of Intercultural Relations, 20*(3–4), 371–383. https://doi.org/10.1016/0147-1767(96)00024-7

Adams-Bass, V. N., Stevenson, H. C., & Kotzin, D. S. (2014). Measuring the meaning of black media stereotypes and their relationship to the racial identity, black history knowledge, and racial socialization of African American youth. *Journal of Black Studies, 45*(5), 367–395. https://doi.org/10.1177/0021934714530396

Alejandro-Wright, M. N. (2013). The child's conception of racial classification: A socio-cognitive developmental model. In M. B. Spencer, G. K. Brookins, & W. R. Allen (Eds.), *Beginnings: The art and science of planning psychotherapy* (pp. 185–200). Psychology Press.

American Psychological Association. (2013). *Physiological & psychological impact of racism and discrimination for African-Americans*. https://www.apa.org/pi/oema/resources/ethnicity-health/racism-stress

Anderson, A., Dobbins, B., Sugland, H., Groff, J., Barris, K., Smith, K., Wilmore, L., Young, P., Fishburne, L., Principato, P., & Russo, T. (Executive Producers). (2014–present). *Black-ish* [TV series]. ABS Studios, Khalabo Ink Society, Cinema Gypsy Productions, Principato-Young Entertainment, Artists First.

Anderson, A., Ross, T. E., Dobbins, B., Sugland, H., Barris, K., Saji, P., Fishburne, L., Winston, R., & Gist, K. (Executive Producers). (2019–present). *Mixed-ish* [TV series]. ABC Studios, Khalabo Ink Society, Cinema Gypsy Productions, and Artists First.

Anderson, R. E., McKenny, M. C., Mitchell, A., Koku, L., & Stevenson, H. C. (2018). EMBRacing racial stress and trauma: Preliminary feasibility and coping responses of a racial socialization intervention. *Journal of Black Psychology, 44*(1), 25–46.

Anderson, R. E., McKenny, M. C., & Stevenson, H. C. (2019). EMBRace: Developing a racial socialization intervention to reduce racial stress and enhance racial coping among black parents and adolescents. *Family Process, 58*(1), 53–67.

Anderson, R. E., & Stevenson, H. C. (2019). RECASTing racial stress and trauma: Theorizing the healing potential of racial socialization in families. *American Psychologist, 74*(1), 63–75.

Anyon, Y., Bender, K., Kennedy, H., & Dechants, J. (2018a). A systematic review of Youth Participatory Action Research (YPAR) in the United States: Methodologies, youth outcomes, and future directions. *Health Education & Behavior, 45*(6), 865–878. https://doi.org/10.1177/1090198118769357

Anyon, Y., Lechuga, C., Ortega, D., Downing, B., Greer, E., & Simmons, J. (2018b). An exploration of the relationships between student racial background and the school sub-contexts of office discipline referrals: A critical race theory analysis. *Race Ethnicity and Education, 21*(3), 390–406. doi:10.1080/13613324.2017.1328594

Anyon, Y., Zhang, D., & Hazel, C. (2016). Race, exclusionary discipline, and connectedness to adults in secondary schools. *American Journal of Community Psychology, 57*(3–4), 342–352. https://doi.org/10.1002/ajcp.12061

Appleby, J. (1998). *Becoming critical friends: Reflections of an NSRF coach.* The Annenberg Institute for School Reform at Brown University.

Ashe, B. D. (2007). Theorizing the post-soul aesthetic: An introduction. *African American Review, 41*(4), 609–624.

Baker, J. L., Stevenson, H. C., Talley, L. M., Jemmott, L. S., & Jemmott, J. B. (2018). Development of a barbershop-based racial socialization violence intervention for young Black emerging adult men. *Journal of Community Psychology, 46*(4), 1–13. https://onlinelibrary.wiley.com/doi/full/10.1002/jcop.21971

Balk, G. (2016, August). Seattle's multiracial identity evolves with the census. *The Seattle Times.* https://www.seattletimes.com/pacific-nw-magazine/seattles-multiracial-identity-evolves-along-with-census

Bambino, D. (2002, March). Redesigning professional development: Critical friends. *Educational Leadership, 59*(6), 25–27.

Banks, T. L. (2000). Colorism: A darker shade of pale. *47 UCLA Law Review, 217,* 1705–1749.

Bar-Haim, Y., Ziv, T., Lamy, D., & Hodes, R. M. (2006). Nature and nurture in own-race face processing. *Psychological Science, 17*(2), 1159–1163.

Bazzaz, D. (2019, August 1). A white Seattle teacher told police she felt unsafe around a black fifth-grader who she says threatened her. *The Seattle Times.* https://www.seattletimes.com/seattle-news/education/a-white-seattle-teacher-told-police-she-felt-unsafe-around-a-black-fifth-grader-who-she-says-threatened-her

Bentley, K. L., Adams, V. N., & Stevenson, H. C. (2009). Racial socialization: Roots, processes, and outcomes. In H. Neville, B. Tynes, & S. O. Utsey (Eds.), *The handbook of African American psychology* (pp. 255–268). Sage.

Bentley-Edwards, K. L., & Stevenson H. C. (2016). The multidimensionality of racial/ethnic socialization: Scale construction for the cultural and racial experiences of socialization (CARES). *Journal of Child and Family Studies, 25,* 96–108.

Bigler, R. S., & Liben, L. S. (1993). A cognitive developmental approach to racial stereotyping and reconstructive memory in Euro-American children. *Child Development, 64*(5), 1507–1518.

Blair, I. V., & Judd, C. M. (2011). Afrocentric facial features and stereotyping. *Science of Social Vision, 18,* 306–320.

Blair, I. V., Judd, C. M., Sadler, M. S., & Jenkins, C. (2002). The role of Afrocentric features in person perception: Judging by features and categories. *Journal of Personality and Social Psychology, 83*(1), 5–25.

Bonilla-Silva, E. (2002). The linguistics of color blind racism: How to talk nasty about blacks without sounding "racist." *Critical Sociology, 28*(1–2), 41–64.

Bottiani, J. H., Bradshaw, C. P., & Gregory, A. (2018). Nudging the gap: Introduction to the special issue "closing in on discipline disproportionality." *School Psychology Review, 47*(2), 109–117.

Bottiani, J. H., Bradshaw, C. P., & Mendelson, T. (2014). Promoting an equitable and supportive school climate in high schools: The role of school organizational health and staff burnout. *Journal of School Psychology, 52*(6), 567–582. https://doi.org/10.1016/j.jsp.2014.09.003

Bowman, P. J., & Howard, C. (1985). Race-related socialization, motivation, and academic achievement: A study of black youth in three-generation families. *Journal of the American Academy of Child Psychiatry, 24*(2), 134–141.

Bradshaw, C. P., Pas, E. T., Bottiani, J. H., Debnam, K. J., Reinke, W. M., Herman, K. C., & Rosenberg, M. S. (2018). Promoting cultural responsivity and student engagement through double check coaching of classroom teachers: An efficacy study. *School Psychology Review, 47*(2), 118–134.

Bratter, J. (2007). Will 'multiracial' survive to the next generation? The racial classification of children of multiracial parents. *Social Forces, 86*, 821–849.

Bronson, P., & Merryman, A. (2009). *NurtureShock: New thinking about children.* Twelve.

Brown, E. (2016, September 27). Yale study suggests racial bias among preschool teachers. *The Washington Post.* https://www.washingtonpost.com/news/education/wp/2016/09/27/yale-study-suggests-racial-bias-among-preschool-teachers

Brown, T. D., Dane, F. C., & Durham, M. D. (1998). Perception of race and ethnicity. *Journal of Social Behavior and Personality, 13*, 295–306.

Brunsma, D. L. (2005). Interracial families and the identification of mixed-race children: Evidence from the early childhood longitudinal study. *Social Forces, 84*(2), 1131–1157.

Brunsma, D. L. (2006). Public categories, private identities: Exploring regional differences in the biracial experience. *Social Science Research, 35*(3), 555–576. https://doi.org/10.1016/j.ssresearch.2004.10.002

Byum, M. S., Burton, E. T., & Best, C. (2007). Racism experiences and psychological functioning in African American college freshmen: Is racial socialization a buffer? *Cultural Diversity and Ethnic Minority Psychology, 13*(1), 64–71.

Caraballo, L., Lozenski, B. D., Lyiscott, J. J., & Morrell, E. (2017). YPAR and critical epistemologies: Rethinking education research. *Review of Research in Education, 41*(1), 311–336. https://doi.org/10.3102/0091732X16686948

Carter, G. (2013). *The United States of the united races: A utopian history of racial mixing.* New York University Press.

Cauce, A. M., Hiraga, Y., Mason, C. A., Aguilar, T., Ordonez, N., & Gonzales, N. (1992). Between a rock and a hard place: An examination of bi-racial early adolescents. In M. P. P. Root (Ed.), *Racially mixed people in America* (pp. 131–162). Sage.

Centers for Disease Control and Prevention. (2009). *School connectedness: Strategies for increasing protective factors among youth*. U.S. Department of Health and Human Services. https://www.cdc.gov/healthyyouth/protective/pdf/connectedness.pdf

Chang, S. (2015). *Multiracial Asian children in a postracial world*. Routledge.

Chang, T., & Karl Kwan, K.-L. (2009). Asian American racial and ethnic identity. In N. Tewari & A. N. Alvarez (Eds.), *Asian American psychology: Current perspectives* (pp. 113–133). Routledge/Taylor & Francis Group.

Christle, C. A., Jolivette, K., & Nelson, C. M. (2007). School characteristics related to high school dropout rates. *Remedial and Special Education, 28*(6), 325–339. https://doi.org/10.1177/07419325070280060201

Chun, W. H. K. (1999). Unbearable witness: Toward a politics of listening. *Differences: A Journal of Feminist Cultural Studies, 11*(1), 112–149.

Clark, K. B., & Clark, M. P. (1950). Emotional factors in racial identification and preference in negro children author(s). *The Journal of Negro Education, 19*(3), 341–350.

Coard, S. I., Wallace, S. A., Stevenson, H. C., Jr., & Brotman, L. M. (2004). Towards culturally relevant preventive interventions: The consideration of racial socialization in parent training with African American families. *Journal of Child and Family Studies, 13*, 277–293.

Cook, C. R., Duong, M. T., McIntosh, K., Fiat, A. E., Larson, M., Pullmann, M. D., & McGinnis, J. (2018). Addressing discipline disparities for black male students: Linking malleable root causes to feasible and effective practices. *School Psychology Review, 47*(2), 135–152.

Cornell, D., Maeng, J., Huang, F., Shukla, K., & Konold, T. (2018). Racial/ethnic parity in disciplinary consequences using student threat assessment. *School Psychology Review, 47*(2), 183–195.

Crosnoe, R., Johnson, M. K., & Elder, G. H. (2004). School size and the interpersonal side of education: An examination of race/ethnicity and organizational context. *Social Science Quarterly, 85*(5), 1259–1274.

Cross, W. E., Jr. (1991). *Shades of Black: Diversity in African-American identity*. Temple University Press.

Cross, W. E., Jr. (1995). *The psychology of nigrescence: Revising the Cross model*. In J. G. Ponterotto, J. M. Casas, L. A. Suzuki, & C. M. Alexander (Eds.), *Handbook of multicultural counseling* (pp. 93–122). Sage.

Cushman, K. (1998, May). *How friends can be critical as schools make essential changes*. Coalition of Essential Schools.

Dagbovie-Mullins, S. A. (2013). *Crossing b(l)ack: Mixed-race identity in modern American fiction and culture*. University of Tennessee Press.

Daniel, G. R. (2002). *More than black: Multiracial identity and the new racial order*. Temple University Press.

Davenport, L. (2016). Beyond Black and White: Biracial attitudes in contemporary U.S. politics. *American Political Science Review, 110*(1), 52–67. doi:10.1017/S0003055415000556

Davis, G. Y., & Stevenson, H. C. (2006). Racial socialization experiences and symptoms of depression among black youth. *Journal of Child and Family Studies, 15*, 293–307.

Denevi, E., & Richards, M. (2018). Frequently asked questions about affinity groups in K–12 schools. *Diversity and equity best practices 2018*. https://www.pps.net/cms/lib/OR01913224/Centricity/Domain/4870/2018%20Denevi%20Richards%20Affinity%20Groups%20FAQ.pdf

Derlan, C. L., & Umaña-Taylor, A. J. (2015). Brief report: Contextual predictors of African American adolescents' ethnic-racial identity affirmation-belonging and resistance to peer pressure. *Journal of Adolescence, 41*, 1–6. https://doi.org/10.1016/j.adolescence.2015.02.002

Dixon, T. L. (2017). Good guys are still always in white? Positive change and continued misrepresentation of race and crime on local television news. *Communication Research, 44*(6), 775–792. https://doi.org/10.1177/0093650215579223

Dixon, T. L. (2019). Media stereotypes: Content, effects, and theory. In M. B. Oliver, A. A. Raney, & J. Bryant (Eds.), *Media effects: Advances in theory and research* (4th ed., pp. 243–257). Taylor & Francis.

Dixon, T. L., & Williams, C. L. (2015). The changing misrepresentation of race and crime on network and cable news. *Journal of Communication, 65*(1), 24–39. https://doi.org/10.1111/jcom.12133

Doyle, A. B., & Aboud, F. E. (1995). A longitudinal study of White children's racial prejudice as a social-cognitive development. *Merrill-Palmer Quarterly, 41*(2), 209–228.

Dreher, T. (2009). Listening across difference: Media and multiculturalism beyond the politics of voice. *Continuum: Journal of Media & Cultural Studies, 23*(4), 445–458. http://dx.doi.org/10.1080/10304310903015712(link is external)

Durlak, J. A., Weissberg, R. P., Dymnicki, A. B., Taylor, R. D., & Schellinger, K. (2011). The impact of enhancing students' social and emotional learning: A meta-analysis of school-based universal interventions. *Child Development, 82*, 405–432.

Eberhardt, J. L. (2019). *Biased: Uncovering the hidden prejudice that shapes what we see, think, and do*. Penguin Random House.

Elam, M. (2011). *The souls of mixed folk: Race, politics, and aesthetics in the millennium*. Stanford University Press.

Erikson, E. H. (1993). *Childhood and society*. Norton.

Essi, C. (2017). "Mama's baby, papa's, too"—Toward critical mixed race studies. *Zeitschrift für Anglistik und Amerikanistik 65*(2), online. https://doi.org/10.1515/zaa-2017-0018

Federal Bureau of Investigation (n.d.). *Hate crimes*. https://www.fbi.gov/investigate/civil-rights/hate-crimes

Feiler, B. (2013). *The secrets of happy families: Improve your mornings, tell your family history, fight smarter, go out and play, and much more*. HarperCollins.

Feliciano, C. (2015). Shades of race: How phenotype and observer characteristics shape racial classification. *American Behavioral Scientist, 60*(4), 390–419. https://doi.org/10.1177%2F0002764215613401

Fields, K. E., & Fields, B. J. (2012). *Racecraft: The soul of inequality in American life*. Verso.

Foreman, P. G. (2002). Who's your mama? "White" mulatta genealogies, early photography, and anti-passing narratives of slavery and freedom. *American Literary History, 14*(3), 505–539.

Freeman, J. B., Penner, A. M., Saperstein, A., Scheutz, M., & Ambady, N. (2011). Looking the part: Social status cues shape race perception. *PloS One*, 6(9), e25107. https://doi.org/10.1371/journal.pone.0025107

Gaither, S. E. (2015). "Mixed" results: Multiracial research and identity explorations. *Current Directions in Psychological Science*, 24(2), 114–119. https://doi.org/10.1177/0963721414558115

Gaither, S. E., Babbitt, L. G., & Sommers, S. R. (2018). Resolving racial ambiguity in social interactions. *Journal of Experimental Social Psychology*, 76, 259–269.

Gaither, S. E., Fan, S. P., & Kinzler, K. D. (2019). Thinking about multiple identities boost children's flexible thinking. *Developmental Science*, 23(1), 1–11.

Gaither, S. E., Pauker, K., & Johnson, S. P. (2012). Biracial and monoracial infant own-race face perception: An eye tracking study. *Developmental Science*, 15(6), 775–782.

Gaither, S. E., Remedios, J. D., Sanchez, D. T., & Sommers, S. R. (2015). Thinking outside the box: Multiple identity mind-sets affect creative problem solving. *Social Psychological and Personality Science*, 6(5), 596–603.

Garg, S., Kim, L., & Whitaker, M., et al. (2020). Hospitalization rates and characteristics of patients hospitalized with laboratory-confirmed Coronavirus disease 2019—COVID-NET, 14 states, March 1–30, 2020. *Morbidity and Mortality Weekly Report (MMWR)*, 69, 458–464. doi:http://dx.doi.org/10.15585/mmwr.mm6915e3

Gerbner, G. (1972). Violence in television drama: Trends and symbolic functions. In G. A. Comstock & E. A. Rubinstein (Eds.), *Television and social behavior, volume 1: Media, content and control* (pp. 28–65). U.S. Government Printing Office.

Gerbner, G., & Gross, L. (1976). Living with television: The violence profile. *Journal of Communication*, 26(2), 172–199. https://doi.org/10.1111/j.1460-2466.1976.tb01397.x

Gerbner, G., Gross, L., Morgan, M., & Signorielli, N. (1980). The "mainstreaming" of America: Violence profile no. 11. *Journal of Communication*, 30(3), 10–29. https://doi.org/10.1111/j.1460-2466.1980.tb01987.x

Gilligan, C. (1982). *In a different voice: Psychological theory and women's development*. Harvard University Press.

Gilligan, C., & Richards, D. A. J. (2018). *Darkness now visible: Patriarchy's resurgence and feminist resistance*. Cambridge University Press.

Gilligan, C., Rogers, A. G., & Tolman, D. L. (Eds.). (1991). *Women, girls, and psychotherapy: Reframing resistance*. Haworth Press.

Gocłowska, M. A., & Crisp, R. J. (2014). How dual-identity processes foster creativity. *Review of General Psychology*, 18(3), 216–236.

Goff, P. A., Jackson, M. C., Di Leone, B. A. L., Culotta, C. M., & DiTomasso, N. A. (2014). The essence of innocence: Consequences of dehumanizing black children. *Journal of Personality and Social Psychology*, 106(4), 526–545.

Gong, L. (2013). Walking in "Chindian" shoes: An interview with Louie Gong. In L. Kina & W. M. Dariotis (Eds.), *War baby/love child: Mixed race Asian American art* (pp. 169–175). University of Washington Press.

Gopnik, A., Meltzoff, A. N., & Kuhl, P. K. (1999). *Scientist in the crib: What early learning tells us about the mind*. HarperCollins.

Gossett, T. F. (1963). *The history of an idea in America*. Oxford University Press.

Greenwald, A. G., McGhee, D. E., & Schwartz, J. L. K. (1998). Measuring individual differences in implicit cognition: The implicit association test. *Journal of Personality and Social Psychology, 74*(6), 1464–1480. http://dx.doi.org/10.1037/0022-3514.74.6.1464

Gregory, A., Hafen, C. A., Ruzek, E. A., Mikami, A. Y, Allen, J. P., & Pianta, R. C. (2016). Closing the racial discipline gap in classrooms by changing teacher practice. *School Psychology Review, 45*, 171–191.

Gregory, A., Huang, F. L., Anyon, Y., Greer, E., & Downing, B. (2018). An examination of restorative interventions and racial equity in out-of-school suspensions. *School Psychology Review, 47*(2), 167–182. doi:10.17105/SPR-2017-0073.V47-2

Guevarra, R. P., Jr. (2012). *Becoming mexipino: Multiethnic identities and communities in San Diego*. Rutgers University Press.

Hall, S. (1998). New ethnicities. In H. A. Baker Jr., M. Diawara, & R. H. Lindeborg (Eds.), *Black British cultural studies: A reader* (pp. 114–119). University of Chicago Press.

Hamako, E. An Introduction to monoracism (2014, Nov. 13) [Conference presentation] Critical Mixed Race Studies Conference Chicago, IL, United States.

Harris, A. P. (2008). From color line to color chart: Racism and colorism in the new century. *Berkeley Journal of African-American Law & Policy, 10*(1), 52–69.

Harris, C. I. (1993). Whiteness as property. *Harvard Law Review, 106*(8), 1707–1791.

Helms, J. E. (1995). An update of Helm's White and people of color racial identity models. In J. G. Ponterotto, J. M. Casas, L. A. Suzuki, & C. M. Alexander (Eds.), *Handbook of multicultural counseling* (pp. 181–198). Sage.

Herman, M. R. (2010). Do you see what I am? How observers' backgrounds affect their perceptions of multiracial faces. *Social Psychology Quarterly, 73*(1), 58–78.

Huang, E., Kasdan, J., Khan, N., & Mar, M. (Executive Producers). (2015–2020). *Fresh off the boat* [TV series]. Fierce Baby Productions, The Detective Agency, and 20th Century Fox Television.

Hughes, D., & Johnson, D. (2004). Correlates in children's experiences of parents' racial socialization behaviors. *Journal of Marriage and Family, 63*(4), 981–995.

Hughes, D., Smith, E. P., Stevenson, H. C., Rodriguez, J., Johnson, D. J., & Spicer, P. (2006). Parents' ethnic-racial socialization practices: A review of research and directions for future study. *Developmental Psychology, 42*(5), 747–770.

Hughes, J. M., Bigler, R. S., & Levy, S. R. (2007). Consequences of learning about historical racism among European American and African American children. *Child Development, 78*(6), 1689–1705.

Hughey, M. W., & Jackson, C. A. (2017). The dimensions of racialization and the inner-city school. *The ANNALS of the American Academy of Political and Social Science, 673*(1), 312–329.

Ibrahim, H. (2012). *Troubling the family: The promise of personhood and the rise of multiracialism*. University of Minnesota Press.

Ifekwunigwe, J. O. (Ed.). (2004). *'Mixed race' studies: A reader*. Routledge.

Itzigsohn, J. (2009). *Encountering American faultlines: Race, class, and the Dominican experience in Providence*. Russell Sage Foundation.

Jackson, K. F., & Samuels, G. A. (2019). *Multiracial cultural attunement*. NASW Press.

Jackson, K. F., Wolven, T., & Crudup, C. (2019). Parental ethnic-racial socializa-tion in multiracial Mexican families. *Journal of Ethnic & Cultural Diversity in Social Work, 28*(2), 165–190.

Jolivétte, A. J. (2014). Critical mixed race studies: New directions in the politics of race and representations. *Journal of Critical Mixed Race Studies, 1*(1), 149–161.

Jones, L. (1994). *Bulletproof diva: Tales of race, sex, and hair.* Anchor books.

Joseph, R. L. (2013). *Transcending blackness: From the new millennium mulatta to the exceptional multiracial.* Duke University Press.

Joseph, R. L. (2017). What's the difference with 'difference'? Equity, communica-tion and the politics of difference. *International Journal of Communication, 11*, 3306–3326.

Katz, P., & Kofkin, J. (1997). Race, gender and young children. In S. S. Luthar, J. A. Burack, D. Cicchetti, & J. Weisz (Eds.), *Developmental psychopathology: Perspectives on risk and disorder.* Cambridge University Press.

Keith, V. M. (2009). A colorstruck world skin tone, achievement, and self-esteem among African-American women. In E. N. Glenn (Ed.) *Shades of difference: Why skin color matters* (pp. 25–39). Stanford University Press.

Keith, V. M., & Herring, C. (1991). Skin tone and stratification in the black com-munity. *The American Journal of Sociology, 97*(3), 760–778.

Kelly, D. J., Quinn, P. C., Slater, A. M., Lee, K., Smith, M., Ge, L., & Pascalis, O. (2005). Three-month-olds, but not newborns, prefer own-race faces. *Develop-mental Science, 8*(6), F31–F36.

King-O'Riain, R. C., Small, S., Mahtani, M., Song, M., & Spickard, P. (Eds.). (2014). *Global mixed race.* New York University Press.

The Kirwan Institute. (2017). *State of the science: Implicit bias review.* The Ohio State University Kirwan Institute for the Study of Race and Ethnicity. http://kirwan institute.osu.edu/wp-content/uploads/2017/11/2017-SOTS-final-draft-02.pdf

Larson, K. E., Pas, E. T., Bradshaw, C. P., Rosenberg, M. S., & Day-Vines, N. L. (2018). Examining how proactive management and culturally responsive teach-ing relate to student behavior: Implications for measurement and practice. *School Psychology Review, 47*(2), 153–166.

Lee, R. E. R. (n.d.). Affinity group resource page. *Seattle Girls' School professional outreach.* https://sites.google.com/a/sgs-wa.org/sgsprofessionaloutreach/affinity -group-resource-page

Lloyd, C., & Levitan, S. (Executive Producers). (2009–2020). *Modern family* [TV series]. Lloyd-Levitan Productions, Picador Productions, Steven Levitan Pro-ductions, 20th Century Fox Television.

Marcia, J. E. (1966). Development and validation of identity ego status. *Journal of Personality and Social Psychology, 3*(5), 551–558.

Matsuoka, N. (2008). Political attitudes and ideologies of multiracial Americans: The implications of mixed race in the United States. *Political Research Quar-terly, 61*(2), 253–267. https://doi.org/10.1177/1065912907313209

Mazama, A., & Lundy, G. (2012). African American homeschooling as racial pro-tectionism. *Journal of Black Studies, 43*(7), 723–748. https://doi.org/10.1177 /0021934712457042

McIntosh, P., Badger, Chen, J., P. Gillette, P., Gordon, B., Mahabir, H., & Men-doza, R. (2015). *Teacher self-knowledge: The deeper learning. Independent School Magazine, 74*(4).

McKibbin, M. L. (2018). *Shades of gray: Writing the new American multiracialism.* University of Nebraska Press.

Mitchell, J. (2020). *Imagining the mulatta: Blackness in the U.S. and Brazilian media.* University of Illinois Press.

Morris, E. W. (2005). "Tuck in That Shirt!" Race, class, gender, and discipline in an urban school. *Sociological Perspectives, 48,* 25–48.

Mosely, M. (2018). The black teacher project: How racial affinity professional development sustains black teachers. *Urban Review, 50,* 267–283. https://doi.org/10.1007/s11256-018-0450-4

Murray, C., & Greenberg, M. T. (2000). Children's relationship with teachers and bonds with school. An investigation of patterns and correlates in middle childhood. *Journal of School Psychology, 38*(5), 423–445. https://doi.org/10.1016/S0022-4405(00)00034-0

Myers-Scotton, C. (1993). Common and uncommon ground: Social and structural factors in codeswitching. *Language in Society, 22*(4), 475–503.

Neblett, N. W., Jr., White, R. L., Ford, K. R., Philip, C. L., Nguyên, H. X., & Sellers, R. M. (2008). Patterns of racial socialization and psychological adjustment: Can parental communications about race reduce the impact of racial discrimination? *Journal of Research on Adolescence, 18*(3), 477–515.

Neville, H. A., Lilly, R. L., Duran, G., Lee, R. M., & Browne, L. (2000). Construction and initial validation of the color-blind racial attitudes scale (CoBRAS). *Journal of Counseling Psychology, 47*(1), 59–70.

Nishime, L. (2014). *Undercover Asian: Multiracial Asian Americans in visual culture.* University of Illinois Press.

Okonofua, J. A., Paunesku, D., & Walton, G. M. (2016a). Brief intervention to encourage empathic discipline cuts suspension rates in half among adolescents. *PNAS, 113*(19), 5221–5226.

Okonofua, J. A., Walton, G. M., & Eberhardt, J. L. (2016b). A vicious cycle: A social–psychological account of extreme racial disparities in school discipline. *Perspectives on Psychological Science, 11*(3), 381–398. https://doi.org/10.1177/1745691616635592

Omi, M., & Winant, H. (1986, 2015). *Racial formation in the United States.* Routledge.

Pabón Gautier, M. C. (2016). Ethnic identity and Latino youth: The current state of the research. *Adolescent Research Review, 1,* 329–340. https://doi.org/10.1007/s40894–016-0034-z

Parham, T. A. (1993). *Psychological storms: The African-American struggle for identity.* African American Images.

Parker, K., Horowitz, J. M., Morin, R., & Lopez, M. H. (2015, June). *Multiracial in America: Proud, diverse and growing in numbers.* Pew Research Center. https://www.pewsocialtrends.org/2015/06/11/multiracial-in-america

PBS. (2003). *Interview with Beverly Daniel Tatum.* https://www.pbs.org/race/000_About/002_04-background-03-04.htm

Peters, F. (2016). *Fostering mixed race children: Everyday experiences of foster care.* Palgrave Macmillan.

Phinney, J. S. (1993). A three-state model in ethnic identity development in adolescence. In M. E. Bernal & J. P. Knight (Eds.), *Ethnic identity: Formation and transmission among Hispanics and other minorities* (pp. 61–80). State University of New York Press.

Plaut, V. C. (2010). Diversity science: Why and how difference makes a difference. *Psychological Inquiry, 21*, 77–99. http://dx.doi.org/10.1080/10478401003676501

Pollock, M. (2004). Race bending: "Mixed" youth practicing strategic racialization in California. *Anthropology & Education Quarterly, 1*(35), 30–52.

Poston, W. C. (1990). The Biracial Identity Development Model: A needed addition. *Journal of Counseling & Development, 69*(2), 152–155. https://doi.org/10.1002/j.1556-6676.1990.tb01477.x

Pour-Khorshid, F. (2018). Cultivating sacred spaces: A racial affinity group approach to support critical educators of color. *Teaching Education, 29*(4), 318–329.

Priest, N., Walton, J., White, F., Kowal, E., Baker, A., & Paradies, Y. (2014). Understanding the complexities of ethnic-racial socialization processes for both minority and majority groups: A 30-year systematic review. *International Journal of Intercultural Relations*, 1–17.

Qian, Z. (2004). Options: Racial/ethnic identification of children of intermarried couples. *Social Science Quarterly, 85*(3), 746–766.

Qian, Z., & Lichter, D. T. (2007). Social boundaries and marital assimilation: Interpreting trends in racial and ethnic intermarriage. *American Sociological Review, 72*(1), 68–94. https://doi.org/10.1177/000312240707200104

Ratcliffe, K. (2005). *Rhetorical listening: Identification, gender, whiteness.* Southern Illinois University Press.

Rauktis, M. E., Fusco, R. A., Goodkind, S., & Bradley-King, C. (2016). Motherhood in liminal spaces: White mothers' parenting black/white children. *Affilia: Journal of Women & Social Work, 31*(4), 434–449. https://doi.org/10.1177/0886109916630581

Rockquemore, K. A., & Brunsma, D. L. (2002). *Beyond black: Biracial identity in America.* Sage.

Rockquemore, K. A., Brunsma, D. L., & Delgado, D. J. (2009). Racing to theory or retheorizing race? Understanding the struggle to build multiracial identity theory. *Journal of Social Issues, 65*(1), 13–44.

Root, M. P. P. (Ed.). (1992). *Racially mixed people in America.* Sage.

Root, M. P. P. (Ed.). (1996). *The multiracial experience: Racial borders as the new frontier.* Sage.

Roth, W. D. (2005). The end of the one-drop rule? Labeling of multiracial children in black intermarriages. *Sociological Forum, 20*, 35–67.

Roth, W. D. (2012). *Race migrations: Latinos and the cultural transformation of race.* Stanford University Press.

Ruiz, A. S. (1990). Ethnic identity: Crisis and resolution. *Journal of Multicultural Counseling and Development, 18*(1), 29–40. https://doi.org/10.1002/j.2161-1912.1990.tb00434.x

Sangrigoli, S., Pallier, C., Argenti, A. M., Ventureyra, V. A., & de Schonen, S. (2005). Reversibility of the other-race effect in face recognition during childhood. *Psychological Science, 16*, 440–444.

Saperstein, A. (2013, May 21). Race in the eye of the beholder. *Made in America: Notes on American life from American history.* https://madeinamericathebook.wordpress.com/2013/05/21/race-in-the-eye-of-the-beholder

Scott, L. D. (2004). Correlates of coping with perceived discriminatory experiences among African American adolescents. *Journal of Adolescence, 27*, 123–137.

Sexton, J. (2008). *Amalgamation schemes: Antiblackness and the critique of multiracialism*. University of Minnesota Press.

Skiba, R. J., Chung, C. G., Trachok, M., Baker, T. L., Sheya, A., & Hughes, R. L. (2014). Parsing disciplinary disproportionality: Contributions of infraction, student, and school characteristics to out-of-school suspension and expulsion. *American Educational Research Journal, 51*, 640–670.

Sollors, W. (1997). *Neither black nor white yet both: Thematic explorations of interracial literature*. Oxford University Press.

Song, M. (2010). Does 'race' matter? A study of 'mixed race' siblings' identifications. *The Sociological Review, 58*(2), 265–285.

Song, M. (2017). *Multiracial parents: Mixed families, generational change, and the future of race*. New York University Press.

Song, M., & Parker, D. (Eds.). (2001). *Rethinking 'mixed race.'* Pluto Press.

Spencer, M. B., Dupree, D., & Hartmann, T. (1997). A phenomenological variant of ecological systems theory (PVEST): A self-organization perspective in context. *Development and Psychopathology, 9*(4), 817–833.

Spickard, P. (1989). *Mixed blood: Intermarriage and ethnic identity in twentieth-century America*. University of Wisconsin Press.

Spickard, P. (2020). Shape shifting: Reflections on racial plasticity. In L. A. Y. W. Tamai, I. Dineen-Wimberly, & P. Spickard (Eds.), *Shape shifters: Journeys across terrains of race and identity* (pp. 1–56). University of Nebraska Press.

Spillers, H. (2011). Mama's baby, papa's too. *Trans-cripts, 1*, 1–4.

Steele, C. (1997). In the air: How stereotypes shape intellectual identity and performance. *American Psychologist, 52*, 613–629.

Stevenson, H. C. (1994a). Racial socialization in African American families: The art of balancing intolerance and survival. *The Family Journal, 2*(3), 190–198. https://doi.org/10.1177/1066480794023002

Stevenson, H. C. (1994b). Validation of the scale of racial socialization for African American adolescents: Steps toward multidimensionality. *Journal of Black Psychology, 20*(4), 445–468. https://doi.org/10.1177/00957984940204005

Stevenson, H. C. (1995). Relationship of adolescent perceptions of racial socialization to racial identity. *Journal of Black Psychology, 21*(1), 49–70. https://doi.org/10.1177/00957984950211005

Stevenson, H. C. (1998). Managing anger: Protective, proactive, or adaptive racial socialization identity profiles and African American manhood development. *Journal of Prevention & Intervention in the Community, 16*(1–2), 35–61. doi: 10.1300/J005v16n01_03

Stevenson, H. C. (2008). Fluttering around the racial tension of trust: Proximal approaches to suspended black student-teacher relationships. *School Psychology Review, 37*(3), 354–358.

Stevenson, H. C. (2014). Promoting racial literacy in schools: Differences that make a difference. Teachers College Press.

Stevenson, H. C. (2017). "Dueling narratives": Racial socialization and literacy as triggers for re-humanizing African American boys, young men and their families. In L. M. Burton, D. Burton, S. M. McHale, V. King, & J. Van Hook (Eds.), *Boys and men in African American families, 7*, 55–84. National Symposium on Family Issues. doi:10.2007/978-3-319-43847-4_5

Stevenson, H. C., & Arrington, E. G. (2009). Racial/ethnic socialization mediates perceived racism and the racial identity of African American adolescents. *Cultural Diversity and Ethnic Minority Psychology, 15*(2), 125–136. https://doi.org/10.1037/a0015500

Stevenson, H. C., Cameron, R., Herrero-Taylor, T., & Davis, G. Y. (2002). Development of the teenager experience of racial socialization scale: Correlates of race-related socialization frequency from the perspective of black youth. *Journal of Black Psychology, 28*(2), 84–106. https://doi.org/10.1177/0095798402028002002

Stevenson, H. C., McNeil, J. D., Herrero-Taylor, T., & Davis, G. Y. (2005). Influence of perceived neighborhood diversity and racism experience on the racial socialization of black youth. *Journal of Black Psychology, 31*(3), 273–290. https://doi.org/10.1177/0095798405278453

Stevenson, H. C., Reed, J., & Bodison, P. (1996). Kinship social support and adolescent racial socialization beliefs: Extending the self to family. *Journal of Black Psychology, 22*(4), 498–508. https://doi.org/10.1177/00957984960224006

Stevenson, H. C., Reed, J., Bodison, P., & Bishop, A. (1997). Racism stress management: Racial socialization beliefs and the experience of depression and anger in African American youth. *Youth & Society, 29*(2), 197–222. https://doi.org/10.1177/0044118X97029002003

Stonequist, E. V. (1937). *The marginal man: A study in personality and culture conflict.* Charles Scribner's Sons.

Streeter, C. (2003). The hazards of visibility: "Biracial" women, media images, and narratives of identity. In L. I. Winters & H. L. Dbose (Eds.), *New faces in a changing America* (pp. 301–322). Sage.

Suárez-Orozco, C., & Suárez-Orozco, M. M. (2001). *The developing child: Children of immigration.* Harvard University Press.

Sue, S., Zane, N., Hall, G. C. N., & Berger, L. K. (2009). The case for cultural competency in psychotherapeutic interventions. *Annual Review of Psychology, 60,* 525–548.

Tafoya, S., Johnson, H., & Hill, L. E. (2004). *Who chooses to choose two?* Russell Sage Foundation and Population Reference Bureau.

Tatum, B. D. (1997/2017). *Why are all the black kids sitting together in the cafeteria? And other conversations about race.* Basic Books.

Tauriac, J. J., Kim, G. S., Sariñana, S. L., Tawa, J., & Kahn, V. D. (2013). Utilizing affinity groups to enhance intergroup dialogue workshops for racially and ethnically diverse students. *The Journal for Specialists in Group Work, 38*(3), 241–260. doi:10.1080/01933922.2013.800176

Tenenbaum, H. R., & Ruck, M. D. (2007). Are teachers' expectations different for racial minority than for European American students? A meta-analysis. *Journal of Educational Psychology, 99*(2), 253–273. https://doi.org/10.1037/0022-0663.99.2.253

Tervalon, M., & Murray-García, J. (1998). Cultural humility versus cultural competence: A critical distinction in defining physician training outcomes in multicultural education. *Journal of Health Care for the Poor and Underserved, 9*(2), 117–125.

Thomas, A. J., & Blackmon, S. M. (2015). The influence of the Trayvon Martin shooting on racial socialization practices of African American parents. *Journal of Black Psychology, 41*(1), 75–89. https://doi.org/10.1177/0095798414563610

Thomas, D. E., Coard, S. I., Stevenson, H. C., Bentley, K., & Zamel, P. (2009). Racial and emotional factors predicting teachers' perceptions of classroom behavioral maladjustment for urban African American male youth. *Psychology in the Schools, 46*(2), 184–196. https://doi.org/10.1002/pits.20362

Thornton, M. C., & Wason, S. (1995). Intermarriage. In D. Levinson (Ed.), *Encyclopedia of marriage and the family* (pp. 396–402). Macmillan.

Townsend, S. S. M., Markus, H. R., & Bergsieker, H. B. (2009). My choice, your categories: The denial of multiracial identities. *Journal of Social Issues, 65*(1), 185–204. https://doi.org/10.1111/j.1540-4560.2008.01594.x

Trent, M., Dooley, D. G., & Dougé, J. (2019). The impact of racism on child and adolescent health. *Pediatrics, 144*(2), 1–14.

Turner, A. (2015). Generation Z: Technology and social interest. *The Journal of Individual Psychology, 71*(2), 103–113. doi:10.1353/jip.2015.0021

United States Census Bureau. (2012, May). *Most children younger than age 1 are minorities, Census Bureau reports.* https://www.census.gov/newsroom/releases/archives/population/cb12-90.html

Urrieta, L., Jr., & Noblit, J. W. (Eds.). (2018). *Cultural constructions of identity: Meta-ethnography and theory.* Oxford University Press.

U.S. Department of Education. (2016, July). *The state of racial diversity in the educator workforce.* https://www2.ed.gov/rschstat/eval/highered/racial-diversity/state-racial-diversity-workforce.pdf

Voight, A., Hanson, T., O'Malley, M., & Adekanye, A. (2015). The racial school climate gap: Within-school disparities in students' experiences of safety, support, and connectedness. *American Journal of Community Psychology, 56,* 252–267.

Walton, G. M., & Brady, S. T. (2017). The many questions of belonging. In A. Elliot, C. Dweck, & D. Yeager (Eds.), *Handbook of competence and motivation: Theory and Application* (2nd ed., pp. 272–293). Guilford Press.

Walton, G. M., & Wilson, T. D. (2018). Wise interventions: Psychological remedies for social and personal problems. *Psychological Review, 125*(5), 617–655. https://doi.org/10.1037/rev0000115

Washington, M. (2017). *Blasian invasion: Racial mixing in the celebrity industrial complex.* University of Mississippi Press.

Washington State Office of Financial Management. (2019, December 23). *Under 18 child population by race/ethnicity in Washington.* The Annie E. Casey Foundation KIDS COUNT Data Center. https://datacenter.kidscount.org/data/tables/4490-under-18-child-population-by-race-ethnicity#detailed/2/any/false/37,871,870,573,869,36,868,867,133,38/3,724,142,2,4533,71,1,13/10512,10513

Waters, M. C. (1994, December 1). Ethnic and racial identities of second-generation Black immigrants in New York City. *International Migration Review, 28*(4), 795–820. https://doi.org/10.1177%2F019791839402800408

White-Johnson, R. L., Ford, K. R., & Sellers, R. M. (2010). Parental racial socialization profiles: Association with demographic factors, racial discrimination, childhood socialization, and racial identity. *Cultural Diversity and Ethnic Minority Psychology, 16*(2), 237–247. https://doi.org/10.1037/a0016111

Williams, K. M. (2006). *Mark one or more: Civil rights in multiracial America.* University of Michigan Press.

Winchell, M., Kress, T. M., & Tobin, K. (2016). Teaching/learning radical listening: Joe's legacy among three generations of practitioners. In M. F. Agnello &

W. M. Reynolds (Eds.), *Practicing critical pedagogy: The influences of Joe L. Kincheloe* (pp. 99–112). Springer International Publishing.

Winn Tutwiler, S. (2016). *Mixed-race youth and schooling: The fifth minority.* Taylor & Francis.

Woolley, M. E., Kol, K. L., & Bowen, G. L. (2009). The social context of school success for Latino middle school students: Direct and indirect influences of teachers, family, and friends. *The Journal of Early Adolescence, 29*(1), 43–70. https://doi.org/10.1177/0272431608324478

Wyness, M. (2012). Children's participation and intergenerational dialogue: Bringing adults back into the analysis. *Childhood, 20*(4), 429–442.

Yeager, D. S., Purdie-Vaughns, V., Garcia, J., Apfel, N., Brzustoski, P., Master, A., Hessert, W. T., Williams, M. E., & Cohen, G. L. (2014). Breaking the cycle of mistrust: Wise interventions to provide critical feedback across the racial divide. *Journal of Experimental Psychology, 143*(2), 804–824.

Zack, N. (Ed.). (1995). *American mixed race: The culture of microdiversity.* Rowman & Littlefield.

Index

About the Authors

Ralina Joseph is Presidential Term Professor of Communication, director of the Center for Communication, Difference, and Equity, and associate dean of diversity, equity, and inclusion at the University of Washington, Seattle.

Allison Briscoe-Smith is a clinical psychologist and director of diversity, equity, and inclusion at The Wright Institute.